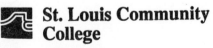

GANGBANGS AND DRIVE-BYS

SOCIAL PROBLEMS AND SOCIAL ISSUES

An Aldine de Gruyter Series of Texts and Monographs

SERIES EDITOR

Joel Best

Southern Illinois University at Carbondale

Joel Best (*editor*), **Images of Issues: Typifying Contemporary Social Problems**

Joel Best (*editor*), **Troubling Children: Studies of Children and Social Problems**

James A. Holstein, **Court-Ordered Insanity: Interpretive Practice and Involuntary Commitment**

James A. Holstein and Gale Miller (*editors*), **Reconsidering Social Constructionism: Debates in Social Problems Theory**

Gale Miller and James A. Holstein (*editors*), **Constructionist Controversies: Issues in Social Problems Theory**

Philip Jenkins, **Intimate Enemies: Moral Panics in Contemporary Great Britain**

Philip Jenkins, **Using Murder: The Social Construction of Serial Homicide**

Valerie Jenness, **Making It Work: The Prostitutes' Rights Movement in Perspective**

Stuart A. Kirk and Herb Kutchins, **The Selling of *DSM*: The Rhetoric of Science in Psychiatry**

Bruce Luske, **Mirrors of Madness: Patrolling the Psychic Border**

Leslie Margolin, **Goodness Personified: The Emergence of Gifted Children**

Dorothy Pawluch, **The New Pediatrics: A Profession in Transition**

William B. Sanders, **Gangbangs and Drivebys: Grounded Culture and Juvenile Gang Violence**

Wilbur J. Scott, **The Politics of Readjustment: Vietnam Veterans since the War**

Wilbur J. Scott and Sandra Carson Stanley (*editors*) **Gay and Lesbians in the Military: Issues, Concerns, and Contrasts**

Malcolm Spector and John I. Kitsuse, **Constructing Social Problems**

GANGBANGS AND DRIVE-BYS
Grounded Culture and Juvenile
Gang Violence

William B. Sanders

ALDINE DE GRUYTER

New York

ABOUT THE AUTHOR

Wiliam B. Sanders is Professor of Sociology and Associate Dean, College of Liberal Arts, University of Texas, El Paso. Dr. Sanders began studying gangs in San Diego, Great Britain, and El Paso during the 1980s. He has published *Detective Work* (a C. Wright Mills Award Nominee), *Rape and Women's Identity*, and eight other books in sociology.

Copyright © 1994 Walter de Gruyter, Inc., New York
All rights reserved. No part of this publication may be reproduced or transmitted in any form, or by any means, electronic or mechanical, including photocopy, recording, or any information storage or retrieval system, without permission in writing from the publisher.

ALDINE DE GRUYTER
A division of Walter de Gruyter, Inc.
200 Saw Mill River Road
Hawthorne, New York 10532

This publication is printed on acid-free paper ∞

Library of Congress Cataloging-in-Publication Data
Sanders, William B., 1994–
    Gangbangs and drivebys : grounded culture and juvenile gang violence / William B. Sanders.
        p.   cm. — (Social problems and social issues)
    Includes bibliographical references and index.
    ISBN 0-202-30536-8 (alk. paper). — ISBN 0-202-30537-6 (pbk.)
    1. Gangs—California.   2. Violence—California.   3. Juvenile delinquency—California.   4. Gang rape—California.   5. Juvenile justice, Administration of—California.   I. Title.   II. Series.
HV6439.U7C26   1994
302.3'4—dc20   93-50050
                                                                        CIP

Manufactured in the United States of America

10 9 8 7 6 5 4 3 2 1

This book is dedicated to Bill Campbell and John Davis, two friends who encouraged me in every way.

CONTENTS

PREFACE

Anyone who has studied gangs over a period of time will admit that the more one studies them, the more complex they are. At best, we can come to understand a bit about certain features of gangs at given points in time. Gangs are dynamic, flexible, and ever-changing. At the same time, they have certain features that transcend gang cohorts and even generations, giving them permanent features. Gang violence is the feature of interest in this book.

In order to put together data that were gathered over a period of twelve years, it was necessary to organize the book into digestible chapters. The beginning, Chapters 1–3, deal with introductory and general materials concerning gang violence. They set the contextual backdrop for the rest of the book and provide an overview of patterns of gang violence. In Chapters 4–6, I examine the major forms of gang violence. These forms reflect the particular kind of violent behaviors that were the focus of the study. Chapters 7–9 examine the different styles of gangs in terms of their ethnic makeup. Just as there are different types of gang violence, there are different types of gang styles, and the styles tend to be associated with the ethnic groups who made up the gangs. Chapter 10 is a single chapter describing how the police attempt to deal with the gangs. Since the police constitute the nexus between society and crime, they not only serve as a major social control agency, they are instrumental in defining what is and is not a gang and gang incident. As such their procedures are important to understand in the context of their societal role and interaction with gangs. An Appendix rounds out the book with a description of the methodology used.

ACKNOWLEDGMENTS

There are several people who helped out immensely in getting this book completed. Those who helped in collecting data included police, research assistants, and even some current and former gang members; so I'll just mention a lot of people whose specific affiliation will be left unstated so as not to upset anyone who wants to remain professionally anonymous. Sine the data-gathering process spanned over a decade, I may have forgotten some key people, and I hope they will understand. William Campbell, Jose Broz, William Howell, Tamara Plak, and Paul Salamando were most helpful in this respect.

Fellow sociologists at San Diego State University and the University of Texas at El Paso also assisted in one way or another. I am especially grateful to Jim Wood and Kenji Ima at SDSU. Howard Daudistel and Fernando Rodriguez at UTEP provided helpful suggestions as well. At Cambridge University, Richard Wright provided some needed introductions. Likewise, other faculty at the Institute of Criminology at Cambridge helped as well. One such contact they provided was Jimmy Boyle, who gave me some needed insights into the gangs that once existed in the Gorbals in Glasgow, Scotland.

Joel Best at Southern Illinois University did his utmost to help me reorganize, untangle, and clarify what I was trying to accomplish. His efforts were appreciated in the long run, and I'm glad nobody saw the book before his suggestions were incorporated. Likewise, Richard Koffler and Arlene Perazzini at Aldine de Gruyter were most supportive and helpful. But as in all such projects, the deficiencies must remain the responsibility of the author.

1

Introduction: The Problem

It was a typical fall evening in San Diego, cool and comfortable. A young man and his girlfriend were sitting in his car, a private place away from their families. The area, called Del Sol, is a subdivision just north of San Ysidro not too far from the border. North of Del Sol is Otay and Las Palmas, and Imperial Beach is to the west, right on the ocean. In the gerrymander that is San Diego, the city limits stop to the north of Otay where Chula Vista and National City insert themselves along Interstate 5 (I-5, to the locals) before the city of San Diego starts up again in areas called Shelltown and Paradise Hills.

The important area at the moment was San Ysidro since the gang there was at war with the gang in Del Sol (as they always had been), and a carload of three gang youths, two from San Ysidro (the Sidro gang) and one from Calexico, were driving over to "mess up" Del Sol. (The guy from Calexico was visiting some friends in San Ysidro, and they wanted to show him how bad Sidro was—hence the excursion into Del Sol.) They were driving down the streets of Del Sol breaking out the windows of Del Sol cars. The boy in the car with his girlfriend "claimed" the Del Sol gang, and when he saw what was happening, he immediately took his girlfriend into her house and ran and got a hoe. He attacked the San Ysidro car with the hoe breaking windows and denting it. In response, the youths in the car knifed the Del Sol boy and killed him.

One of the youths in the car ran and hid in a drainage ditch, and the other two panicked when they realized the rest of the Del Sol gang was coming out to get them. They accidentally ran the car into a chain link fence and became so entangled they couldn't get away. The Del Sol gang called an ambulance for their fallen comrade and then proceeded to attack the two young men in the car.

The police were summoned to a "hit and run" accident. The dispatcher, who apparently got something wrong, kept requesting backup police for the accident. The head of the gang detail, with whom I was riding, listened to the calls for assistance and realized that something other than a simple accident had occurred. On the hunch that the incident was gang related, given the location and the increasing panic with which the dispatcher kept requesting additional police units, the sergeant headed down the freeway to the South Bay region of Del Sol.

Upon arrival in Del Sol, I saw the police unsuccessfully attempting to keep the Del Sol gang away from the Sidro boys who were sitting bleeding next

1

to the car. The Sidro boys had that dumb groggy look of people who have
been badly beaten and were attempting to maintain consciousness so that
they could ward off attacks and not die then and there. The Del Sol gang
members would break away from the police and run and kick or hit the
Sidro boys. Finally, the police were able to separate everyone, and I started
interviewing witnesses.

The above episode occurred in 1981 during the first phase of my
research on gangs. Ten years later in 1991, I was finishing up the research by gathering data on Southeast Asian–American gangs—gangs
that didn't even exist when the research began. Like sociologists before
me, I was attempting to understand the phenomenon of gangs, and this
book relates what was found.

For years, sociologists have attempted to understand gangs as social
organizations. From Thrasher's (1928) classic work in the 1920s to Jankowski's (1991) examination of gangs of the 1980s, a major focal point
has been to find what it is about a gang's structure that leads to patterns
of gang violence and other delinquent behavior. This book attempts to
turn that question around to see how the situation of gang violence
shapes the groups we call gangs.

My focus is the *situation* of gang violence. We will attempt to ask what
makes juvenile gang violence occur in the way it does. The answer
begins with an examination of the violent situation and expands outward to the gang. In this way, we hope to understand not only gang
violence, but the phenomenon of gangs themselves.

AN ETHNOGRAPHY OF SITUATIONS

An Appendix describes the research methodology in further detail,
but we should begin with an overview of the research. The basic question for this study was, What's going on when a gang or gang members
engage in violent behavior? To get as close as possible to gang situations,
I chose to spend time with the police unit whose major function was to
deal with gang members. Whenever a gang event was reported, this
police unit was called to handle the situation. In these situations, and in
reports of these situations, I gathered details about what occurred before, during, and after the gang violence, based on my observations and
interviews. Police reports of these situations, based on their observations and interviews, complemented and supplemented my own. In
addition, research assistants and I interviewed and took written accounts from gang informants. (I use the term *informants* in the anthro-
pological and ethnographic sense, in that they simply provided

information. They were not police informants nor were their identities passed on to the police.)

The great bulk of the data were collected from a 100 percent sample of all gang-related crimes handled by the police department's gang unit in 1981 (144 cases) and 1988 (184 cases). However, data were also collected from several months of 1980 (80 cases), and 100 percent of the cases involving Southeast Asian–Americans gangs in 1990 and through September 1991 (20 additional cases.)

Both quantitative and qualitative data were taken from the situations based on observations, interviews, and written reports. Virtually all of the quantitative data can be considered nominal in that my focus was on getting descriptions of events in violent situations to develop an understanding of what typically occurred. The goal was to provide an overall picture of the situations of gang violence—an *ethnography of situations.*

GROUNDED CULTURE

This book's sociological perspective involves studying the interactional structure of the situation in the tradition of Erving Goffman. However, at the same time, it recognizes the importance of the phenomenological tradition, especially that of Harold Garfinkel (1967) and the ethnomethodologists. On the one hand, Goffman treats situations as "little institutions" in a fairly positivistic manner. On the other hand, ethnomethodology takes contextual embeddedness (indexicality) as a condition of social behavior, and contends that all meaning relies on context for its exact and specific sense. Furthermore, there is a reflexive (mutually elaborating) relationship between interpretation and the phenomenon in the world. The interpretation of the phenomenon characterizes the phenomenon in a certain way that gives it a specific sense while simultaneously justifying that very interpretation in terms of the phenomenon being interpreted (Garfinkel 1967).

To some extent, this work also reflects some aspects of the more recent postmodern scholars in the area of law and society (Milovanovic 1993). The postmodernists acknowledge the embeddedness of interpretive work in even the most behavioralistic and positivistic positions. The point of reality creation is in the process of interacting with social structure, and the social structure does not exist independent of the interpretive work of that interaction.

Together, these perspectives provide a research focus on the social situation while at the same time acknowledging the interpretive work that creates a sense of situation. This is unlike Goffman, since he treats situations as a *reality sui generis*—a social fact in the Durkheimian sense. In this book, social situations are treated as reflexive constructions in the phenomenological sense. Goffman's concepts will be employed with the understanding of an underlying social construction not necessarily held by Goffman.

Reflecting this background, the key concept used in this book to account for the nature of gang violence and patterned behavior of gangs is *grounded culture*. Rather than separating culture and structure, with culture hovering over social structure like a cloud, culture's *specific sense* is viewed as grounded in the social structure. (By *specific sense* I mean how talk is used and understood in a given context.) As typically used in sociology, culture is a "gloss" to explain behavior relating to a set of shared values, norms, and world view. Culture is somewhat vague even though the content of culture is explained in terms of key values. However, the key values tend to be further glosses that only become sensible when pointing to specific instances of behavior. In an attempt to cull the specific sense of culture as related to behavior, rather than simply naming and defining a value for one and all in a given society, it is necessary to show how a certain value term is used in a specific situation. For example, a cultural concept such as *loyalty* must be located in a specific instance for it to have a social reality. The concept *loyalty* is woven into the day-to-day experiences of those who live in the structure. Loyalty gets its exact meaning from life in the structure and not simply as a verbal tradition handed down independent of the structure. Hence, while in middle-class society loyalty may be viewed in terms of patriotism to back military actions taken by the government, it can be viewed in gang areas in terms of standing up for your gang. While some experiences and senses of culture are held in common, others, grounded in different structures, are very different. Thus, in talking about grounded culture, we are talking about how a certain cultural value is used in the context of a group, organization, or subculture.

By examining the social situations of violence, we can see not only the patterns of violence, we can examine what sense is made of these situations. *The meaning of the actions in the situations constitutes the culture.* That is, culture is embedded in the situated meaning of events and actions. The violence elaborates the culture, and at the same time is explained by the culture. That is, gang violence tells us something about the culture (or subculture) while we use the culture to explain the violence. It is a reflexive relationship.

Since our focal point is the violent gang situation, it is necessary to first examine what we mean by gangs and gang activities. In attempting to account for patterns of gang behavior, there are different, often contradictory, conceptions of gangs. So to proceed, we need to sort out what the subject matter is.

DEFINING GANGS AND GANG ACTIVITIES

To define gangs and gang activities, we must consider both the sociological and the social contexts of the meaning of gangs. Social definitions are commonsense definitions that make up the social discourse of groups. Any sociological definition must first examine how various segments of the community perceive gangs, and then develop a definition that can be used to examine the socially defined phenomenon. Since there are different social realities, there are competing definitions of gangs. This section examines these definitions and their basis.

Political and Social Conceptions of Gangs

In 1978, I called the police to get some information about gangs in San Diego. The response was that San Diego had no gangs. There were street groups and other delinquent groups, but there were no gangs. The official policy was to deny that San Diego had a gang problem. In part, the police reluctance to acknowledge gangs may have been due to San Diego's multimillion-dollar tourist industry. The image of a city with gangs hardly fit the image of a fun place to visit. (Similar image problems plagued Florida in 1993 as an alarming number of foreign tourists were murdered in that state.) Moreover, there was a widely held belief that *any* publicity about gangs would encourage gang activity. Ignoring gangs or gang activities in the newspapers or on television might cause gangs to wither and die for lack of attention. When the gang problem increased to a point beyond denial, news items began mentioning that some shootings and assaults were "gang-related." Nevertheless, the press did keep the names of gangs out of the paper most of the time.

The official view sponsored by city boosters, politicians, and others with a practical concern for keeping gang activity out of the limelight contrasted with the conception of gangs by those who lived in the communities who were victims of gang activities. Drive-by shootings by gang members had been taking place, school kids had been giving up their lunch money to gang extortion, and gang members had been robbing community merchants since at least the early 1970s. All the while a lively drug trade thrived among gang members. As a result, members of the community where gang activity was the greatest felt that the power structure was intentionally ignoring their problems. Since the communities with the gang problems were largely Mexican- and African-American, the victims felt it was simply another example of neglect of problems suffered by minorities.

Police Criteria

By 1979, a police Border Task Force was disbanded due to the international political problems it generated. The task force had been established to protect illegal aliens from the border bandits that preyed on the aliens in the canyons along the border. Since most of the robbers were from Mexico, it was inevitable that the American police would be involved in an international incident. Not only were there incidents involving Mexican bandits, but there were also incidents with Mexican police operating on both sides of the border. [For an excellent description of the rise and fall of the Border Task Force, see Joseph Wambaugh's *Lines and Shadows* (1985).]

The remnants of the disbanded Border Task Force became the kernel of the San Diego Police Department's gang detail. The police saw gangs as a practical problem to be solved by law enforcement. That is, when the gang detail was established to cope with gangs, the issue of defining a gang was a matter of differentiating gangs from nongangs for the allocation of resources and formulating a plan of action. Like all police plans of action, it required:

1. identifying the criminal element;
2. locating the criminal element;
3. stopping the crime committed by the criminal element using arrest or other measures (e.g., proactive intervention).

Identification involved designating as gang members any youth who:

- claimed a gang (i.e., said he/she was in a gang);
- had gang tattoos;
- associated with gang members;
- was involved in gang activities;

Claiming territory and fighting over territory with groups who did likewise was also part of what the police defined as gangs. So, through the exigencies of doing their job, the police derived a definition of gangs. A more formal police definition provided the following characteristics:

A youth gang by definition is a group of individuals between the ages of 8 and 24 years who associate on a continuous basis. The gang is without formal organization or leadership. A street gang has a name, claims a particular territory or neighborhood, and directs its criminal activity towards rival gangs and the general populations. (San Diego County Deputy Sheriffs' Association 1990:22)

There were a number of problematic elements in the police definition, but the police resolved conceptual problems by practical considerations. For example, one group of youths, who called themselves the *Morely Street Boys*, claimed to be a gang, and patrol officers brought the group to the attention of the gang detail. The gang detail sergeant pointed out that the group had not been involved in gang activities, such as assaults, extortion, or drive-by shootings. Also, they had not been the target of rival gangs. He described them as "wannabes" and even though they claimed a gang identity, that identity was denied by the police. Thus, while the police used self-identification as a gang criterion, they also used the practical criterion of gang activity.

The police did have a process of designating gang members. This "documentation," as the police called it, involved photographing gang members, describing their gang affiliation, and recording other potentially useful information. For example, police would record an automobile a youth owned or had access to with the idea that if such a vehicle were involved in a drive-by shooting, they would have a link between the auto and a person.

In responding to calls involving gang activities, primarily gang violence, the police also derived a sense of "active" and "inactive" gangs. Active gangs were involved in frequent gang activities. To be an active gang, a gang had to be identified as being involved, either as victim or perpetrator, in a violent gang activity or selling drugs. After a period of no reports of a given gang, the police would assume that enough gang members had been arrested, killed, or intimidated, by the police or other gangs, to the point of inactivity. Then the gang would be informally placed into an inactive category until it did something to draw attention to itself.

The police ignored inactive gangs, treating them as nongangs. Few members of inactive gangs were documented, there was virtually no proactive action against them, and the police simply assumed there was no active core to lead them in gang actions. So the police criteria for gangs were very much based on activities and not structure.

Interestingly, though, the police assumed that most inactive gangs would at some later time become active again. That is, they assumed *some underlying structure* in the community where the gang existed. The "structure" was a type of tradition that acknowledged a certain gang to have some claim over the area. That structure would allow a younger group of boys to reinitiate *gangbanging* (a term used to refer to general gang activities). So while the police definition of gangs focused on the immediate practical concerns of gang activities, they assumed gangs had an underlying shell or structure.

SOCIOLOGICAL CONCEPTUALIZATIONS

In the sociological literature, not only are there different definitions of gangs, but most researchers have defined different types of gang. Reviewing other research leads to one of two conclusions: Either there are several very different types of youth gangs, or there are very different definitions of what constitutes a gang (Horowitz 1990:37–54). There is a confusion between delinquent gangs and delinquent groups.

Based on this study's findings, some sociologists seem to have not an "overorganized" conception, but a "wrongly organized" conception of gangs. That is, some researchers seem to borrow certain organizational concepts from sociology and superimpose them on gangs. The conceptions do not fit very well, and the gangs appear to seem either almost wholly disorganized or almost bureaucratic. Yablonsky's (1962) concept of the "near-group" virtually defines what a gang *is not* because such a concept implies too loose a structure and transitory a group. On the other hand, Miller's (1969, 1975) list of structural elements in gangs, even though useful as a comparative tool, provides an overorganized sense of gangs. Jankowski (1991), while clearly describing a non-bureaucratic organization, talks about leadership roles that are far more structured than seems to be the case with the gangs observed in this study. Finally, Thrasher's (1928) conception of gangs is so broad that it virtually equates group delinquency by youths with gang behavior.

In order to clarify the tradition of gang notions used in this book, I would like to examine Malcolm Klein's (1971) and Walter Miller's (1975) definitions. Klein seems to have found gangs similar to those observed in this study. Gang structure and activities, as described by Klein, most closely fit what I saw. Miller's conception was grounded in the social definitions of those who worked with gangs. While the elements Miller used to define gangs did not coincide with the findings of this study, they serve as good sociological guidelines to clarify another sociological conception of gangs.

After examining what Klein and Miller have found, I will offer my own conceptualization. This definition is more exclusive in that it focuses on the violent component of gang situations, but I believe that gangs are dynamic, and at this point in history, they have a particularly violent edge that must be a part of any gang conceptualization. Not only do gangs change, but so too does what society considers gang behavior, and so rather than attempting to clarify what gangs are once and for all, I attempt to do so only for this particular point in time.

Malcolm Klein's Definition

First of all, Klein provides a general focus that incorporates most of what seemed to characterize the delinquent groups considered as gangs in this study:

> [W]e shall use the term *gang* to refer to any denotable adolescent group of youngsters who (a) are generally perceived as a distinct aggregation by others in their neighborhood, (b) recognize themselves as a denotable group (almost invariably with a group name) and (c) have been involved in a sufficient number of delinquent incidents to call forth a consistent negative response from neighborhood residents and/or enforcement agencies. (1971:13)

Klein's definition rests on lay assumptions and provides a good grounding in that it recognizes that the community has a hand in defining a gang. However, it would probably include more delinquent groups in the gang definition than either the police or the neighborhood would. That is because there are a lot of delinquent groups, especially "doper groups," who meet all of Klein's criteria, but are not considered delinquent gangs.

The best example of this encountered in the research was a group who called themselves North Park Stoners. They were recognized as a distinct group in the neighborhood, they recognized themselves as distinct, including their name, and the community and law enforcement saw them as a delinquent group. However, their primary delinquency was drug use. They were not violent, they did not force others from their territory, and they did not respond to violent attacks on their group.

In one telling incident, a gang called the Lomas murdered one of the Stoners. Some of the Lomas boys were having a party. A North Park Stoner became involved in a verbal argument with one of the Lomas members when several others of the gang at the party physically attacked and killed the Stoner. No one, including the police, the Lomas gang, and least of all the North Park Stoners, felt there would be a retaliation or what was commonly called a "payback."

Some sociologists might assume that the North Park Stoners are a good example of a *retreatist gang* (Cloward and Ohlin 1960:178–86). First, we would have to assume all that is implied by the retreatist adaptation

and drug use. Juvenile drug use in general, and gang drug use in particular, has transformed since Cloward and Ohlin outlined their concept of
a *retreatist subculture*; the amount, type, distribution, and social conceptions of drugs have changed. Larger segments of society have adopted
certain "recreational" drugs, and drug use among gangs has not sig-
naled the end of gang fighting and/or violence by the gang members.
Second, even if we accept the notion of drug use as a retreatist adaptation, Cloward and Ohlin never really emphasized that groups in a retreatist subculture were *gangs*. In fact, Cloward and Ohlin (1960:179–84)
point out that the retreatist adaptation is possible due to a *double failure*:
failure to achieve success goals through both legitimate *and* illegitimate
means. A conflict gang that was routinely defeated by other conflict
gangs was likely to drop out of gang fights and into drug use. In effect, it
threw in the towel as a gang and took up dope or alcohol.

So, while it can be argued that groups like the North Park Stoners are
a type of gang, it does little good to do so. In the lay understandings
among peers and neighborhoods, such groups are simply *doper groups*.
The police referred to them and similar groups as "just a bunch of
dopers." In contrast, *gangs* that routinely use large amounts of drugs
and alcohol are treated in a qualitatively different manner, and key
elements of their behavior are different as well. In order to understand
some of these key elements, we will turn to Miller's definition of gangs.

Walter Miller's Definition

As part of a nationwide study of gangs in the 1970s, Walter Miller
developed the following definition:

> A gang is a group of recurrently associating individuals with identifiable
> leadership and internal organization, identifying with or claiming control
> over territory in the community, and engaging either individually or col-
> lectively in violent or other forms of illegal behavior. (Miller 1975:9)

From this definition, we can identify five key elements of gangs:

1. violent or criminal behavior as a major activity of group members;
2. group organization with functional role division, chain of
   command;
3. identifiable leadership;
4. group members in continuing recurrent interaction; and
5. group identification with and claiming control over identifiable
   community territory.

Examining these five elements of gangs by Miller, we can see more precise definition than that developed by Klein. Since Miller's definition was derived largely from a consensus of people who worked with gangs across the country, it would appear it would have validity by that consensus. However, Miller's definition may be too narrow in some parts and too broad in others. Rather than reflecting a consensus, the emergent criteria really reflected a very broad spectrum of what people considered to be a gang. Among those who developed the criteria, there was a high estimate of 2,700 gangs and a low estimate of 760 gangs for six cities across the United States (Miller 1975). The various agents, including social workers, probation officers, and police, did not agree on exactly what constituted gangs or gang behavior. Given the range of gang estimates, some agents estimated there were three times as many gangs as other agents. So, while Miller provides a valuable insight into the disagreement surrounding the parameters of a gang, there is no consistent or consensual formulation that is useful for clarifying exactly what is and is not a gang.

Comparing Miller's criteria for gangs to what was found in this study, there seem to be three key areas of divergence; violence, structure, and leadership. The recurrent interaction and territoriality of the gangs was clearly evident in those gangs in this study. However, violence, structure, and leadership are key elements that need to be redefined.

Violence. First of all, Miller's reference to criminal *or* violent activities is too broad. Returning to the example of the North Park Stoners, criminal activity (drug use) was a major activity of the group, but violence was not. I think a better definition of gangs would include criminal *and* violent behavior as major activities. The violence is connected to the fifth criterion, territoriality. If a group is going to claim territory *seriously*, it is going to have to be willing to use violence to defend it. Otherwise, it has no way to sustain claims over the public domain. It is virtually contradictory to say that a gang is territorial and not violent. (One *could* argue that a group is territorial by repeatedly using the same area, but even Miller's definition of territoriality includes *control* over the area. Without the willingness to use coercive force, there is no control.)

Other researchers of California gangs have also noted violence as a defining criterion. Joan Moore, in a study of Chicano gangs states "all Chicano gangs are fighting gangs" (1978:36). She also notes, "there is one type of gang-related violence that is exhibited by all gangs— intergang conflict" (p. 40). This implies that all gangs engage in some kind of violence. Along the same lines, Quicker (1983), in discussing Chicana (girl) gangs, points out the use of violence by female gang members. Likewise, most other studies of gangs including Keiser (1969),

Allen (1977), Yablonsky (1962), Geis (1967), Jankowski (1991), and even Klein (1971) and Miller (1958), note elements of violence in gangs.

Klein (1971) and Miller (1969) both contend, though, that too much has been made of gang violence. It is overplayed in the press, and much of the research on gangs gives violence too much emphasis. Miller points out that the vast majority of gang activities is *not* violent.

Even though a time and motion study of gangs would show there is *exceedingly* little time devoted to violence, it is the *willingness to do violence* that makes a gang a gang. No one who understands gangs expects daily, weekly, or even monthly drive-by shootings. But the knowledge that the group will use violence sets it apart from other juveniles, whether they are delinquent or not, who do not use violence. Violence itself is proof of the willingness to do violence.

So while it is important to note that Klein and Miller are perfectly correct in cautioning us away from an overviolent conception of gangs, it would be equally wrong to ignore the key role that violence plays in gangs. As we will see, while the actual number of violent acts may be small in comparison to the nonviolent ones, violent acts have much more effect than anything else the gangs do and far transcend the occasion of the violence.

Structure. A second point of contention in Miller's definition of gangs is the idea that there is group organization with functional role division and chain of command. This image suggests a highly organized group on an almost bureaucratic model. Some gangs appear to approach this level of structure and organization. Lincoln Keiser's study of Chicago's Vice Lords suggests such a structure. The Vice Lord Nation was guided by an eight-member board, and each of the Vice Lords gangs had a president, vice-president, secretary-treasurer, supreme war counselor, war counselor, gunkeeper, and sergeant-at-arms. The president along with the supreme war counselor and war counselor made up the war council, which decided whether or not and with whom the Vice Lords would fight (Keiser 1969:17–19).

Compared to what Keiser found, the gangs examined in this study were far less structured. Like the Vice Lords and other gangs in other studies, the San Diego gangs were divided along age and gender lines. There were cliques within the gangs and even cliques within age cohorts, but otherwise there was not much differentiation as far as a chain of command was concerned. For example, one gang called Shelltown had a clique called Gamma Street, which was made up of a cohort of close friends within the Shelltown gang. The Gamma Street clique was not on a hierarchy, but instead was recognized simply as a group that spent a lot of time together.

At the other end of the continuum, Lewis Yablonsky describes violent gangs as *near-groups*. A near-group is characterized by diffuse role differentiation, limited cohesion, impermanence, minimal consensus on norms, shifting membership, emotionally disturbed leadership, and limited definition of membership expectations (Yablonsky 1962). And while a few studies have found similar groups as Yablonsky (Cummings 1993:49–73), the near-group does not appear to match what most other researchers have observed in gang structure, and certainly not the gangs I observed in San Diego. Gangs originally observed in 1980, such as the West Coast Crips, Red Steps, Pirus, 70s, VELs, and Sidro, among others, were still active in 1991. This hardly fits the near-group characteristic of impermanence. The longevity of the San Diego gangs also suggests something more than minimal consensus on norms and shifting membership. In fact, some of the gang members traced their membership back to their fathers' involvement in gangs. So while Miller's conception of gangs tends to provide an "overstructurized" model, Yablonsky errs far more with an "understructurized" model.

The model that most closely approximates what was observed in San Diego has been provided by Malcolm Klein. Klein uses the concept of a gang *cluster* to describe a gang structure:

> A gang "cluster," as we will use the term, consists of from two to five age- and sex-related groups that are somewhat distinct in structure but are clearly aligned as *subgroups* of a larger whole. (1971:62)

Within the cluster there are different levels of involvement, defined as *clique, core,* and *fringe*. The clique membership is made up primarily of core members, and most subgroups within the cluster are age-related. The gang structure, according to Klein, is more a matter of complex companionship patterns and levels of involvement than division of labor and chain of command (1971:65).

The San Diego gangs may have been virtually identical to what Klein describes, but the level of involvement was described a bit differently by both gang members and the police. The San Diego gangs were described as having a *hard-core* nucleus that initiated most of the gang delinquency. This hard core was considered to be the most dedicated to the gang, the most reliable, and the most willing to engage in violence. On a second level was an *affiliate* group, which identified with the gang but was not considered as committed to the gang or as reliable when there was danger. An affiliate would sometimes fight and back up his *homeboys* (fellow gang members), but he was not considered to have the heart of a core member. Finally, there were the *fringe* members, and what the core members often referred to as "wannabes." These were kids in the neighborhood who would claim affiliation with the gang, attend gang parties, wear gang colors, and hang out with gang members, but who would not engage in gang violence.

Like Klein's gang cluster, there were some companion connections between the hard-core and the fringe members. In one telling case, a group of three hard-core members and a fringe member were driving in a car together with a gun. They drove by a rival gang's house and found several rival gang members standing in the driveway "like sitting ducks." Continuing down the street, they pulled the gun out, made a U-turn and began back down the street to shoot the rival gang. At this point, according to my informant, the fringe member became hysterical crying, "You can't do this! You just can't go and shoot people." The hard-core members were dissuaded primarily because of the attention they believed the fringe member was drawing to their car in the middle of hostile territory. As they drove by the rival gang a second time, they were still unnoticed, and they returned home without incident. This illustrates how members with different involvement levels (e.g., hard core and fringe) in a gang can end up in the same gang situation. With a slight twist in the event, a fringe member would have been involved in a gang killing. However, because of their dissimilarity in violent situations, fringe and hard-core members were less likely to forge such links as those who were involved at the same level.

To summarize the gang structure as found in this study, the gangs are age- and sex-graded with graduated levels of involvement and commitment to the gangs. The subgroupings in gangs are cliquelike, and not hierarchical. There is only informal division of labor and chain of command.

Leadership. A final and thorny problem in understanding gangs is leadership. On the one hand, it is clear that some gangs such as the Vice Lords described in Keisler's study had identifiable leadership almost precisely in the way that Miller defines it. On the other hand, several studies indicate that there are multiple leaders and their authority is largely informal. In his autobiography, Washington, D.C., gang leader John Allen described himself as being *one of the bosses* and later being *the boss* (1977:42). When Allen was one of the bosses, it was because of his ability to steal. When he became *the* boss, it was because he shot the former boss in the leg in a power play.

Most other studies of gang leadership emphasize interpersonal skills over toughness, though. Diplomacy, coolness, and charisma appear to dominate over being *loco* or crazy in a fight. For example, one of the Gamma Street boys of the Shelltown gang had a street name of El Cyco (an innovative spelling of *psycho*). He was an acknowledged threat to rival gang members because he was considered crazy enough to attack anyone regardless of the odds against him. However, no one considered El Cyco a leader. He may have been a human weapon a leader might use, but he was considered too unstable to be a leader. This did not mean that he lacked status in the gang; he was looked upon as an asset. Other gangs who considered attacking Shelltown knew they would have to deal with El Cyco. So while high status in a gang can be gained by being a *puro loco* (real crazy), high status and leadership are two very different things.

This is in sharp contrast to what Yablonsky described in his work on violent gangs. Yablonsky argued that members of violent gangs were too unstable to have a single leader, and anyone who became one of multiple leaders was likely to be a sociopath and psychopath (1962). Like many of his other assertions, Yablonsky appears to be in a small minority in his description of gang leadership.

Turning again to Klein, instead of attempting to identify a gang leader it is better to understand the concept of *leadership* in a gang (1971:92). Leadership is conceived as providing a functional role in a given situation. That is, instead of a *position* in a gang, leadership is a collection of *functions* in a gang. A number of different members can fill the functional leadership role at different times depending on the exigencies of the situation.

Given Klein's conception, identifiable leadership is almost an impossible task. The police in this study were under no illusion that there was a single leader in a gang, and when a core member was arrested they did not think they had broken the gang by arresting its leader. Likewise, in interviews with gang members, any reference to *a leader* would be rejoined with the comment, "It's not like that." The best way to describe gang leadership appears to be in terms of the following:

- *multiple*—more than a single leader at any one time;
- *informal*—choice of leader is not structured;
- *situational*—leadership role may only be in certain situations; and
- *functional*—situated leadership is based on a particular function.

By such a definition, instead of gang leadership being identifiable, it is dynamic, fluid, and unstructured.

Violence and Defining Characteristics of Gangs

In one of the stories of gang lore in San Diego, a small gang called Las Palmas was attacked by a much larger gang, the Imperiales. The damage to the Las Palmas was minimal, but their retaliation was maximum. They killed two Imperiales and let it be known in no uncertain terms that the same fate would befall anyone else who attacked them. After that incident the Las Palmas were left alone by all the other gangs. In fact, their involvement in gang violence and crime was almost nonexistent after the double homicide.

The point is that violence by gangs, no matter how infrequent, is at the core of their definition. Even Miller, who warned against an overemphasis on gang violence, differentiated gangs from "street groups" on the basis of violence (1975:9). So rather than arguing that gangs cause violence, I think it is prudent to consider the thesis that violence causes, or at least defines, gangs.

Deadly Violence. Further on we will examine the group structure that goes with violence, but the first consideration in examining violence as a defining criterion of gangs is the severity, in quality and quantity, of the violence. Are groups who get into occasional fistfights gangs? If a group uses a gun once, is it a gang? If a group uses sticks and bats but not knives and guns, is it a gang? All of these issues are relevant, but we cannot examine every nuance of violence, every combination of weapons, and the number of times violence is done.

To simplify—and I believe accurately portray—the level of violence needed to define a gang, I propose that for a group to be a gang, it must use *deadly force*. That is, if a group is willing to use enough violence to kill others, whether in defense or in aggression, then it should be considered a gang. A good example of how the use of deadly force can differentiate a gang from a nongang can be seen in a group called the PB Rats and later PB Vermin. The PB Vermin were a permanent fixture at the beach in the Pacific Beach (PB) area of San Diego. They were variously described as *beach bums, surfer bums, beach dopers,* and *skateboarder bums.* On occasions, they would get into fights with others who came into their area. However, deadly force was never used, and there were no records of the police being notified by hospitals of serious wounds inflicted due to altercations with the PB Vermin. The police knew of their existence, and the special beach patrols kept an eye on them. However, the gang detail and other gangs never considered the PB Vermin a gang. Other gangs who came to the beach and fought each other never attacked or were attacked by the Vermin. So, while the Vermin were violent on occasions, they never used deadly violence.

Violence in the Name of the Gang. A second element of gang violence is the use of group violence in the name of the gang. A group of kids might get together and use a gun to commit a robbery. In fact they might actually kill someone in the process. However, unless the group identifies with a gang, and understands that the violence is for or with the gang, we are not talking about the violence as a defining element in the gang.

The clearest type of gang violence in the name of the gang is when one gang attacks another, typically in a drive-by shooting. Often during such shootings, the attacking gang will call out its name. For example, a Shelltown boy was shot and killed in a drive-by shooting by members of the Spring Valley Locos gang, who shouted the name of their gang while making the attack.

To the extent a gang member feels an obligation to use deadly force because of his affiliation with a gang, we can understand that violence as gang-defining violence. At the same time that the violence defines the gang, the gang obligation generates the violence. This points to the *reflexive* nature of such a definition. The violence and the gang are mutually elaborating (Garfinkel 1967). The violence defines the situation as a gang event and structure, and the gang is seen as the generating force behind the violence, thereby specifying the nature and cause of the violence.

Violence and Gang Solidarity. Another function of violence in defining gangs is the effect of violence on gang cohesion or solidarity. A Durkheimian axiom notes that group solidarity increases with an external threat to the group. Likewise, Klein and Crawford (1967:259–61) argue that gangs have precious few sources of internal cohesiveness, and they rely on external threats such as rival gangs and the police to maintain gang cohesion.

Deadly violence visited on gangs is a clear source of external pressure. However, violence by a gang against another gang or nongang also generates external pressures. When one gang attacks another, it can expect a payback in the form of further violence. Likewise, any gang violence is going to bring police attention. Whether the gang sees the response to its violence as appropriate or not, it generates the external pressure that increases solidarity.

There is a necessary caveat to the idea that external pressure increases internal solidarity. Enough pressure, in the form of arrests and deaths, can destroy the gang or at least cripple it to the point that it is no longer the target of other gangs or the police. In 1981 the Del Sol gang suffered three homicides. This generated concern in the community, especially among the parents and girlfriends of the Del Sol gang members, that being a *cholo* was not such a good idea. In particular, a girlfriend of one of the homicide victims had been a big supporter of the tough gang image of Del Sol. After the death of her boyfriend, she proclaimed that gangbangers were losers and she would henceforth have nothing to do with them. While these incidents did not wholly destroy the gang, they did put a damper on the its activities. In later years, while Del Sol was still recognized as a distinct gang, the number of incidents involving it fell significantly.

A gang called the 70s killed a police officer in the 1970s. After that incident, police pressure increased so much that there was almost no gang activity by the 70s for years. The external pressure did not eradicate the gang, but it did subdue it. Whether gang cohesiveness increased during this period is unknown, but it does not seem likely.

In a related case, two police officers were shot and killed by a Filipino youth, described as a "wannabe" member of the Lomas, a Mexican-American gang. The incident occurred while a Lomas gang member was sitting in the car with the Filipino boy. In no uncertain terms, the Lomas members disassociated themselves from the incident, and the Lomas gang member who was in the car when the shooting took place actively helped in the arrest and conviction of the Filipino. The gang members did not think that outside pressure generated by a police crackdown would help either their reputation or their cohesiveness. In fact, they could have recognized massive police pressure as a blow from which they might not recover.

Perhaps a better example of the negative effect of external pressure on a gang involved a gang with the unlikely name of The Insane Family. Several of this gang's key members were killed or arrested in a short period of time. Then it simply disappeared.

While some external pressure can increase cohesiveness, excessive external pressure can break gang cohesiveness. The belief that "We gotta stick together to help one another" is a strong source of solidarity in gangs, and external pressure from rival gangs and even the police increases such beliefs. However, when the belief becomes "We're getting shot at or arrested everywhere we go", the gang can become viewed as a source of problems and disunity.

Violence and Territory.   As pointed out earlier, for a gang to be territorial, it virtually has to be violent. That is because a gang cannot lay any legitimate claim to public areas otherwise. However, by being willing to use violence against rival gangs who come into their area, they can maintain a claim. So, in talking about gang territoriality as a defining characteristic of gangs, it is necessary to define territoriality as the *willingness to use violence to maintain territorial integrity.* Groups willing to do so can be considered gangs.

Individual Members and Violence.   A seemingly contradictory element must be introduced into gang violence. While it is important to understand that, to be a gang, a group must demonstrate the willingness to use deadly force, it is not important that such force be used all the time or by all the members. We have already seen that a gang consists of members of varying degrees of involvement and commitment. The fringe members or wannabes were observed not to use violence. Even an affiliate member may not use violence if he demonstrates commitment to the gang in other ways, such as by stealing or providing drugs for other members.

The frequency and intensity of violence may also vary considerably. Sometime a gang may not have displayed violence for years, but its reputation as a gang can be made in a single incident where it demonstrates the willingness to use deadly force. In fact, when gang members feel their reputation has to be renewed, they often resort to violence to make such a statement. For example, an on-again, off-again gang called Varrio Market Street, after a period of noted inactivity, suddenly shot-gunned some members of the VELs (Varrio Encanto Locos) to let others know it was a serious gang.

Other gangs use far more violence on a routine basis. In 1988, the Crips and Pirus were shooting one another and at a Los Angeles–based branch of the Crips who were attempting to muscle in on the crack cocaine trade in San Diego. During that period, there were a high number of violent incidents, including several homicides.

So while there may be an ebb and flow of violence in gangs and only certain members engage in the bulk of the violence, the violence has be to part of the gang's current or historical makeup. Otherwise, the gang will drift into a street group status or disappear altogether as a coherent group.

Gangs and Transpersonal Membership.   An important feature of a gang as a *social fact* in the Durkheimian sense is transpersonal membership. That is, a gang as a group should not be dependent on a single set of individuals and personalities. It must transcend any cohort and be treated as a phenomenon beyond the individuals that make it up at any one time. This helps to differentiate gangs from ad hoc groups based on a particular set of personalities. Such groups, I believe, could usefully be called near-groups in exactly the way Yablonsky defined the concept. They are impermanent and transitory, and while they are of interest by comparison, they are not gangs.

Once such near-group that came and went fairly quickly in San Diego was a gang of mixed ethnic groups called Four Corners of the World. What made this near-group interesting was its suicide pact. The members decided that rather than being taken prisoner by the police they would commit suicide. After a robbery, they were cornered by the police, and the leader committed suicide, but the other members did not.

Thus, while I do not think Yablonsky's concept of near-group is useful for defining violent gangs, it is very useful for specifying what groups are not gangs. The near-groups are transient aggregates based on certain persons being together at a certain place and time. They may or may not be violent, they are unstable as a group, and their existence is temporary. This contrasts with gangs that are transpersonal, territorial, and violent.

Gangs Defined

From the foregoing discussion we are now in a position to define youth gangs:

> A youth gang is any transpersonal group of youths that shows a willingness to use deadly violence to claim and defend territory, and attack rival gangs, extort or rob money, or engage in other criminal behavior as an activity associated with its group, and is recognized by itself and its immediate community as a distinct dangerous entity. The basic structure of gangs is one of age and gender differentiation, and leadership is informal and multiple.

This definition differentiates gangs from near-groups, street groups (or *hanging groups*), and hate groups. The near-groups are transitory and not transpersonal. The street groups are not willing to use deadly violence in either fighting rival groups or defending territory. The hate groups, such as the skinheads, are not territorial. (The skinheads will be discussed in Chapter 9 to contrast them with the gangs.)

Gang-Related Incidents

With a focus on gang violence as a major defining element of gangs, there is a very real problem of running into a tautology. To wit, if a youth group, with the attending criteria discussed above, is violent, it is a gang. The fact that it is a gang means it is violent. Identifying what the police call *gang-related* incidents is important to differentiate gang activities from non–gang activities. As we will see, though, it is not always clear when an incident is correctly identified as gang-related.

As far as the police were concerned, if an incident involved a gang member, it was gang-related. In one shooting, for example, a gang member shot a rival in a love triangle. The violence was not in the name of the gang, the victim was not a rival gang member, and the action involved a single member.

Some sociologists have been quick to point out that because the police call an incident gang-related does not make it so. Jack Katz (1989:11) argues that even though a criminal has been identified as a gang member it does not mean that the crime was caused by his gang involvement. The example above involving the love triangle and the gang member shooter would be the kind of incident that Katz would use to question the label of gang-related. Similar types of shootings occur all the time, with none of the involved parties having anything to do with gangs. Such shootings typically are attributed to such mundane motives as jealously.

In Spergel and Chance's definition of *gang crime incidents*, we can see how a crime, such as robbery, would be very difficult to classify as a gang or non–gang activity by gang members.

> A *gang crime incident* is an incident in which there was gang motivation, not mere participation by a gang member. If a gang member engages in nongang-motivated criminal activity (e.g., crime for strictly personal gain), the act should not be considered a gang incident. However, since gang members are likely to be serious offenders as well, information systems should record all types of crime but at the same time distinguish gang from nongang crime. (1991:23)

Spergel and Chance's conceptualization is a nice, neat differentiation, but it is a very difficult distinction in reality. Robbery by a group of gang members looking for some money may be for personal gain in that each receives an equal share of the spoils, but were it not for the gang affiliation, the crime may never have occurred. Gang life generates certain delinquent occasions, both directly and indirectly, and to specify which are gang- and non-gang-motivated may not be possible. Gang-related incidents can be viewed as part of the gang life, and while it may be of some abstract interest to divide the incidents into gang and nongang, it probably would not shed any light on gang criminality to do so.

A lot of gang violence has been centered around the sale of illicit drugs, notably crack cocaine. Before the youth gang involvement in drug dealing, there were always killings surrounding the sale and distribution of illegal drugs. Did the violence in the drug trade lead to increased gang violence as the gangs became involved in drug dealing, or did gang violence lead to increased violence in the drug trade?

In a way, these are empirical questions. By examining the events where gang members were involved, we can see if the gang is or is not a key to the crime and/or violence. To the extent to which the actions are defined as part of a gang event and to the extent to which gang member-

ship is required to participate in the event, we can account for it as a
gang-related incident.

GANGS AND GROUNDED VALUES

A major sociological explanation of gang behavior centers around the
idea of a *delinquent subculture*. More specifically, Cohen (1955) and
Cloward and Ohlin (1960) argue that in the world of the gangs, there are
distinct values that are in opposition to the dominant values of society.
These values, in short, say that it is all right to kill, steal, use dope and
commit all of the other negative behavior associated with gangs. Boys
growing up in such subcultures are socialized into these oppositional
values as solutions to structural problems in achieving legitimate success
goals. What's more, there is peer pressure to accept the delinquent
values.

In an insightful critique of the delinquent subculture thesis, David
Matza (1964:48–50) pointed out that anybody who bothered to look
would find that the most commonly expressed values in areas defined as
subcultures of delinquency were *conventional* values. Delinquency, when
it occurred, was a matter of negating the evil in the offense so that,
under a given set of circumstances, it was permissible to break the law.
This neoclassical approach argues that a subculture of delinquency generates understandings that have more exceptions for legitimately breaking the law than does the legal code. For example, it is perfectly legal to
punch an attacker in the nose to stop the assault. So Matza (1964:59)
argued that the typical subcultural delinquent was not one full of delinquent values, but rather was one who came to understand that there
were *extenuating conditions* where breaking the law was in line with
conventional morality. The subcultural delinquent, through *subterranean
convergence*, was able to define more situations as extenuating conditions
where breaking the law would not break the true spirit of conventional
morality (Matza 1964:62–64).

The existence of *techniques of neutralization* and *negations of the offense*,
for Matza, proved that conventional morality was the dominant set of
values in subcultures of delinquency. Were it the case that delinquent
values were dominant, there would be no need for the neutralizing work
done to create the proper extenuating circumstances justifying the exception to conventional morality. In other words, if it was perfectly
acceptable to commit crimes, then there would be no need for neutralizing work to make it acceptable. The crimes would be committed on any
and all occasions.

What Cohen, Cloward and Ohlin, as well as Matza all have in common is a positivistic notion of values. For Cohen as well as Cloward and Ohlin, the values became internalized, even though the subculture was a functional response to blocked legitimate success goals. The delinquent values were the subcultural delinquent's values, held and sanctioned in the same way that conventional values would be. Since these values *determined* the bulk of the juvenile's behavior, the behavior naturally would be delinquent.

Matza's (1964:7–12) positivism, described as "soft" positivism, is a bird of a much different feather, but it maintains certain basic assumptions of positivism that are held in common with Cohen and Cloward and Ohlin. The major difference between the hard and soft positivists is that the soft positivists have the neoclassical rational actor as a fundamental model for human choice. The hard positivists' social actor is driven by forces of determinism that he cannot see or control, while the soft positivists' actor has certain deterministic elements in his life, but can also make rational choices. Matza describes his conception of the delinquent as follows:

> The image of the delinquent I wish to convey is one of drift; an actor neither compelled nor committed to deeds nor freely choosing them; neither different in any simple or fundamental sense from the law abiding, nor the same; conforming to certain traditions in American life while partially unreceptive to other more conventional traditions; and finally, an actor whose motivational system may be explored along lines explicitly commended by classical criminology—his peculiar relation to legal institutions. (1964:28)

Value Meanings and Contexts

While Matza's conception of soft positivism and delinquency separates his position from that of Cohen and Cloward and Ohlin, it is still grounded in a very basic assumption: *Expressed values have the same meaning.* Cohen, Cloward and Ohlin, *and* Matza do not question that expressed values that say the same thing may not have very different meanings. Values expressed in words such as *honesty, loyalty, integrity, bravery,* and *industry* may not mean the same thing at all. Any word's or utterance's specific sense is derived from its context (Garfinkel 1967). The comment, "That's bad!" can mean several different things depending on the context of its use. In the context of a mother admonishing a child for hitting a playmate, the statement is one of negative moral judgment. For a youth listening to a sound system in an automobile that can be heard several blocks away, the same statement means admiration and approval. Other contexts can generate still further meanings.

What is important is that we acknowledge that values are context-dependent. When we turn to larger contexts, such as the community or neighborhood, we should expect that as these structures differ, the specific sense of the values in them will differ as well.

Grounded Values

At this point we can talk about *grounded values*. Since the specific meaning of expressed values is dependent on the context of their use, we can talk of values as grounded in a given context. Treating the community structure as a context, we can examine values as grounded in the community. For example, take the expressed value of hard work. In a middle class community, hard work for a youth would likely mean putting off immediate gratification by being diligent in school in order to go to college to get a good job. In a lower class community hard work may mean getting a job picking strawberries in the fields.

Taking the different grounds for the meaning of hard work in the different communities, we can also see that the grounds are based on what the individual is likely to experience. A middle-class youth who dropped out of school so that he could spend the rest of his life as a berry picker would be seen as a moral failure. From a positivistic point of view, we could argue the middle-class berry picker was indeed involved in hard work, but the sense of hard work in middle-class communities does not include stoop labor outside of manicuring one's lawn or garden. However, in a lower class community where a youth may join his parents routinely in agriculture work, the sense of hard work could very well be grounded in stoop labor.

Turning to an example of a conventional value in a delinquent context, consider the value of loyalty. As a general conventional value, loyalty refers to maintaining allegiance to family, school, friends, and company. As one grows up, he or she comes into different affiliations. The specific sense of loyalty depends on the group with whom one associates. People have been known to have avid loyalties to everything from their church to the type of car they drive.

When one's focal structure is the gang in the neighborhood, the sense of what loyalty means may be grounded primarily in the gang. The school may be grounds of failure, the straight kids may be grounds of rejection, and the family may be grounds of indifference. What loyalty means to the youth is developed in the gang. When a youth sticks with the gang on occasions when the gang is threatened, he is told he is a loyal person. His understanding of loyalty has an empirical base in the gang. Loyalty is grounded in the gang.

So when we talk of values in high-delinquency areas, we cannot assume that the same expressed values have the same meaning as they do in low-delinquency areas. We must examine the situations in which any values are grounded to understand their specific meaning. In this way, we can better tie the meaning of the values to the social structure in which the values are grounded.

SUMMARY

In this chapter it has been necessary to cover a great deal of material in a very little space. First, I attempted to review several nuances in defining a gang. This should give the reader a feeling for certain complexities in studying gangs without overwhelming him or her with all of the various arguments of what properly constitutes the subject matter of gang study. The definition developed in this chapter is one that seemed to best reflect what was examined and is not necessarily what others have found or will find in the future. Gangs are *dynamic*.

Second, I wanted to introduce a theoretical orientation to values and the idea of subculture. The idea of grounded values will be developed further in later chapters, but I wanted to introduce it here to provide an orientation to the approach the book will take to this important element in gang study. As the book develops, we will be melding situations of gang violence and grounded values into an explanation of gang behavior.

2

Situations and Gang Violence

SITUATIONS TO TRY ONE'S METTLE

This chapter examines the circumstances in which gang violence actually occurs and gang identities are established. Beginning with the sociological understandings of situations, we will proceed to see how situations provide the norms for directing behavior and grounding for an understanding of social values. These values, in turn, justify and generate forms of gang violence. Further, we will see how identities develop in gang situations and how the gang is attractive in that it provides the situations where youths can demonstrate valued attributes of identity. Finally, I will attempt to show how an examination of gang situations provides the key to understanding the basis of gang organization and the values that justify and perpetuate gang activities.

Situations and Occasions

Erving Goffman (1959, 1961, 1963a, 1963b, 1967, 1969) explored and developed structural concepts at the interaction level of analysis more thoroughly and thoughtfully than any other sociologist. His key concept is that of the *situation*. A *gathering* refers to two or more people in one another's immediate presence, and a situation is "the full spatial environment anywhere within which an entering person becomes a member of the gathering that is (or does then become) present" (Goffman 1963a:18). The wider social affair that typically encompasses situations is the *social occasion*, which is bounded by time and space, has fairly regular features, and is recognized as an identifiable kind of event by its participants (p. 18). A party, a school day, a workday, a wedding, and a dance are social occasions. For Goffman,

a social occasion provides the structuring social context in which many situations and their gatherings are likely to form, dissolve, and re-form, while a pattern of conduct tends to be recognized as the appropriate and (often) official or intended one—a "standing pattern of behavior." (p. 18)

The range of occasions is wide, and their normative character varies with levels of formality, focus, and specificity. A scheduled lecture is a relatively formal, focused, and specific occasion, while an afternoon at the mall is more diffuse and unfocused. What can be expected at the lecture is fairly predictable. There is little leeway for deviance in such occasions, and those experienced with such events know what is expected from them. More diffuse events have a looser set of expectations, and the sense that the event is structured may be lost on the participants. Where there are diffuse circumstances, even though clearly located in time and space, Goffman (p. 19) suggests that the concept of *behavior setting* may best conceptualize the form of the event. For example, a bar constitutes a behavior setting where various situations and occasions arise and dissipate over time.

To determine patterns of situations, I gathered data by observing situations of gang-involved crime and going over police reports. (Later on, I and my assistants interviewed gang members and asked them to write up situations as they perceived them.) Setting up categories of situations, it was possible to record data on an observation schedule set up much like a questionnaire. The situation variable was broken into five categories:

- hanging out
- party/picnic
- school
- drive-by
- other

Each case was checked off as being of a certain category on the observation schedule. Most gang occasions involving violence were very diffuse (Table 2.1). In fact, since the two most common occasions, hanging

Table 2.1.   Occasions of Gang Violence, 1981 and 1988

	1981 (N = 140)	1988 (N = 178)
Hanging out/other	75.0	81.3
Party/picnic	8.6	2.3
School	0.7	0.6
Drive-by	15.7	15.9
Total	100.0	100.0

out and "other", were so diffuse that it became virtually impossible to differentiate them, they were collapsed into a single category. In looking at the two years where it was possible to collect a 100 percent sample of all cases categorized as gang incidents, we can see the breakdown.

As an occasion, hanging out was defined as those circumstances when the gang members would come together, typically at a specified location in their area, and talk, play, drink, use drugs and engage in general socializing. For example, the *70s* (Seven-ohs or *Setentas*) would routinely gather at a park in the middle of their neighborhood and socialize. Similarly, the West Coast Crips would gather at the corner of thirtieth and Imperial streets, talking, drinking, and socializing. These occasions were clear instances of what was recognized as "just hanging out."

However, I later found that occasions placed in the *other* category were sometimes described as hanging out as well. For example, if a group of gang members were on their way either to a specific or unspecified place, they would sometimes describe it as hanging out. At other times, the seemingly identical behavior would be described as a purposeful, goal-directed action. The reply to "What were you doing?" for a group of gang members on the way to a movie varied from "We were just hanging out" to "We were going to the movies."

The important point is not that violent gang youth behavior could not be located in crisp, cleanly delineated occasions, but rather that the occasions where gang violence took place were typically diffuse and unfocused. Relatively few instances of gang violence took place in less diffuse occasions, such as parties, picnics, or school.

Defining drive-by shootings as unique occasions resolved another analytic problem. There were two reasons why the notion of a drive-by shooting *as an occasion* makes sense for purposes of analysis. First, when a drive-by shooting occurred, it was difficult to argue that the occasion *of the shooting's target* structured the behavior of those who did the shooting. In one case, a party was going on when a drive-by shooting occurred. The party may have been the occasion of the targets, but the shooting gang *did not* subject itself to the party occasion's structure. Therefore, in order to focus on the behavior of the attackers, drive-by shootings were treated as occasions in their own right.

Second, treating drive-by shootings as occasions forces attention to situations surrounding the actual shooting. The drive-by shooting is an incident with a past, which led to and structured the incident itself. Thus, the key event of the shooting is treated as a by-product of a larger occasion.

The primary analytic difficulty with defining an occasion around a specific act is that if one type of gang violence is defined as an occasion, why not define all of them that way? In other words, why not define

other assaults, robberies, and rapes as occasions in their own right as
well? If the occasion is treated as the independent variable, and the
action as the dependent variable, there is a problem of defining the
independent variable *as* the dependent variable. Thus, to say that drive-
by shootings are caused by drive-by shootings is tautological.

Actually, the problem is more in the name of the occasion than in the
analytic treatment. The *drive-by occasion* is not the same thing as a *drive-by
shooting*. The occasion and the act are separate analytic entities. The
occasion begins with the decision to get into a car with guns and culmi-
nates with exiting the car. A drive-by occasion can occur without an
actual shooting; gang members go looking for a rival target and, failing
to find one, return home without discharging their weapon. My focus
will be on the drive-by occasion as it structures the situations within the
occasion, including the situated behavior of shooting at rival gang members or their property.

Norms and Situations

Goffman speaks of (1963:24) *situational proprieties,* norms that regulate
communication in situations. Goffman differentiates situational proprieties from other types of norms and moral codes, including codes of
honor, law, and ethics. Situational proprieties regulate communication
in face-to-face interaction, where codes of honor regulate relationships,
legal codes mold political and economic matters, and ethical codes regulate professional life.

Situational proprieties can and do come into play when gang members are in face-to-face situations where intentional breaches of proprieties become cause for assault. In certain types of gang clashes, violating
the situational proprieties constitutes a way of challenging opponents.
Situations provide the grounding for norms. When anyone, gang member or not, announces that an act is right or wrong, the judgment has a
situational context. The judgment may be considered universal and not
situated, but it is a specific behavior in a specific situation on which
judgment is passed.

My point is not to argue that norms are situational as opposed to
universal. However, when we talk about norms (or values), we must
somehow locate and identify them in a situation. They must be
grounded in some way so that we can understand why a person violated
a norm or expressed a value. The statements "Ya gotta back up your
homeboys" and "Ya gotta do what's right" may both express identical or
opposite sentiments. Doing "what's right" is far vaguer than "back up
your homeboys," but the situation where the words are uttered provides

the specific sense of what the meaning is for both. For example, suppose a gang member reports to his fellow gang members (homeboys) that he was attacked by a rival gang and demands that he be avenged. In the ensuing discussion, *in that situation*, the comments "Ya gotta back up your homeboys" and "Ya gotta do what's right" can be understood as agreements on values or loyalty.

However, identical utterances in different circumstances can have opposite meanings. The statements "Ya gotta back up your homeboys" and "Ya gotta do what's right" also can be arguments against one another. Suppose one member does something especially horrendous, bringing pressure from the community and police: One comment might be that loyalty of the gang to its members is more important than the reaction of the community ("Ya gotta back up your homeboys"). On the other hand, if the act is so offensive and/or generates so much pressure that loyalty to a fellow member is eclipsed by preserving the well-being of the gang, the sense of "doing what's right" may not include saving the skin of an offending gang member. For example, in a drive-by shooting where a baby was the only victim, the community outrage may so great that the gang members feel no obligation to save the shooter.[1] "Doing what's right" may be providing the name of the shooter to the police. In Chapter 1, we saw that the Lomas gang turned on a fringe member when he murdered two police officers. They demonstrated gang loyalty by distancing themselves from the killer, not protecting him. As a *universal* norm and value, gang loyalty is high, but whether that loyalty means protecting a fellow member or turning in a fellow member depends on the *situation* for the way in which the norm is used.

Gang members often discuss universalistic values and norms when speaking of feats of members who demonstrate valued attributes. However, while the discussion may be universalistic, the examples are grounded in specific situations where the attribute was demonstrated. In one such tale of *heart* (bravery, composure, and staying power all together), a boy called Weasel was described as frail and small but wholly fearless. He would wade into a fight slashing at opponents with a knife even though the opponents were much larger and even more numerous.

The important point is that gangs ground norms and values in the gang environment and the situations of the gang life. Non–gang members may speak of the same values, but they have a wholly different meaning since they are grounded in non–gang situations. Whether a grounded norm or value is directly observed or part of the neighborhood lore, the fact remains that there is a specific referent for it. In middle-class neighborhoods, tales of true grit are not grounded in gang fights and drive-bys, but in athletic, scholastic, professional, and business successes. The son or daughter who is accepted to Harvard provides situated grounds for values of hard work and perseverance. Young people *live* the business successes of their parents and the accompanying norms and values that are espoused for such success. Being *tough* is an expressed middle-class value, but it is grounded in athletic achievements or scholarship for youths and business or professional situations for the parents instead of gang fights.

So the differences between gang and non–gang environments is not necessarily the norms and values espoused. Instead it is in the different types of situations generated in different social milieus that provide the grounds for expressing the norm or value. As a result, there can be very different senses for the same values in the different environments.

Identities and Situations

Just as norms and values are grounded in situations; so are identities. Goffman (1967:149–270) offers an elaborate and compelling concept of *character* bounded to *fateful* situations. Basically, he traces the ways in which people come to judge themselves and others in situations that test various character attributes. Identities that are presented in safe social interaction are subject to question, especially when those identities claim strength in the face of adversity. However, actions that *demonstrate* resourcefulness, bravery, integrity, coolness, and other valued behavior in situations that test those very attributes provide unequivocal evidence of *strong* character and the associated identity. Likewise, the incapacity to behave effectively when the chips are down and the heat is on, shows *weak* character (p. 217).

Generically, when a situation is both consequential and problematic, we can call it *fateful*. *Consequentiality* is defined as the capacity of a payoff to flow beyond the bounds of the occasion in which it is delivered and to influence objectively the later life of the bettor (Goffman 1967:159–60). A problematic situation is simply one where a person cannot be reasonably certain of the outcome. A gang member who places himself in a situation where he may be stabbed, shot, or later arrested is in a consequential and problematic set of circumstances. He is in a fateful situation.

A good example of a fateful gang situation occurred when three rival gang members attacked the Del Sol gang (described at the start of Chapter 1). The assault on the vehicles, the murder, and the counterattack all reveal the fateful nature of gang violence. It was problematic, in that the original attackers knew there was a chance that they would be caught in the act and attacked themselves, and it was consequential for the future lives of the attackers (who went to prison) and the homicide victim.

At the same time that we can see the Del Sol incident as fateful, we can see it as a situation where character was established. The youth who was killed received posthumous glory from fellow gang members for attacking three rivals with only a hoe. The two attacking gang members who were trapped in the car and severely beaten never cried for mercy and, even in a stupor, kept fending off repeated attacks. They had demonstrated their character as strong against overwhelming odds. The third member of the attacking trio, who escaped retaliation by hiding in a ditch, was judged to have weak character for while his homeboys were being assaulted he did nothing to help them.

One cannot predict with any certainty when and where fatefulness will occur. An alternative to waiting around for fateful situations to randomly crop up is to seek them out or create them. Goffman (1967:185) refers to this type of fatefulness as *action*. The attack was fateful for the Del Sol gang although they did not seek out risk even though they expected attacks from rival gangs from time to time as a random danger of gang life. The rivals, on the other hand, sought the risky business, and for them it was action, intentionally creating a situation where they could demonstrate they had the strength of character to look fate in the eye and not waver.

Between times of action or fatefulness, there are identities to maintain and claims to be made. These identities Goffman (1959:22–30) calls *fronts*, presentations people make for others in terms of a given situation. A gang boy in the presence of his peers at a party presents himself as fun and sociable. At a family get-together, the same boy acts as the dutiful nephew or grandson.

In situations of gang activities, not necessarily delinquent ones, there is the *possibility* of the gang front. Gang colors, a hair net, bandana pulled low just above the eyes and black-dark glasses, a Pendleton over a T-shirt with just the top button buttoned and khaki baggy pants pulled up high, or some other combination of attire make up the gang front. (Pendleton is the brand name of a high-quality woolen shirt, but any woolen shirt that had a similar cut was called a Pendleton.) Tattoos are a more permanent (and committed) sign of gang identity. Likewise, stances, manners of walking, and making gang hand signals are all ways in which a gang member can present a gang front. So in that sense, the gang provides an identity for its members whether or not the member actually engages in gang delinquency.

A useful differentiation between fronts and character is that fronts show who one would *like* to be, and character shows who one *really* is. As noted in Chapter 1, there are different levels of commitment to a gang. Fringe, affiliate, and hard-core members all had gang identities to a greater or lesser degree; however, the hard-core members had more than a gang front. They had established gang character by dint of having put themselves in situations that tested the claims inherent in the gang front. The affiliates had gang character of sorts since they had shown under peril that they would stand up with the gang. However, the affiliate-level members' reluctance to renew their claims of gang character on a regular basis left the strength of their gang character in question.

The consequences of a gang front can be just as perilous as gang character. In one case, a boy who claimed a Filipino gang called the Be Down Boys was murdered because of his enthusiastic representation of a gang member. Fellow gang members referred to him as a "motor mouth," who was always "talking big" and displaying the gang's hand signals. However, he never knowingly put himself in a fateful situation for the gang and had the reputation of being a "wannabe" member. On the day the boy was killed, members of a Mexican-American gang called the Paradise Hills Locos saw him flashing his gang's hand signs at them. In a rare cross-ethnic alliance, the Locos had aligned themselves with a small Filipino gang called Da Boys against the much larger Be Down Boys. The Mexican-American gang members chased the boy down and shot him to death. It is unlikely that the victim realized that he was in mortal danger until the Locos began shooting at him. Thus, the presentation of a gang front generated the fateful situation resulting in a gang killing. (Almost exactly a year later, the Be Down Boys retaliated by killing a Paradise Hills Loco, who by all accounts was also a fringe member who had nothing to do with the killing of the Be Down Boy.)

Attractions to Gangs

Adolescence is a time for developing identities. Identities are generated in situations where one can either present a front of some valued attribute or establish character, and gangs provide such situations.

Charles Horton Cooley ([1902] 1964) put his finger on the social process of becoming someone in society in his concept of the "looking-glass self." Basically, we see ourselves as others see us. However, Goffman (1959) pointed out that people are well aware of identity being a mirror of other's views. Therefore, they engage in various types of impression management to generate the front necessary to get the reaction, and identity, they want. With enough resources, generating an identity is not too difficult. The very wealthy can show off the right clothes, homes, boats, automobiles, and bejeweled companions simply by having enough money. Middle-class youths, with the right tutoring, encouragement, and resources have a much better chance of excelling academically, implying later success, and successful identities, in the business or professional world. Athletic ability can provide opportunities for a wide range of social and ethnic classes, but the positions on the school teams are limited; so not even all of those with some athletic ability can find a position, and identity, on the team. Besides, academic ability, to a varying degree, may limit access to an athletic identity due to schools' scholastic requirements for team eligibility.

The gang offers a wide variety of identities to be claimed or established. A youth can be respected and feared by non–gang youth. He can claim or show he has courage, gameness, integrity, loyalty, and coolness in gang situations. In other words, the gang provides resources in the form of identity-generating situations so that the youth can be *somebody*.

Character Contests.   The very identities that attract members to gangs are the source of gang conflict and violence. Horowitz and Schwartz (1974) maintained that challenges to the self in the form of questioning one's honor are a primary source of gang violence. Likewise, Jankowski (1991) points out that "respect" and "honor," can be achieved, maintained or reestablished through violence. In fact "gang members generally directed aggression at those individuals whom they perceived to show a lack of respect or to challenge their honor" (p. 142). Furthermore, Jankowski (p. 140) cites *ambition* and *personal/group testing of skills* as factors in both individual and group violence in gangs. Both are aspects of identity that can be understood in terms of *face*, "the positive social value a person effectively claims for himself by the line others assume he has taken during a particular contact" (Goffman 1967:5). Face is the positive aspect of identity, situated in contacts where others acknowledge those positive aspects claimed by a person. An ambitious move or a test of skill is an effort to gain or maintain face. In the context of the gang, it is a cause for violence.

A good example of a gang using violence to establish face occurred in 1981 when the Spring Valley Locos attacked the Shelltown gang. During a Shelltown party, the Spring Valley Locos drove up to Lolo, a fringe Shelltown member, and shot him with a rifle seven times, mortally wounding him. After the shooting, I was interviewing Shelltown boys, and they told me that the Spring Valley Locos were just trying to establish themselves. They were shocked and dazed by the shooting of Lolo, but it seemed perfectly clear to them that it had been done by an ambitious gang to enhance its reputation. They had done it to gain face at Shelltown's expense.

Goffman describes *character contests* as those situations where "[e]ach person will be at least incidentally concerned with establishing evidence of strong character, and conditions will be such as to allow this only at the expense of the character of the other participants" (1967:240). For gang violence, I would like to broaden this notion to include *face* along with *character* as the prize at stake. Also, I would like to point out that character contests may not necessarily be zero sum games. A gang member who is beaten severely in a fight may have established character by standing up to overpowering adversaries. At the same time, those adversaries also have established character by demonstrating their fighting ability. Some face may have been lost by the vanquished and gained by the victor, but all parties can claim some positive traits of identity by virtue of participating in the fateful situation.

GROUNDED VALUES, GANG SITUATIONS, AND GANG SUBCULTURES

The social situation is a micro-structure, the nexus between the individual and society. Individuals both participate in and create situations. At the same time that situations *create* identities, the identities that individuals bring to a situation give situations different nuances. However, situations are independent of individuals; we can recognize situations independent of those individuals who happen to be participating in a situation at any particular time.

As we have seen in this chapter, identities—like norms and values—are grounded in situations. Goffman (1961:26–29) shows that situations provide world-building attributes in the form of *realized resources*. A realized resource is what people can expect to get out of situations. Realized resources in gang situations include various gang identities (*cholo, vato loco*, player), grounding of values and norms (loyalty, courage, integrity), and gang events (parties, fights, drive-by shootings). These identities, values, norms, and events make the gang recognizable as an entity, and in turn the gang provides gang situations that generate the realized resources that provide the members with grounds for their actions and understandings of themselves and others.

There is a mutually elaborating relationship between the gang *as an organization* and *gang situations*. The standard sociological relationship takes the organization as the independent variable and the gang behavior as a dependent variable: The gang *causes* the gang fights. However, without gang fights, how would we recognize gangs? Gang behavior *causes* gangs; without recognizable gang situations, the gang would be lost as an entity.

Jankowski's major emphasis was the gang as an organization rather than gang situations. Jankowski notes that, "policy makers must understand that situations are not the root cause of violence [even though] situations do affect the level (intensity and extent) of gang violence" (1991:176). However, throughout his work, Jankowski shows how situations are used to define and maintain the gang. The fear of a gang's decline, for example, is cited as cause for attacking a rival gang (p. 163). From the perspective developed here, a gang fight situation shores up the gang. It redefines it and the identities of the gang members. Likewise, Jankowski (p. 162) points out that loyalty can be grounded in a gang assault. New gang members' loyalty is tested by having them attack another gang. Loyalty is thereby grounded in a specific gang situation. The specific sense of what *loyalty* means was *not* an abstract gang organizational value, but rather it was a *grounded gang situation* value.

My point is not to deny any organizational or relational connections between gang members. Rather it is to point out that gang activities and the organization mutually define and elaborate one other. Both exist in the larger context of certain types of communities, opportunities, and expectations. This larger context generates a set of experiences that are handled with resources, language, ideologies, and folklore available to the individuals who live there. The worldview or outlook is grounded in the situations generated and experienced in this context, not in the abstract with general, universalistic norms and values that are applied independent of the members' experience.

This returns us to the idea of grounded values. The gang, as a phenomenon, is grounded in the community realities. In turn, the gang provides a set of situations for understanding and dealing with those realities. This is not an oppositional subculture; rather it is simply another set of situations through which a set of values may be grounded. Schools and the media present American norms and values. However, as Sutherland (1947) so brilliantly noted, the majority of value learning occurs in intimate personal groups, as opposed to watching television or listening to a teacher. That is because intimate personal groups share experiences in situations where those values are made real. Their reality, in turn, is grounded in the community of their common experiences and situations.

Thus, in discussing a subculture, especially a delinquent one, we should not seek to discover the source of *delinquent values*. Instead, we should look to see how common, conventional values are grounded in the experience of community members. A situation-generating and situation-defined structure is the gang. By examining the situations that most clearly distinguish the gang—gang violence—not only can we understand the gang, but we can understand how the values are grounded and used.

NOTES

1.   Where babies or other non–gang members are victims of gang violence, there is often community outrage, but it is rarely sufficient to move gang members. They usually view non–gang victims as unintended casualties but nothing about which they should feel remorse or that should otherwise give pause to gang violence.

3

Patterns of Gang Violence

This chapter examines the general patterns of gangs and gang activities in San Diego from 1980–1990. The purpose of the chapter is to provide an overview of gangs in San Diego for comparative purposes and outline the context of the gangs and gang activities. The broad patterns show the different groups involved in gang activity and when they came into play, characteristics of the situations of gang violence, and a general idea of the communities.

As we will see, there is a good deal of leeway for interpreting the data. This is especially true with police data. Different investigative units (e.g., homicide, robbery) would often investigate gang-related crimes and not pass on the information to the gang detail, and some gang crimes did not end up in police records on gang-related activities. Likewise, patrol units might not indicate on their reports that a gang-related crime had occurred, and organizational changes, both within the gang unit and within the police department, led to changes in recording procedures.

HISTORICAL OVERVIEW OF SAN DIEGO GANGS

Interviews with former gang members indicate that gangs developed in San Diego in the early 1970s. These were Mexican-American gangs living in the working- and lower-class barrios, especially those in the South Bay area near the Mexican border. In the early 1970s, San Ysidro, Otay Mesa, Imperial Beach, and Del Sol had fighting gangs. There also may have been Mexican-American gangs in what is called Southeast San Diego, especially the Logan Heights area, but there is no solid evidence that they were around until the latter part of the decade.

The origin of African-American gangs can be traced to Los Angeles. In the late 1960s and early 1970s, African-American gangs were active in the south-central Los Angeles and Compton areas. In the 1970s the gangs developed into two distinct groups, the Crips and the Piru gangs.

The Crips were first to emerge as a major force, with many different gangs taking on Crips as part of their names, such as the Kitchen Crips, 5 Deuce Crips, and Rollin 20 Crips. Each individual Crips gang was called a *set*.

The initial reaction to the Crips was a group of gangs that were "anti-Crip." Later, on West Piru Street in Compton, a gang called the Compton Pirus formed. Wearing the color red, they came to be known as Bloods, and they were quickly recognized as the only gang powerful and ruthless enough to stand up to the Crips.

By the mid- to late 1970s, gang members from both the Crips and Pirus began showing up in San Diego, and by 1980 there were a number of distinct Crips and Piru gangs. The West Coast Crips and Neighborhood Crips were early San Diego Crips gangs, and a group called the Skyliners changed its name to Pirus, and later to Skyline Pirus to distinguish itself from other Piru gangs that later developed.

In the late 1980s, Filipino groups began gang activity in the Paradise Hills area. The Be Down Boys were especially active and had the dubious distinction of being the first Filipino gang with a member murdered by another gang. Other Filipino gangs began developing in more middle-class areas in the northern part of the city, an area that had never had a serious gang problem. Mira Mesa and Rancho Peñasquitos are mixed areas, but they are primarily middle-class suburban developments.

An interesting twist in the Filipino gangs is the use of African-American gang names and colors. The Rancho Peñasquitos gang, for instance, call themselves the Northside Blood and their primary rivals in Mira Mesa had the name of the Ruthless Possee Crips. The Northside Blood sport the color red, while the Crips show blue. Even the Filipino gangs that have Filipino names, such as the Bahala Na-Barkada, consider themselves in the Crips faction and use blue as their color. However, other than the names and colors, there seems to be no other connection between the Filipino and African-American gangs.

The final major group of gangs that developed at the time of this writing were the Southeast Asians. They came into being as a major identifiable force in about 1989–1990 and, by 1991, they were routinely being reported to be involved in gang violence. These gangs are made up of the children of Laotian, Khmer (Cambodian), Hmong, and to some extent Vietnamese refugees. Some, like the Tiny Oriental Crips, took on the names of African-American gangs, while others, Oriental Killer Boys and Oriental Boy Soldiers did not. However, their gangs are all unique in using the word *Oriental* in their names. The Oriental Boy Soldiers are primarily Khmer, while the other gangs are mainly Lao and Hmong. There are a smattering of Vietnamese in these gangs and even some reported whites, but the bulk are Laotian and Khmer.

Creation of Gangs

The sociological literature on gang origins generally traces them to poverty and its attending conditions. Thrasher's (1928) classic work on gangs concluded that gangs exist to fill the void of social disorganization in lower-class communities. Cohen (1955) and Cloward and Ohlin (1960) saw gangs as an adaptation to lack of access to legitimate success goals in the lower class. Joan Moore (1978) argued that the Chicano gang was an innovative adaptation to being on the bottom of a dual—Chicano and Anglo—stratification system. The Chicano gang represented a stylistic and symbolic challenge to being deemed the lowest status in the community (Moore 1978:38–41).

At this writing, the most recent theory of gang formation is Jankowski's. He argues that even though the gang communities are not disorganized, the low-income milieu is responsible for the formation of gangs. Specifically, Jankowski says that gangs "are organized around an intense competition for, and conflict over, the scarce resources that exist in these areas" (1991:22). Jankowski concludes that boys and young men in low-income areas seek to improve their competitive advantage in gaining access to the scarce resources by forming into gangs. He describes those who join the gangs as having *defiant individualist* characters. This type of character differentiates those in the low-income areas who join gangs from those who do not (pp. 21–28).

The problem with most current sociological theories of gang formation is the vast number of low-income areas in the United States, and the dearth of gangs and gang members relative to this poverty. To borrow from Matza's (1964:21–27) characterization, such theories of gang origin suffer an embarrassment of riches. That is, given the theorized conditions that spawn gangs, we should expect to see far more gangs than in fact exist.

Jankowski's remedy to the overprediction of gangs due to low-income life-styles is to suggest that only those with a character of defiant individualism join. Therefore, some juveniles in areas with gangs do not join gangs because they lack the special character. However, Jankowski simply sends the argument back one more level. What generates defiant individualism? If the same conditions that are likely to create gangs *also* create defiant individualism, then we must ask again why there are not *more* such defiant individuals.

Virtually all gang researchers note the relationship of low-income areas and gangs. We must clearly define what the relationship is. Almost all gangs are found in low-income areas. However, it *is not* true that all low-income areas have gangs. It is only a one-way relationship. A number of small- and medium-sized towns in Oklahoma have grinding poverty but not gangs. Likewise, gangs did not form in the hollows of Appalachia even though Appalachia and poverty are almost synonymous.

Another element in the formation of gangs seems to be an urban setting. At one time this setting was the high-density tenement buildings and projects of New York, Boston, and Chicago. However, the lower-density developments in California, especially in Los Angeles and San Diego, also saw gangs develop. While we can still posit a possible relationship between urban settings and gangs, it is important to understand that urban density is variable. Some of the gang areas in San Diego, in fact, would look downright suburban to a visitor from the East Coast.[1]

We have the facts that where we find gangs we also find (1) a low-income area and (2) an urban setting. What we lack is a good explanation as to why some low-income urban settings have no gangs. In the United States, several cities, such as Spokane, Washington, have been spared a gang problem. Likewise, when we look cross-culturally, we have a big problem explaining why European cities have no gangs.

As part of the research for this book, I spent time in London in 1984, working with a contact I had through Cambridge University, attempting to locate gangs. The police were unable to locate a gang that met my criteria. They had a horrendous problem with violence at football matches (soccer games), a behavior they called *hooliganism*. But at the time, they simply did not have the gang problem as found in San Diego.

The lack of gangs in London was not because gangs and gang violence were unknown in Great Britain. In the late 1950s and early 1960s Jimmy Boyle described gangs in the Gorbals area of Glasgow, Scotland, that were very much like the contemporary ones in the United States:

> There were lots of gangs in Glasgow and this seems to have been the case since I can remember. In the Gorbals alone there were two "Cumbie" gangs, "The Beehive," "The Hammer," "The Dixy," "The Valley," "The Clatty Dozen," "The Skull," "The Stud," "The Kay" and one or two others that I can't recall. (1977:50)

In 1984, when I interviewed Boyle about gangs in Glasgow and the Gorbals in particular, he said that the gang boys had all turned to heroin and were no longer fighting gangs. However, the gangs during Boyle's youth were violent; in fact, Boyle went to prison for a gang-related murder. So, while the primary conditions associated with gang violence—low income and urban settings—are present, the fighting gangs are not.

It might well be argued that we cannot compare British and American society. Their history and culture are different, and guns are far less available in Great Britain. Nevertheless, the fact that violent youth gangs *did develop* in the Gorbals and were virtually identical to their American cousins suggests that the gang phenomenon can be transcultural. The tricky problem is in identifying exactly what leads to the formation of the violent gang in low income, urban areas independent of the cultural setting.

Origin of Del Sol

Rather than speculating on how gangs form by inference or deduction, I want to take a specific instance of gang formation and examine it for clues. Then, by looking at this example, we can make some inferences. My focus will be the situations surrounding the formation of the gang to see how these situations gave impetus to the gang formation.

The gang being examined is Mexican-American, Del Sol. Its name derives from a low- to medium-income development in the South Bay area of San Diego, not far from the Mexican border. Located between San Ysidro, Otay Mesa, and Imperial Beach, Del Sol was a newer subdivision built in the middle of established communities and gangs.

One of the original members of Del Sol explained how he and a number of other boys formed their gang. In their teenage years, they began going to parties. Other youths at the parties would ask them, "Where are you from?" Such queries can be challenges or simple questions. However, when asked by members of other gangs, the questions are typically challenges. To avoid conflict, the reply "I'm not from anywhere" means the respondent does not claim a gang—at least not at the moment. It is also a way of losing some face and may result in being attacked anyway for being a punk (a weakling).

After being roughed up at several such encounters, a group of Del Sol boys decided that the next time they went to a party together, they would "carry" (bring weapons). If anyone asked them where they were from, they would reply, "*Del Sol. Y que?*" The use of "*Y que?*" in the context of Mexican-American gangs means, "And what are you going to do about it?" It is an unequivocal challenge. If they were attacked, they would bring out their weapons and fight back.

After a number of encounters where challenges were made and answered, Del Sol became recognized as a gang. The recognition was informal, but it was as valid as an organizational charter. The Sidros, and to a lesser extent the Imperiales, Chula Vista Locos, and Otay Locos, immediately became their rivals. Further clashes between Del Sol and other gangs merely verified Del Sol's legitimate claim to a gang.

Like Goffman's *character* that is only realized in a situation that *tests* one's mettle, a gang is only as good as the situations in which it can be defined. Without situations where a gang either must fight or crawl off with its collective tail between its legs, there is no social validation. A gang is initially formed in its willingness to do violence in situations that call on a collective courage or even recklessness. Such situations forge and validate the gangs, and we can see the origin of gangs in such situations. To study gangs, we must understand how fateful circumstances make gangs social realities. Goffman pointedly summarizes the relationship between the situation and the people who inhabit them: "Not, then, men and their moments. Rather moments and their men" (1967:3). In this context, we can understand the origin of gangs.

Before going on, it is important to comment on some implications of the track being followed here. If a gang's origin is in situations created by other gangs, we must eventually seek the cause of the original gang. For now, it is enough to point out that once gangs come into being as a *possible adaptation*, they generate situations that spawn further gangs. In the same way that differential association theory (Sutherland 1947) explains how criminal behavior patterns pass on from one group to another, we can say that gangs generate situations that provide circumstances for further gangs to form. We can speculate that the original gangs may have formed in a similar manner, as groups of youths discovered it was prudent to band together in violent situations where collective efforts won out over individual ones.

Gang Areas

Not surprisingly, most gangs and the great bulk of gang activities occur in low-income areas. The more urban areas had more gang activities, but many of the areas where gang situations occurred are characterized by suburban sprawl.

Socially and economically, San Diego can be divided roughly into two major parts, north and south, with Interstate Highway 8 (I-8) the line of demarcation (see Figure 3.1). North of I-8 within the city limits are numerous suburban communities with light industry and professional employment. The communities include Mission Beach, Pacific Beach, Bay Park, La Jolla, Kearney Mesa, Linda Vista, University City, Scripts Ranch, Mira Mesa, Clairmont, Mission Beach, Rancho Peñasquitos, Carmel Ranch, and Rancho Bernardo. South of I-8 is the city center, the shipyards, and heavier industry. Along the southern rim of I-8 above Mission Valley runs a line of middle- and upper-middle-class communities extending to the ocean and south to Point Loma. South of Balboa

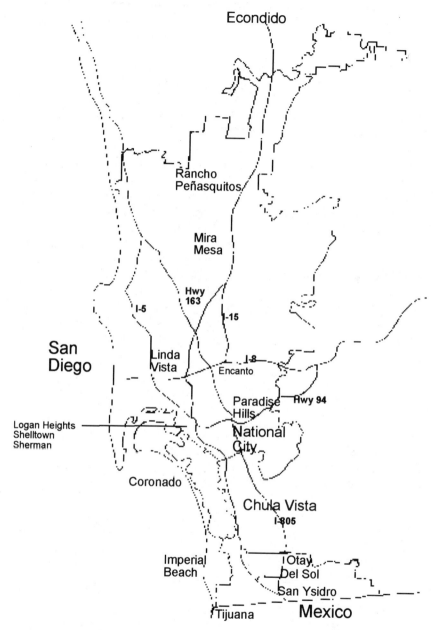

Figure 3.1.　Map of the San Diego area.

Park and south of University Avenue and east of Balboa Park, most of
the communities are working-class and lower-income areas. This area is
generally called Southeast San Diego, encompassing the communities of
Logan Heights, East San Diego, Paradise Hills, Golden Hills, Lomita,
and Encanto. South of Logan Heights are National City, Imperial Beach,
and Chula Vista, separately incorporated cities. The city of San Diego
starts up again south of Chula Vista and East of Imperial Beach. This
area, generally referred to as South Bay, includes the communities of San
Ysidro on the Mexican border, Del Sol, Otay Mesa, Nestor, and Palm
City.

The gang areas within San Diego city limits, are primarily south of I-8.
Linda Vista, Mira Mesa, and Rancho Peñasquitos, north of I-8, had some
gang activity in the later part of the 1980s, primarily Filipino gangs in
Mira Mesa and Rancho Peñasquitos that came into being around 1987. A
group from Clairmont called themselves Varrio Clairmont, but they rarely caused problems other than graffiti. Linda Vista had a sporadic gang
history, but there was relatively light activity in that area until the late
1980s when Southeast Asian–American, Mexican-American, and
African-American gangs appeared. Most of the gangs north of I-8 were
considered "wannabes," and even though there were some instances of
serious gang violence, they paled compared to Southeast San Diego and
South Bay.

ETHNIC COMPOSITION OF SAN DIEGO AND ITS GANGS

San Diego's ethnic composition is rich and complex. The data from
1987 and 1990 give a rough idea of what the ethnic composition looked
like by the second half of the decade (Table 3.1). As can be seen, there is
a trend toward greater minority makeup of the population.

Table 3.1.   San Diego Ethnic Composition (%)
            1987 and 1990

Ethnic group	1987	1990
White	69.2	59
Hispanic	16.9	21
Asian/other	8.5	11
African-American	5.4	9

Source: SANDAG (San Diego Association of Governments).

San Diego's Hispanic population is essentially Mexican-American, with different generations and groups representing different degrees of assimilation and orientation. There are Puerto Ricans, Cubans, and other non-Mexican Hispanics, but they make up a small minority. There were no juvenile gangs that identified with Hispanic origins other than Mexican.

The African- and European-American groups are largely nonethnic Americans. That is, while there are Jamaican blacks and Swedish whites who identify with their country of origin, they are exceptional and do not make up any sizable population of the city.

The most interesting and complex ethnic group in San Diego is the Asian-Americans. They can be divided into three major groups: native Asian-Americans, Filipinos, and refugee Southeast Asian–Americans. The native Asian-Americans, largely of those of Japanese and Chinese ancestry, are generally integrated into American society. This group is heavily represented in the professional and business community and enjoys a higher than average standard of living.

The Filipino-Americans in San Diego represent a post–Vietnam War phenomenon. In exchange for citizenship, many Filipinos served in the U.S. military. After the war, they moved to the United States, many to San Diego. Likewise, many Filipino women received special immigration status to fill a nursing shortage. They are largely middle class, with big populations in Mira Mesa and Rancho Peñasquitos. A lower-income group of Filipinos lives in the Paradise Hills area.

Filipinos represented ideal immigrants for San Diego. They had a low crime rate, their youths excelled in school, and they prided themselves in being good, productive citizens. While they did not assimilate to the extent of losing their Filipino identity, assimilation was relatively smooth.

The refugee Southeast Asians include several dissimilar groups. Their immigration was either forced or chosen after the Vietnam War. Many Chinese-Vietnamese fled Vietnam on overcrowded boats. They and other "boat people," including Hmong, Laotians, Cambodians, and ethnic Vietnamese, who came to San Diego with little or nothing. (There were also a number of Vietnamese who worked for the United States and were able to leave with some financial resources, but they were in an earlier immigration at the very end of the Vietnam War.)

A large refugee population settled in the Linda Vista area and in an area between Southeast San Diego and the southern rim communities of I-8. The poorer Asian refugees ended up in Linda Vista and East San Diego, including many Hmong, Laotians, and Cambodians. Vietnamese refugees came to dominate the area between East San Diego and the Kensington-College area financially.

Gang Ethnicity

In the early 1980s, gang activity was about a 40–60 split between African-Americans and Mexican-Americans. When other ethnic groups were involved in gang incidents, it was usually as victim. By 1988, there were a sizable number of reports of Filipino-American gang incidents, but the vast majority of the gang violence was African- and Mexican-American (see Table 3.2).

Near the end of the decade, the picture had changed by the inclusion of the Filipino-American gangs and the slight relative reduction of the Mexican-American gangs. Nevertheless, the gang scene was dominated by the African- and Mexican-American gangs. By 1990, the Southeast Asian–American gangs also came to be part of the ethnic picture of gang activity in San Diego.

Before continuing, we must consider why other low-income urban groups were not involved in gang activity. We will first examine the low-income whites, of whom there were plenty, and then the Asian-Americans.

Lack of White Gangs.   A problem with structural explanations of gang formation is that not all cohorts with the same structural situation have gangs. The white youths who live in Southeast San Diego and South Bay share the same low-income, urban setting as the Southeast Asian–, Afri-can-, and Mexican-American youths, but they do not form white gangs and generally do not join the few mixed ethnic gangs found in San Diego.

The single white group identified in a Sheriff's Office publication was a group called the Death Wish Kids. This group's major claim to being a gang was spraying DWK on sidewalks and walls. (Members of other gangs referred to DWK as standing for any "dumb white kid" with a spray can.) They were not involved in any reports of violence nor identified as victims of violence by other gangs. The police did not list them as a gang and saw them as an occasional nuisance, like doper groups and other amorphous clusters.

This is not to say that white violent youth gangs do not exist, but they

Table 3.2.   1988 Reported Incidents of Gang Activity (%) by Ethnic Background (N = 184)

Hispanic	44
African-American	42
Filipino	14

simply were not found in San Diego. Jankowski, who studied gangs at virtually the same time as I, identified both Irish- and Italian-American youth gangs on the East Coast. Likewise, the violent fighting gangs identified in Glasgow were white.

One explanation for the lack of white gangs in San Diego is the lack of white ethnic group identity. In Boston, New York, Philadelphia, and other Eastern cities, there are communities that identify with an Irish, Polish, or Italian heritage. Lower-class boys in these identifiable white ethnic groups can share a common belief that they are the victims of discrimination by a dominant group of whites, usually identified as WASPs (white Anglo-Saxon Protestants). Jankowski (1991:84–86) noted that the Irish-American gangs of Boston saw themselves victimized by the white, Brahmin, blue bloods who paid them low wages and gave unfair competitive advantages to nonwhite minorities. Certainly Irish as well as Polish and Italian history documents discrimination by dominant whites, fostering a "we versus them" ideology.

San Diego poor white youths lacked the ideology or the history of being singled out for their membership in a white ethnic group. They may have been very conscious of being white, especially those who shared poverty with a majority who were black or brown, but they themselves did not see whites as a despised ethnic or nationality group.

There was no love lost between the poor whites and poor nonwhites. Indeed there is a long history of fistfights between the "surfers" (mostly white) and "beaners" (derogatory term for Mexicans) in Southern California. However, a former Chicano gang member, who still professed a hatred of surfers, said that the clashes between the whites and Mexican-Americans typically did not involve weapons. They were fistfights, even when they involved Mexican-American gang members. They were episodic, and they did not involve either side seeking out the other. White youths from the Huntington Beach area in Orange County (north of San Diego) reported similar nonlethal clashes between themselves and Mexican-American youths.

Although there was some conflict between white youths and nonwhite youths in low-income areas, the whites did not form gangs. What's more, the ethnic groups that did form gangs reserved severe violence for members of rival gangs from their own ethnic background; the occasional encounters they had with groups of white youths resulted in largely unreported fistfights.

Rise of Filipino and Southeast Asian Gangs. While we can argue that poor whites lacked a strong ethnic identity, the same cannot be said for Asian-American groups. The first Oriental group that generated gang activity to any extent was the Filipinos. Except for the Asian-Americans who had been in the country several generations, the Filipinos were better off than other Asian-Americans. Several Southeast Asian refugee groups that arrived as boat people, were poor, highly identifiable, unable to speak English, and targets of discrimination at the hands of just about everyone, including other Asian refugee groups. By 1990, the Lao, Khmer, and Hmong also had gangs, but the Vietnamese did not.

Kenji Ima,[2] who has studied Asian refugees in San Diego for years, offers a cultural explanation: The Chinese-Vietnamese and Vietnamese have a certain cultural pride, even arrogance, that does not need a role model in the American gangs. They feel themselves culturally superior not only to the Filipino-, African-, and Mexican-Americans, let alone the Hmong, Laotians, and Khmers, but also to whites. As a result, they stick closely to their own cultural patterns with the confidence that they will overcome the temporary obstacles of low income. What's more, compared to the situation they left in Vietnam, the Asian refugees are relatively better off. Also, the Chinese-Vietnamese do not suffer the Chinese-specific discrimination they did in Vietnam, and so they see their relative opportunities as much better.

Ima also notes that the Hmong, Laotians, and Cambodians desperately seek role models, which they found in the gangs in their neighborhoods. The African- and Mexican-American gangs, who picked on them as "chinks" and "gooks" provided them with the models of gang violence. They adopted the styles of violence in drive-by shootings, but they did not adopt the *cholo* style of the Mexican-Americans. The Southeast Asian gang style was their own, with certain characteristics of the African-American gangs.

However, if we use cultural explanations to separate gang from nongang groups, we will need to watch for cultural clues in the makeup of existing gangs as well as exceptions in nongangs. In turn, this will help us understand how the specific situations become defined as conditions for gang actions or not, and how culture serves as an interpretive scheme in formulating those definitions.

Inter- and Intraethnic Gang Activity

One of the more interesting patterns among San Diego gangs is their avoidance of interethnic gang rivalries. Both African-American and Mexican-American gang members responded to questions about interethnic gang conflict with "live and let live." African-Americans and Mexican-Americans expressed respect for the other's power. Although Mexican-Americans, outnumbered African-Americans by three to one, they believed that the Crips and Bloods were very powerful. The attitude expressed by both groups was summed up in the sentiment, "Who needs more trouble? We've got enough to handle now."

An exception to the apparent ban on interethnic gang violence is the conflict between Southeast Asian gangs and certain other gangs. The Oriental Boy Soldiers (Khmer) and the East San Diego (Mexican) traded drive-by shootings in 1990. Likewise, Southeast Asian–American gangs attacked black gangs. What little data was available suggested that the Southeast Asian gangs were getting even for past transgressions against them and making their mark in the neighborhood. In one case, some Pirus (African-American) roughed up a Cambodian boy. For the entire following week, Southeast Asian–American gang members went through the Pirus' neighborhood and shot at any African-Americans they saw, whether they were gang members or not. Similarly, in the feud between the Oriental Boy Soldiers and East San Diego, the targets are often non–gang members.

Interethnic gang conflict exists in situations where one ethnic group is targeted by another. African-, Filipino-, and Mexican-American youths are likely to be bullied by gang members of their own ethnic group. From their viewpoint, the situations of violence involve *gang members* not gang members of a particular *ethnic group*. In the case of the Southeast Asian–Americans, they were picked on by gangs of African- or Mexican-Americans. Not only were these gang members of a different ethnic background, but there were no Southeast Asian–Americans in the gangs. So their situations of encounter was viewed as *interethnic*, not just gang related. As a result, when they formed gangs for protection, they protected themselves from gangs of other ethnic origins. Del Sol boys, discussed earlier in this chapter, formed a gang in opposition to *foreign* gangs in San Ysidro, Imperial Beach, and Otay Mesa; the Southeast Asian–Americans formed gangs in opposition to *foreign* gangs. It was incidental that the gangs against whom the Southeast Asian–Americans fought were of a different ethnic background.

For the most part, though, the interethnic conflict was the exception rather than the rule. Moreover, when interethnic conflict did occur, it was not an ethnic or racial matter; it was a matter of money or drugs. For example, a robbery victim's ethnic background is largely irrelevant to gang members.

The lack of interethnic conflict becomes evident in examining the 1988 data. Table 3.3 shows the breakdown in gang-related incidents. The great bulk of gang activity is directed against others of the same ethnic background. About a third of the Filipinos' actions were against Hispanics and whites. However, most of the actions against Hispanics were directed at the Paradise Hills Locos, a Mexican-American gang that affiliated with a Filipino gang.

Table 3.3.   Ethnic Background (%) of Offender
and Victim in 1988 (N = 183)

Black vs.	
Black	32.2
Hispanic	1.1
Asian	0.5
White	2.2
Hispanic vs.	
Hispanic	29.0
Black	2.2
Filipino	2.2
White	4.4
Unknown	0.5
Filipino vs.	
Filipino	7.7
Hispanic	1.6
White	2.2
Unknown	0.5
Asian vs. Asian	0.5
Unknown vs.	
Black	7.7
Hispanic	4.4
Filipino	0.5
Asian	0.5

Actions against whites and most Asian-Americans was not intergang violence. Since the Southeast Asian–American gangs were not active until 1989–1990, their conflict with the Mexican-American gangs is not reflected in the 1988 data. Likewise, much of the intraethnic assaults were on non–gang members. The 1981 data showed that 71.4% of all gang violence was directed at non–gang members. However, by 1988, the number of recorded gang incidents against non–gang members was only about 27.2 percent. This reflected, in part, the lower number of robberies gangs committed in 1988 as they found greater profits in the sale of rock cocaine. Since robbery victims were typically non–gang members, there was a higher proportion of them in the 1981 data compared to the 1988 data.

PATTERNS OF GANG ACTIVITY

This section examines certain general patterns of gang violence. In attempting to understand situations of gang violence, it is necessary to examine several general variables. Included in these variables are month, time of day, day of week, and hours of offense. Sometimes by stepping back and examining such variables, we can infer clues to other features of the violent situations that may have been overlooked from inside the situation. The data are quantified from information gathered in 1981 and 1988 when I got a 100 percent sample of the gang detail's data. These data are based on firsthand observations and information from police reports.

Month

Aside from a dip in September, all the months of gang violence show only a little variation, and month does not seem to be a good predictor (Table 3.4). August is relatively high for both years, and April had the most incidents in 1988. The beginning of school may explain the dip in September as the gang boys come under the renewed formality the *beginning* of school brings. However, as we will see later, most gang kids drop out of school or routinely ditch. So there may be some other reason for the September low in gang violence.

Day and Time

We can better pinpoint the patterns of gang violence by looking at the time and day instead of the month. Table 3.5 shows that the weekend days are relatively high. In part, *but only in part*, this is due to the large

Table 3.4. Percentage of Incidents by Month, 1981 and 1988

Month	1981 (N = 144)	1988 (N = 183)
January	11.8	9.3
February	6.3	8.7
March	6.9	6.6
April	7.6	11.5
May	8.3	7.1
June	7.6	8.2
July	10.4	7.7
August	13.2	10.9
September	3.5	4.4
October	9.0	9.8
November	7.6	9.8
December	7.6	6.0

Table 3.5.   Percentage of Incidents by Day for 1981
         and 1988

	1981 (N = 144)	1988 (N = 183)
Sunday	22.9	21.3
Monday	11.8	12.0
Tuesday	10.4	9.8
Wednesday	15.3	13.7
Thursday	11.8	10.9
Friday	9.7	13.7
Saturday	18.1	18.6

number of youths who are in the controlled situation of school during the week. Goffman (1963:198–215) describes situations on a continuum of *tightness-looseness*. Tightness can be equated somewhat with *formality* and looseness with *informality*. As an occasion, school is fairly tight; its situations are delineated by seating patterns, course content, a rigid timing, and a clear set of sanctions for violations. There is not much room to break out, and while gang violence does occur during school-time, it usually does not. (I hasten to add that one former gang member told me that extortion of lunch money from students was routine, occurring in the loose-behavior settings of the boys' rest room and school yard. The *threat of violence*, though, rarely brought the attention of the police and was usually enough to persuade kids to give up their lunch money.)

Nonschool situations for youths are looser, the boundaries are not as clear, and there are more options for things to get out of hand. Attempts at sanctions are met with demands to *loosen up*, reflecting the nature of the occasion and relatively undefined boundaries of appropriate actions.

The effect of schooltime in controlling gang activities is evident when we consider time of day (Table 3.6). Gang violence rises as school ends, jumps again during the after-dinner hours, peaks during the late evening, and decreases during late night hours after 2:00 a.m.

Surprisingly, a higher proportion of gang violence occurs during the weekdays while school is in session than on weekends. Of the eleven incidents of gang violence that occurred between 6:00 a.m. and 2:00 p.m. in 1988, nine were during school days, and only two on weekends. Likewise, in comparing months and time of gang violence, we found that 91 percent occurred during school months. So, while we found that few incidents of gang violence occurred during schooltime, there were fewer such incidents during weekends and summer months during schooltime hours.

Table 3.6. Time of Gang Offenses (%) for 1981 and
1988

Time	1981 (N = 144)	1988 (N = 183)
0601–1000	4.2	2.2
1001–1400	7.0	3.9
1401–1800	20.3	18.2
1801–2200	26.6	30.9
2201–0200	33.6	33.7
0201–0600	8.4	11.0

A final interesting note concerns gang violence on Sunday. When this was first noted in 1981, the police suspected that it was probably late Saturday night incidents that were officially recorded as Sunday ones. However, the bulk of the Sunday incidents occur *Sunday night*, not late Saturday. This may be due to the culmination of loose occasions that characterize *time-off* or *time-out* periods (Goffman 1961:34–66). Missed opportunities and revenge (paybacks) may simply be coming to a head before the week tightens up with Monday.

PATTERNS OF VIOLENT SITUATIONS

This section is an overview of the general trends of gang violence. We examine the legal offense, type of gang offense, weapons used, and location of offense during 1981 and 1988. These features provide an overall sense of the nature of San Diego gang violence.

Table 3.7 shows that assault, coded under California Penal Code 245

Table 3.7. Typical Gang Offenses 1981 and 1988 as
Percentage of All Known Gang Offenses

Offense	1981 (N = 144)	1988 (N = 183)
Homicide	3.5	14.2
Attempted homicide	5.6	0.5
Assault	41.0	62.3
Shooting	4.2	9.8
Robbery	30.6	4.9
Other	15.3	8.2

Table 3.8.   Types of Violent Incident (%) 1981 and 1988

Type	1981 (N = 144)	1988 (N = 161)
Drive-by	15.3	38.5
Fight	10.4	9.3
Assault	38.9	46.6
Robbery	35.4	5.6

(245 PC), is the most common form of gang violence. Assaults rose from 1981 to 1988. Homicides and shootings also jumped. The offenses coded as shootings under 246 PC typically occurred when shots were fired at a house or vehicle with no clear human target. Sometimes shootings were classified as assaults (245 PC) if there were occupants in the house.

Robberies show the major drop between 1981 and 1988. As noted earlier, this drop was explained by the rise in crack cocaine sales by gangs. Robberies were just not as profitable.

Table 3.8 shows the breakdown of gang violence into more specific types. General assault is the most common form of gang violence. In 1988, the drive-by shooting replaced robbery as the second most common gang attack. Fights between large groups of gang members remained fairly low; they usually occurred when rival gangs met at a commonly used park or the beach. Gangs much preferred drive-by shootings to a melee. The overall trend for gangs to use hit and run tactics, such as drive-by shootings, was noted by Miller (1975:39) in the 1970s. It appears that, as gang use of manufactured guns increased, the melee began declining because the new weapons produced more casualties. Earlier gangs had relied on homemade zip guns, inaccurate, with fairly low muzzle velocity.

Given California's expansive cities, gang territory is not well-suited for treks by a large number of youths to a gang fight. Large groups could be spotted by the police, and if the gang broke up in smaller groups to rejoin for a rumble with a rival, the segments could be attacked en route to the fight. The drive-by shooting is a tactic that lets gangs cope with the spread-out city and survive retaliation. It is a quick in-and-out foray, and it can harm a rival.

Guns were very common in both 1981 and 1988 (Table 3.9). However, by 1988, the use of guns had eclipsed all other weapons. In 1981, only about a third of the violent reported incidents involved guns, but by 1988, over half of gang situations involved some type of firearm.

Table 3.10 shows that the favored location for gang violence did not

Table 3.9. Gang Weapons (%) 1981 and 1988

Type	1981 (N = 144)	1988 (N = 183)
None	3.5	7.1
Pistol	9.0	27.3
Shotgun	2.8	9.3
Rifle	11.8	2.7
Unknown gun	9.7	20.2
Knife	19.4	14.8
Club	6.9	5.5
Rock	1.4	1.1
Body	22.9	5.5
Bottle	3.5	0.5
Multiple	9.0	6.0

change; in 1981 and 1988 the streets provided the setting for most gang violence. School and recreation centers are seldom the place for gang violence. As noted previously, these settings are tighter and more controlled than the wide-open streets. However, private homes are settings for a number of gang incidents; like the streets, homes typically offer loose boundaries for appropriate behavior.

TRENDS

From 1980 to 1988 the rate of violent gang activity showed an overall decline, although incidents began increasing steadily after 1986 (Figure 3.2). During the same period, the police gang detail grew. Critics of

Table 3.10. Location of Gang Violence 1981 and 1988

Location	1981 (N = 137)	1988 (N = 182)
Private home	13.9	20.3
Park	7.3	6.6
Street	54.0	52.7
School	1.5	1.1
Recreation center	0.7	1.6
Other	22.6	17.6

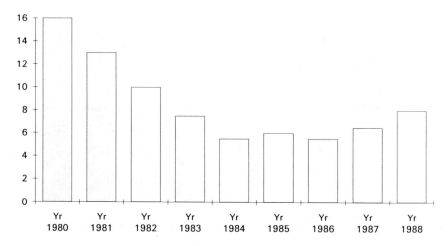

Figure 3.2.   Rates of recorded gang incidents per 100,000 population.

police labeling incidents as *gang related* expected that there would be more reports of gang violence because more personnel were available to locate and record gang activities. However, instead of an increase in police recording of gang activity, there was a decrease. This may be due to refinements in police reporting practices, especially focusing on the more violent crimes, or it could have been due to an actual drop in gang activities.

Another measure of gang violence is to take the most serious cases, gang-related homicides, and compare them over time (Chart 3.3). We

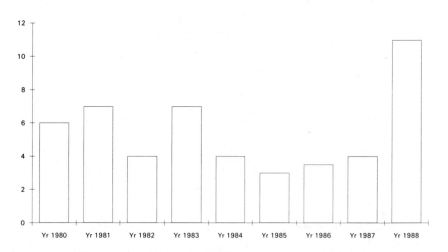

Figure 3.3.   Rate of gang-related homicides 1980–1988.

find a more uneven curve than the incident rate data show; however, it is clear that there was a decline during the middle of the decade and a jump in 1988.

That jump in gang related homicides in 1988 has been largely attributed to the "crack cocaine wars." Most of the wars involved the Crips and Pirus, either against one another or gangs from Los Angeles. Of the gang-related homicides for 1988, 62 percent involved African-American victims, while only 42 percent of the gang activities involved African-American gang members. (In 1988 only 30 percent of the gang-related homicides involved Hispanics as either victims or perpetrators while they accounted for 44 percent of the gang-related incidents.)

It is always a problem to trace trends and patterns in agencies upon whom the researcher is dependent on defining criteria. Moreover, different jurisdictions have different definitions of what constitutes gang incidents and gang-related homicides (Maxson and Klein 1990:71–100). However, since the research data were culled from a single organization in this research, there is more uniformity in recording incidents. While this does not automatically mean there is uniformity over time in a single organization, there is a better possibility of it.

Another counting problem arises when there are a high number of homicides involving the sale of drugs. Some analysts suggest we not treat these killings as gang-related since the driving motive is competition for money in drug transactions and not traditional gang-motivated violence (Moore 1993:36–38). The upswing in drug-gang-related homicides in 1988 then may be discounted by some analysts as a true indication of increased gang violence. I believe there is a confusion between gangs as dynamic organizations with different modes of behavior and a more stable yet unrealistic conception of gangs. The Crips and Pirus were committing violent acts in the early 1980s when they were not involved in crack cocaine sales. When they became involved in crack cocaine distribution, they did it in the same bounded territories they had maintained since their inception. Indeed, they did change, but the change was primarily in adopting crack cocaine, not in giving up everything else the gang was doing. So while the gang had added another activity that may have led to increased violence, it was still gang-related violence.

Active and Inactive Gangs

Is a gang a gang if it is not involved in violent gang activity? The thesis proposed here is that a gang that is not involved in violent gang situations ceases to be a gang. However, there is a gang shell or inactive gang that can perpetuate the name and history of a gang. At a later time, the inactive gang can be rejuvenated by a cohort willing to engage in gang violence. A useful distinction in examining gangs is that of an active and inactive gang. Between 1981 and 1988, the activities of gangs changed. Some gangs became more active and others became less active. Table 3.11 shows a sample of gangs and the different amount of activity they had during the two different years.

A few post-1988 observations and discussions with former gang members indicated that gangs like Del Sol and Sidro, while inactive for a time, were becoming active again. Likewise, the Setentas (70s), who seem to have cut their gang activity way back by 1988, were heavily involved in wars with Paradise Hills Locos and the VELs by 1991. Likewise, the Southeast Asian gangs were active by 1990.

Organizationally, gangs can make the transition between neighborhood street groups (inactive gangs) and fighting gangs (active gangs). The neighborhood constitutes a source of solidarity, and the tradition of the gang is part of the oral history of the neighborhood. Thus, a gang shell, *not core*, can be maintained while no violent gang activity occurs.

Cyclical Activity and Age Cohorts

Gangs changed from inactive to active and back to inactive over time. Without a hard-core element willing to do violence, a gang is inactive.

Table 3.11.   Comparison of Attacking Gangs 1981 and 1988, Number of Incidents

Gang	1981	1988
5/9 Brim Pirus	4	5
70s	5	1
Be Down Boys[a]	—	8
Del Sol	6	0
East San Diego	1	0
Lincoln Park Pirus	6	7
Logan	13	18
Lomas	5	2
Neighborhood Crips	4	5
Shelltown	8	8
Sherman	1	6
Sidro	16	0
VELs	10	3
West Coast Crips	25	10

[a]Gang did not exist in 1981.

With passing generations, new cohorts, tutored in gang lore, come to dominate the central position of a gang. If a cohort has a violent hard core, it defines the gang's violent stance. This cohort does not have to be the older boys but can be a very young group. As one of the Vice Lords from Keiser's study noted,

> The roughest boys I ever met, they was between the ages of 13 and 15— Lil' Lord, Rough-head and them. They was the Midgets—the Midget Lords. And these were the baddest boys I ever went up against! (Keiser 1969:16)

As a new age cohort of boys comes into the gang, the level of activity rises. After a time, they either make their names, become more aware of the risks they are taking, or become cowed by the police or other gangs. When this occurs, the gang's activity subsides.

One gang, Del Sol, was hit so hard in 1981 that it was notably less active in 1988. Three Del Sol homeboys were murdered in 1981, and to some extent this may have turned the community against the gang. Jankowski (1991:32–34) argues that a gang must be accepted by local residents in the community. Local residents can make life more or less difficult for gang members and *vice versa*. When gangs attract undue police attention or other gangs who shoot up the community, the gang is harming the community. After several drive-by shootings, including shootings into family homes, there may have been enough pressure on Del Sol to forgo provoking violent situations that would harm the community.

One gang member who said that the girls in the community acted as catalysts for gang violence also noted that they could serve the opposite purpose. They could shun gang boys and the *cholo* style, and generally serve notice that they would have nothing to do with the gang life-style. Of course a number of "nice girls" in the community did exactly that, but several girls had romantic ideals of the homeboys who were in gangs. They supported the gangbangers through dating and recognition, but they were not *cholas* or gang girls. The boyfriend of one such girl, who was becoming ever more enamored with the gang life-style, was stabbed to death by a rival gang. After that incident, she wholly withdrew her support of the gang life-style, blaming them for her boyfriend's death. Likewise, a girl's parents may put pressure on their daughter's to avoid gang boys.

Thus, in times of low community support, gangs may become less active. The measurement of community support is somewhat problematic. Usually the extent to which community members actively assist the police and provide information to hamper gang business (e.g., report crack houses, locate gang hangouts, identify gang members) support is low. However all-out community cooperation with the police against the gangs may produce a sudden rise in *reported* gang activity, making it appear as through the gang is more active. Eventually, though, we should expect gang activity to wane after loss of community support. A good example of this occurred with the Syndo Mob. After community members became upset over the crack cocaine trade wars and the drug in their community, they worked with the police to run the gang out of the community. After heavy police and community pressure in 1988, the Syndo Mob was notably less active.

Graffiti

Gang graffiti is only tangentially related to gang violence, but it is an important part of gang life. Gang names, the street names of their members, and various self-laudatory and rival-deprecatory comments make up a typical gang sign or *placaso* (or *placa*). Some are quite simple and crude, while others are elaborate artistic affairs.

The terms *gangsters, gang, gangbangers,* and *mob* show up frequently in gang graffiti, telling us something about their self-identity. Crips and Piru graffiti often include the characters C/K, P/K, or B/K, which stand for Crip-killer, Piru-killer, or Blood-killer, respectively. Chicano gangs, though, did not have anything in their *placasos* that derogated rival gangs. Instead, in a very stylized spray-painting or drawing, they would put the name of their gang followed by the street names of their homeboys. Usually, they would only put in the names of their clique, not the entire gang. By 1992, a popular style was to put the numbers of the alphabet representing the first letters of the words of their gang name. For example, the Red Steps used 1819 and Shelltown (or Shell Town) used 1920.

When a gang wants to cause a rival gang to lose face, they paint an X over their rival's *placaso*, and place their own name on the wall. When an "X-ing out" occurred, it was usually taken as a direct challenge by the offended gang.

Gang Names

Like graffiti, gang names are only tangentially related to gang violence. The main characteristic of a gang name is the inclusion of its area. Even names like the VELs include territory (the acronym is for Varrio Encanto Locos; Encanto is a community in San Diego). The VELs' rival gang, the 70s, is named after 70th Street, which divides Lomita Village from Encanto.

Gangs like the Crips and Bloods (Pirus) may or may not have a territorial name. The Lincoln Park Pirus have a definite location in their name, while the West Coast Crips are far vaguer in specifying location. Groups like the Neighborhood Crips have territory in their name, but like *varrio*, the *hood* is a generic name for any African-American gang's neighborhood, even though it has a special meaning for the Neighborhood Crips. Comments such as "Hood rules" refer to the Neighborhood Crips and not just any gang in the hood.

Some gangs, though, such as the Be Down Boys[3] and the 5/9 Brims do not include any territorial claims in their name. And some of the most widely used names, Crips and Bloods, do not have close territorial ties. While the Bloods originated with a high school color, and hence territory, there are Bloods that have no clue as to the origin of their name. Likewise, even though Piru was the name of a street in Compton, there are Pirus all over that do not identify with the territory in Piru Street. There does not seem to be a requirement for territory in a name, but most gangs use it.

Nondelinquent Pastimes

The final topic we should consider in this chapter is how gangs spend their time. In interviews with gang boys, they said that most of the time they were like any other youth groups. They looked forward to going to parties, spending time with friends in situations of pure sociability, and spending time at home with their families. Compared to nondelinquent youth groups, there was probably more drug and alcohol use, involvement in other types of nonviolent delinquency, and higher rates of school dropout and truancy, but overall gangs do not spend most of their time being violent.

Those who have spent a considerable amount of time living among gangs, including Miller (1969), Keiser (1969), Klein (1971), and Jankowski (1991), note that most of what gang boys do is not delinquent. Klein noted,

> What do gang boys do—how do they spend their time? Offhand, I can think of few categories of people who are less exiting to observe than gang members simply because, by and large, they just stand around and do nothing! Certainly, their involvement in delinquent episodes in so infrequent that one must wait many months before sufficient offenses have taken place to provide the grist for the statistician's mill. This is perhaps the most important fact about gang behavior—most of it is nondelinquent. (1971:123)

Before continuing, it should be pointed out that with the heavy use and sale of drugs by gangs now common, it is difficult to be out of some type of delinquent situation for gang members. Selling drugs is often nothing more than hanging out and waiting for customers to come and buy. Thus, while the appearance of doing nothing is still the same, the activity may in fact be selling dope.

It is this juxtaposition between normal adolescent pastimes and the explosive violence that makes understanding gangs so problematic. In my own experiences with gangs, the police and I would stop and talk to them at one of their gathering places. They would be charming, full of bravado, surprisingly talkative, and full of questions about what police and I were doing. Indeed some were sullen and silent, but they were the exception rather than the rule. Soon after such light encounters, the same group of boys may be involved in a shooting or stabbing. So, while the bulk of the situations in which these boys find themselves is common to most adolescents, there is the underlying possibility of deadly violence. It is the attack upon or the defense of their area, the payback, the drive-by shooting, or the chance encounter with rival gang members that was always a possibility. In many ways the gang is something other than a gang until there is a situation present to bring it to life.

NOTES

1.   Jankowski (1991:9) notes that there is higher density in the individual living units in the lower-density low-income areas of the West Coast than the casual observer would readily see.

2.   These comments were based on discussions I had with Dr. Ima, and as of this writing were not published. Elsewhere in the book there are references to published works by Ima.

3.   The name Be Down Boys may have originated from the gang credo, "Being down for the neighborhood."

4

Drive-Bys

INTRODUCTION

This chapter closely examines one of the key violent situations associated with gang life: drive-by shootings. I have attempted to explore this phenomenon from several different angles in order to provide a fully developed understanding of it. First, it is examined in terms of a historical background to see how drive-bys replaced other types of gang violence as a favored tactic. Then, using Erving Goffman's concept of *strategic interaction*, we evaluate drive-bys as a strategy. Further using Goffman's notions of character and identity developed in situations, we see how a gang identity can be found in the context of a drive-by. Finally, we look at the different types of situations where drive-bys develop and how they develop.

THE DRIVE-BY SHOOTING IN THE CONTEXT OF GANG WARFARE

A drive-by shooting occurs when members of one gang drive a vehicle into a rival gang's area and shoot at someone. As used here, the drive by is a hit-and-run tactic and does not include situations where members of one gang, who happen to have guns, arrive at a location in a car, and then later on encounter rival gang members and use their guns. However, drive-bys *do* include situations where gang members drive to a location, find a target, jump out of the car, chase the victim down, and then flee in the car after the shooting. The idea of a drive-by is that it is a hit-and-run maneuver, and whether someone temporarily leaves their car is not considered analytically important. The following examples provide a sense of the range of types of drive-by shootings:

> The victims, some members of Da Boys, were at home. Some Be Down Boys drove up, got out of the car, and shot at the victims, their car,

and dog. After firing several shots, they got back in their car and drove away.

Members of Eastside Piru were hanging out in front of a liquor store when a car drove by. Some Crips in the car said, "What's up, blood?" The Pirus ignored them and walked away. After a Piru member refused to come over to their car, the Crips began firing, hitting the victim three times. Then the Crips drove away.

A member of the Neighborhood Crips was sitting on a wall when he heard a car drive up. He turned to look at the car and then turned back. At this point he was shot in the head. The victim ran into a friend's house, noting only that the shooter was wearing red. [Red is the color of the Crips' rivals, the Bloods/Pirus.]

Some VELs were standing in front of their house when two 70s on a motorcycle drove by and shot a pistol at the house and car, hitting the car.

Some Varrio Market Street boys were standing outside when four VELs drove up and yelled, "Encanto, Encanto!" and asked, "Where are you from?" When the victims replied "Varrio Market!" the VELs started shooting.

Sometime after World War II, gangs introduced the term *japping* to refer to hit-and-run attacks (Klein 1971:24). The term came from certain unorthodox strategies used in the war by Japanese soldiers, especially shooting from hidden positions behind Allied lines. It was an unconventional mobile warfare discovered by the gangs. Walter Miller (1975:36–38) used the term *foray* to characterize these mobile tactics. This type of gang warfare is in contrast to the melee or rumble, where gangs meet at appointed places and times to do battle in large groups.

In the traditional East Coast cities with high-density populations, narrow streets, and congested traffic, a foray was often conducted on foot or bicycle. The neighborhoods are relatively close, and gang members were able to make a quick attack and get back to the safety of their own area before the other gang could mobilize for a counterstrike. It would even be possible to make a hit-and-run attack using public transportation, such as the subway.

On the West Coast, particularly in Southern California, the neighborhoods are further apart, more spread out, more likely to be on the ground level, and have lower density. There is an excellent road system and relatively little public transportation. The automobile is the primary mode of transportation, and using the freeway system, an attacker can quickly return to his home base miles away from the site of the shooting. It was in this type of situation that the drive-by shooting developed.

In San Diego, there was an increasing use of the drive-by shooting from the early 1980s to the end of the decade. Table 4.1 shows the jump in drive-by shootings as a percentage of gang attacks from the early

Table 4.1. Percentage of All Gang Assaults
That Are Drive-By Shootings

Year	Drive-bys
1981	23.7
1988	40.8

1980s to the later part of the decade. As can be seen, the drive-by almost doubled in proportion to non-drive-by assaults from the beginning to the end of the decade.

STRATEGIC INTERACTION AND DRIVE-BY SHOOTINGS

Analytically, we can understand drive-by shootings as a rational reaction to the conditions of gang warfare. Erving Goffman (1969:100–101) describes *strategic interaction* as those situations where people come together under conditions of mutual fatefulness. The *players* in these situations attempt to dope out what the other is going to do, and make the best possible *move* to maximize their chances of surviving the encounter. Since the level of violence used has escalated in the situations of gang warfare, they are literally life-and-death ones.

As situations come to be more and more those of life and death, the notion of chivalry takes on a different tone. In encounters with knives and clubs, one could well spare the life of (or limit the wounds upon) an opponent. It was not only a chivalrous move, it was one that might be repaid later, and as such, was a strategic move. A victor who did not finish off an opponent with a fatal blow or shot could receive as much honor for chivalry as he could for ending the opponent's life. The value was in the honor, not just the victory.

In gang warfare, as it became clear that face-to-face encounters with manufactured guns should be short in duration, the automobile was seen as a resource to make such meetings as brief as possible. Only in situations of pure recklessness would an assembled group stand before opponents who were displaying firearms.

When manufactured firearms began to be used by gangs on a large scale in the 1970s, the old-style rumble was replaced without ceremony by the *foray* (Miller 1975). In the wide-open spaces of Southern California, the drive-by became the adopted style of the foray.

In the context of gang warfare the drive-by shooting is the military equivalent of getting hit by an unseen shell. Since there is an almost constant enemy but there are not constant staged battles, a drive-by is something that can happen anywhere, any time. What's more, a drive-by is hidden in the normal appearances of its surroundings (Goffman 1971:238–82). A car driving down San Diego streets is a normal occurrence, and like all such mundane events is seen but unnoticed. When bullets or shotgun pellets suddenly begin spewing from a car, it is too late. Since about 80 percent of all drive-by shootings were in the evening or at night (between 6 p.m. and 6 a.m.), noting a vehicle belonging to a rival gang is even more problematic. The following case provides an instance where the most mundane of situations can be transformed into a deadly one:

> The victim, a Syndo Mob member, was working inside his car on the back window. He saw a white van back down the alley. When the van's passenger side door came in front of his car, a Piru pointed an Uzi machine gun at him and fired eighteen rounds, hitting his car several times but missing him.

Given the swift and deadly nature of drive-by shootings, gang members live in a very real situation of sudden death. Considering the stances to unpredictable danger, Goffman suggests postures that can be "deer-like, ever ready to be startled, . . . cow-like, slow to be mobilized, or lion-like, unconcerned about predators and wary chiefly when stalking prey" (1971:242–43). One might expect the general stance to be either deerlike, especially when separated from fellow gang members, or lionlike, demonstrating heart to the gang. However, a good deal of the postures of the targets appeared to be cowlike. This could be due to the frequent use of alcohol and drugs by gang members. Since partying was a major pastime for gang members, and parties consisted of drinking, illicit drug use, dancing, and sex, it would be trying indeed to maintain full alert on such occasions. Intoxicated gang members make easy targets. The following illustrates a relaxed interlude being transformed into a situation of high alarm:

> A member of the Neighborhood Crips and his girlfriend were sitting on what was described as an "electrical box" [possibly a phone company switching box]. He heard several shots fired and pulled his girlfriend towards him when he realized she had been shot.

As an aside, we should note that drug use is a general part of gang life. At one time, gangs reportedly would not stand for members who used heroin because they were considered unreliable in gang fights (Bernstein 1957). However, a former Mexican-American gang member active in the 1970s reported in interviews that he had not only been addicted to heroin, but was dependent on other drugs as well. However, he had been considered an active, core member of the gang. When he was sent to Youth Authority, it was for violent activities, not drug addiction. The idea that heroin users are in too much of a stupor to do anything other than nod off or search for more drugs simply is not true. Like other drugs, the context and understanding of heroin use is as important as the pharmacological effects. In the 1950s gangs used marijuana prior to gang fights, while hippies used the same drug in the 1960s for love-ins. The drug was the same, but it was used for very different purposes. In the late 1960s when drug use became more acceptable among the young, its use among gang members also became more acceptable. This was not a gang-specific change, but a generational and societal one.

Jankowski (1991:80–82) found that Chicano gangs in Los Angeles seemed to be the only ones that tolerated heroin. Most of the gangs Jankowski studied did not mind the use of marijuana, cocaine, some amphetamines, and alcohol, but they drew the line at heroin because they considered addicts unreliable. In gangs whose primary purpose was to raise money, a heroin junkie could not be counted upon to help the gang financially since his primary focus would be on spending every cent he had on heroin.

Jankowski (1991:81) noted that Chicano and Irish-American gangs were organized primarily for entertainment, and so financial reliability was not as important to them as it was to gangs interested mainly in raising money. Since the Irish-American gang members were not attracted to heroin, it was not problematic. However, the Chicano gang members did use heroin for entertainment—the same reason they joined the gang. Therefore, according to Jankowski, using heroin was consistent with the gang's primary function.

Moore (1978:36) also noted that a unique feature of Chicano gangs was fighting and heroin. Since fighting, often in the form of shooting at an individual or group from a passing car, does not require a great deal of skill, heroin users were not deemed as unreliable as they would be in the melee style of fighting. Moore (1993:37) even goes so far to suggest that increased violence may be related to increased drug use. Moreover, since the gang was not in business to increase its wealth, a heroin addict was not seen as a drain on manpower or resources. However, as related by a former gang member and heroin user, even the most dedicated homeboy soon learned that loaning a junkie money was not wise if he expected repayment.

Jankowski's findings were verified in my interviews with San Diego gang members regarding drug use. Among Mexican-American gang members, there were virtually no negative sanctions regarding heroin or crack cocaine use. A Red Step Chicano boy replied to questions about gang sanctions against heroin, "We don't get in trouble for using dope. You use from your own money—it's your turn over."

However, the African-American gang members did say they were not allowed to use crack. One sixteen-year-old Piru quoted a drug dealer's axiom, "Never get high on your own supply." When asked what would happen if he used crack, he said, "The big dudes will beat you up." The big dudes he mentioned were older members whose major concern was maximizing profits. Likewise a Neighborhood Crip said, "There is no way we can use when selling. I just smoke a little weed. You would get your ass kicked if you use. The big guys will get you."

So while heavy drugs such as heroin and crack cocaine are not tolerated in gangs with business interests, they are tolerated in active, violent fighting gangs. And since drive-by shootings do not require sobriety, it can be understood how contemporary fighting gangs can allow heavy drug use among their members.

The term *kicking back* was used by gang members to convey a desired stance of relaxing or having fun. Not only was this a general term favored by youth in the area, gang members used it to describe everything from parties to hanging out at their favorite haunts. Jankowski (1991:81) found the identical term and sentiment used among Chicano gangs.

Returning to the relaxed stance that seemed to be a dominant posture of the targets of the drive-by shootings, we can understand their lack of alertness in terms of kicked-back situations. Goffman (1961:37) explains fun in terms of *spontaneous involvement*. To be spontaneously involved is to disattend to all but the unfolding moment. If one must concern oneself with external matters that take attention away from being engrossed in kicking back, then one cannot enjoy the fun of the gathering. At parties, a sure bore is one who brings up unpleasant chores at the office, unfinished homework, a dying relative, or anything else that takes away from being caught up in the moment of the gathering. Constant reminders of the *possibility* of a drive-by and the need for alertness are also undesirable in kicked-back situations, because they put a damper on the spirit of the occasion. Furthermore, one who shows too much alertness may be accused of lacking the heart for gang life. So, for those with a nervous alertness, there is a need to manage the impression that they are indifferent to the dangers of drive-bys, and they may in fact let down their guard in the *performance* of doing so.

To the extent people can disattend to external matters in a situation, we can say they are at *ease* (Goffman 1961:41–45). *Tension* is defined as a "sensed discrepancy between the world that spontaneously becomes real to the individual, or the one he is able to accept as the current reality, and the one in which he is obliged to dwell" (p. 43). For the gang members, kicking back and enjoying any ease contrasts dramatically with the state of alertness necessary to survive a drive-by shooting. Since the weather in Southern California is conducive to year-round outdoor activity, gang members spend a good deal of time outside. In about 90 percent of the cases, the victims were outside when attacked in a drive-by shooting. In several cases, those who were shot outside were spillovers from an indoor party. The following is typical of a kicked-back occasion that was disrupted by a drive-by:

> Some VELs were leaving a party when a car drove by with some boys who yelled "Logan, Logan" and shot them. Later, several other people who were at the party showed up at the hospital with stab and gunshot wounds.

The irony of gangs is that the very kicked-back life-style that is an important part of their life is disrupted by the tension of drive-by shootings, another part of gang life.

In the aftermath of drive-by shootings where someone is actually killed or severely wounded, the reaction of the gang members and others in the neighborhood is disbelief that it really happened. Even though violence is a major part of gang life in terms of topics of conversation, tattoos proclaiming violence, and carrying weapons, the actual situation of violence always produces trauma.

So the unprepared posture often taken in the face of danger appears to be more a matter of denial than it is of either bravery or ignorance. There may be a temporary alertness after a drive-by against a gang, but it seems to be short-lived. In one instance, a boy from the Shelltown gang had been murdered two weeks prior to a drive-by shooting where a second Shelltown member was gunned down. The denial cannot be maintained indefinitely, and some gangs do post sentries and/or have their gatherings in *cul de sacs* or other locations where drive-by shootings are difficult. However, the overall attitude is one that recognizes the drive-by shooting as a possibility, but gangs filter it out as an external matter. To give it too much attention takes away from the *vida loca* (the crazy life), but to be wholly unaware of it can have fatal consequences. So drive-bys are viewed as something to avoid (as a target), hoping oneself is not the victim.

GROUNDED VALUES AND THE DRIVE-BY SHOOTING

Up to this point we have discussed drive-by shootings primarily from the point of view of the target: a contingency in the life of a gang member. Now, I would like to examine drive-by shootings from the point of view of the shooters. How can we understand what it takes to get in a car with one's homeboys and deliberately go hunting for someone to shoot? It is true that some drive-bys seem to be unplanned in that someone just happens to have a gun in a car and starts shooting, but interviews with former gang members show that drive-bys can be fairly deliberate hunting expeditions for human quarry.

One argument explaining deliberate initiated violence is to classify individuals who do such things as sociopaths, psychopaths, or some similar label implying that they are violent and without scruples or conscience. Likewise, we could argue that the core gang members suffer from sociopathic maladies, as did Yablonsky (1962), and that those with these dysfunctions are attracted to the most violent element of gangs. Thus, we would conclude, boys who engage in drive-by shootings are *really* suffering from individual problems and would be violent no matter what.

There are several problems with such individualistic arguments. First of all, they tend to be tautological. To wit, if a person who engages in drive-by shootings must be sociopathic, and sociopaths are defined as those who are involved in drive-by shootings. The same problem existed in preclassical criminological thought. The offensive act and offensive person are wrapped together into a single entity: evil (Sylvester 1972:3). Distinctions between the evil *act* and evil *actor* become blurred. Second of all, gangs are a group phenomenon. If sociopaths are persons without regard for others, they would not be subject to or care about others in their gang. Since observers of gang life report that there is very much a concern for the options of fellow gang members, it would be difficult to argue for a sociopathic personality generating gang behavior. On their own, sociopaths or psychopaths may generate all kinds of bizarre behavior, but involvement in a drive-by shooting in cooperation with fellow gang members in a car hardly seems to fit in with the wholly antisocial nature of this personality type. Finally, those who seem to fit the sociopathic and psychopathic labels tend to be loners, and the nature of their offenses is different from patterned crime.

Gang members involved in drive-by shootings talk about their feats in the same displaced way that bomber pilots talk of hitting targets. The gang boys are proud of that fact that they had the heart to point the gun and pull the trigger at an enemy, *not necessarily that they may have killed someone*. Short and Strodtbeck (1964:25–29), in their examination behind why gangs fight, point out that gang boys need to maintain status. They get the status by performing well in gang-gang encounters. In quoting gang boys' elation after one such encounter, Short and Strodtbeck illustrate the combined pride and tension relief:

> "Baby, did you see the way I swung on that kid?" "Man, did we tell them off?" "Did you see them take off when I leveled my gun?" "You were great, baby. . . ."

The tension was relieved. They had performed well and could be proud. (1964:26)

Those who could not or would not perform by going along on a drive-by were judged as lacking heart. They could still be part of the gang, but like the rear echelon troops in a battle zone, they are given no hero status or meaningful medals.

The gang, as a group or organization, provides the situation of the drive-by shooting. We might say that in the same way that situations have realized resources as described by Goffman (1961:28), gangs too have realized resources. One of the resources that can be realized by gang membership is participation in a drive-by shooting. The guns, the cars, the rivals, and even the accounts (Scott and Lyman 1968:46–62) are gang-provided resources.

Of the gang-provided resources, the least important are the guns and automobiles. Virtually anyone can get cars and guns in San Diego without much trouble. However, coming up with *murderous* rivals and the *accounts* necessary for shooting at them is another matter. The rivals are generated as part of gang lore, accidental encounters, and contingency of ethnic group and location. As part of gang lore, images of rivals as cowardly, venal, dangerous, and worthy of disdain are passed on from one generation to the next. The rivalry between the Crips and Bloods/Pirus in San Diego is traced to a rivalry in Los Angeles, one that had nothing to do with anyone in San Diego. When the gangs in San Diego started using Crips and Blood/Piru in their names, they based their rivalry on the Los Angeles gangs' lore. Within the lore are the accounts for any enmity between the two groups. Likewise, an accidental encounter between nonrival gangs may result in a fight or a killing. Once that occurs, a vendetta may be established that will work into a full-time rivalry. Finally, a rivalry may simply crop up because of the proximity of two gangs. The 70s and VELs are the Mexican-American gangs nearest to one another, and that seems to be the basis for their rivalry. Likewise, since ethnic lines are generally uncrossed boundaries in San Diego gang life, two gangs such as the West Coast Crips (African-American) and the Calle 30 (Mexican-American) are not rivals although they are adjacent and even part of the same area.

Knowing the accounts, justifications, and meanings generated in gang life to participate in a drive-by shootings is core to understanding gang violence. One of the most difficult matters to resolve in this research was how to make sense of a kid sticking a gun out the window of a car and intentionally shooting another human being. Gang members learn accounts or vocabularies of motives (Mills 1940:904–13) in gang situations. For example, a gang boy who is attacked and beaten, shot at, or stabbed has two experiences. First, he has *empirical* evidence of a physically painful and/or frightening experience. Second, he has a *rational* experience in that he seeks a reason—a motive or account—for the experience. The rational account is not an automatic calculation of costs and benefits in the classical or neoclassical sense The rational account is weighing the empirical experience against ways of talking about what has happened.

A middle-class youth who was subject to a near-miss in a drive-by shooting would be given the account that he was in the wrong place. He would be given advice to avoid those situations by avoiding the neighborhoods where gangs exist. Low-income non–gang youths in the community who cannot avoid such neighborhoods will be given advice to avoid certain individuals or places in the neighborhood. However, gang youths who experience being a target of a drive-by are provided with very different accounts. They hear about revenge, heart, courage, balls, honor, and perhaps even how weak the attacker is if no one is harmed. So the rational experience of the gang boy is one of dealing with the problem by means other than avoidance. Even the meekest members of the gang are glad there are other members who have the heart to drive by and "mess up" their rivals. Instead of hearing about the futility of endless vendettas, gang boys come to *understand* that only a powerful counterstrike can thwart future drive-bys. The gang's honor is at stake, but the honor is more than saving face. If a gang is seen to have honor, it is seen as a gang that should not be trifled with. As such, it is a safer, *more rational*, gang. So instead of being merely an act of vengeance, a drive-by shooting is seen as a rational action to protect the gang. Those in the role of drive-by shooters are seen as protecting not only the gangs' honor but also its life and limb.

The accounts and understanding of what a drive-by shooting means as a protective measure are grounded in the gang-generated situations. The values and norms surrounding and justifying drive-bys, either as a rational battle plan in view of the available weapons or as a defensive act to stave off drive-bys in one's own patch, find their specific meaning in the way the gangs talk about the situations of their occurrence. In turn, the *talk* is justified by the empirical reference of what happens in their neighborhoods and to them as gangs.

ACTION AND THE DRIVE-BY SHOOTING

Goffman (1967:185) defines *action* as taking on fatefulness for its own sake. A drive-by shooting clearly has the makings of a fateful situation. It is risky in that those who drive by and shoot at a rival may become the target themselves, or they may be caught by the police. It is consequential since what occurs in the occasion of the drive-by will almost certainly have significant effects on the shooters' future.

Horowitz and Schwartz (1974) argue that honor in gangs is a key to understanding their violence. One can gain honor by acting bravely in a gang encounter, establishing character for oneself and possibly robbing it from an opponent. Since character contests make up a part of gang warfare, both individually and collectively, we must examine the drive-by in this light. As noted above, not all members of a gang have the mettle to sit in a car with a gun and go hunt rival members. Those who do can demonstrate they have character or heart. This is understood in Goffman's (1967:214) use of the term *character*. To wit, a gang boy has the opportunity to demonstrate he has the ability to act coolly and deliberately even though alarms may be going off inside that tell him to get out of the car and away from the danger.

At the same time there is a concrete, grounded situation in which to establish character, there is excitement in taking chances. The adrenaline that pumps through one in the face of danger creates a heightened awareness, but its effects must be kept in check to demonstrate coolness. Once the firing begins, the pent-up feelings can be released in firing the gun or listening to it go off, and there is a spontaneous involvement in the moment. Also, there is the excitement of the recognition of the fellow gang members. Their praise for heart and bravery provide another high in the aftermath of the shooting. All of the excitement is grounded in the drive-by shooting. In the telling of the drive-by, future drive-bys are preordained, for the telling provides the grounds for others to establish themselves and feel the thrill of danger.

NORMATIVE AND STRATEGIC INTERACTION IN DRIVE-BY SHOOTINGS

Goffman (1969:130) notes that while it is possible to conceive of strategic interaction as free of norms, it is usually very difficult in reality. We can examine drive-by shootings as purely tactical moves based on the most efficient way to do in a rival, but upon closer examination, there is a good deal else that goes on and *does not* go on to make the move a purely strategic one.

Above we noted that norms appear *not* to keep gangbangers from blasting away at dwellings with non–gang members inside, but because norms against shooting at dwellings where a rival's family members may be present are not included in the moral code of the gang does not mean that norms do not exist at all. There do seem to be norms against singling out an innocent relative of a gang member and shooting at him or her. The lack of remorse shown by gang members when asked about killing babies, small children, and women is not an attitude of condoning such killings. It is a reflection of their view of reality. They will readily defend themselves by pointing out they were not *trying* to harm innocents, but that is one of the unfortunate side effects of gang warfare—just like any other warfare. In the same way that the rules of war "protect" noncombatants from being shot at *intentionally*, women and children have never been protected from the consequences of area shelling or bombing. As long as they can demonstrate that they did not knowingly and intentionally kill non–gang members, they can maintain a normatively correct posture.

Emergent Norms in a Drive-By

While it was possible to gather data on the events of a drive-by shooting during the immediate time of the shooting, it was not possible to gather much data on what led up to the shooting. In other words, there were few data that show how a drive-by emerges. From the data that were collected, widely different circumstances seem to be involved.

In one case, a police informant was at a party with some Logan gang members. As the party developed, gang members became more intoxicated with alcohol, drugs, or both and decided to "hit" the Sherman gang. It is not clear whether they decided to do the drive-by first and then became intoxicated to bolster their resolve, or after becoming intoxicated the idea of a drive-by seemed like a good one. In interviews with a former gang member, it seemed that he and his fellow gang members were "loaded" a good deal of the time, regardless of the situation. Thus, while drugs and/or alcohol may have been present in drive-by situations, they do not seem to explain how the kernel of the idea of a drive-by developed since the same state of intoxication was present when drive-by shootings were the furthest thing from gang members' minds.

In another shooting where data were available concerning the events that led up to the drive-by, two of the people in the shooting car were literally innocent bystanders. It involved a girl whose boyfriend's brother was a gang member. The following transcript excerpts show how the drive-by evolved:

> [F]irst, it started from my house and it was about four o'clock in the afternoon. Me and my boyfriend were talking inside this car and we decided to go for a ride around the block cause he wanted to drive. And around two blocks away from my house, we saw his brother. And uh, he

asked us to stop the car so he can get in the car with us. So when, uh, we stopped the car, he asked us to go to another block to pick up two of his friends. When we went out there, we saw two of his friends with something in their hands. We . . . picked them up. They asked me to open the trunk of the car. First, I didn't want to but then my boyfriend told me to do it. Cause, uh, well he probably thought it was something else but he didn't know if they had a gun with them. Whatever they had in their hands that was in the back of my car. So they get in the car and we left. So they asked us to go where I live at.

We went down there, and they went across the street to pick up a friend. We stopped the car and [name] got out of the car and went to pick up [name]. So when [he] come out of the house, he had a gun with him. A small gun with him. And then, uh, he got into the car and he told us to drive. I didn't want to. My boyfriend didn't want to either. But then [the boy with the gun] pulled my hair, and he told me to do it. He told me "Come on girl, do it." So my boyfriend, he got out of the car and he said, "Don't be pulling her hair," and [the boy with the gun] said, "Man, don' start nothing with me right now. I'm drunk, I'm loaded right now." So my boyfriend told me, "[girl's name] get in the car and then let's go." But then uh, first, uh, my boyfriend was talking so when we, he found out what they put into the trunk was two guns, a gun, he didn't want to talk no more. He wanted to stay [at the girl's house]. And then, he told me to stay too, I didn't want to. I said "Whatever my car was . . . [the car belonged to the girl.]

And he pointed the gun to him [girl's boyfriend]. I don't know if he mean it to point it to him or not but I know he pointed to him, he said, "Man let's get out of here." So my boyfriend said, "We better go before we get shot." So we go into the car and we started driving around by the park, I don't know the name of the park. And when we saw two guys come. They were coming around by the park, [the boy with the gun] said, "Man, stop. Stop the car." [At this point, the girl narrating the drive-by was in the back seat of her own car with her boyfriend. Two of the boys in the front seat jumped out of the car and began shooting at the boys in the park, hitting one.]

If the girl was telling the truth and was not involved with the gang members from the outset, it appears that the situation for a drive-by was an opportunistic one. That is, it was known that someone had guns and wanted to shoot at a rival gang. When the opportunity of an available automobile came about, the gang members took over the car and went looking for targets. When they found the targets, they simply shot at them.

The transformation of the situation of one from "driving around" to a drive-by started when the guns were brought into the car and the driver and her boyfriend were forced to accompany the shooters. Since the girl and her boyfriend were unwilling participants, they were under the coercive rule of the gun and not the rules of situated norms. The two others in the car who did not participate in the shooting were "along for the ride" and made no attempt to gain the release of the girl and her boyfriend. Their lack of action and failure to indicate they did not want to be along suggests they were nonshooting drive-by participants. It was an exciting outing for them. (Indeed, it may have been an exciting outing for all of them, and after deciding who was going to take the fall for the offense, the others may have openly cooperated with the police.)

More data on the nature of the emergent norms in drive-by shootings are needed. The accounts provided by researchers like Jankowski are reflections of commonsense reasoning by the gang members in the context of their social reality. However, such accounts tell us little of how actual situations of gang violence evolve or about the situations themselves. Like we do with other data that have emerged in the study of crime, we tend to want to know more about the actors than the situations they create and in turn become caught up in. However, since the actors are behaving in the way they are because of the nature of the situation, we need to know more about those situations.

SITUATIONS OF DRIVE-BY SHOOTINGS

In looking at some situations where drive-by shootings occur, we can get an inkling of the strategies and norms behind these attacks. The kinds of situations that occur prior to a drive-by shooting are often vague, but we will attempt to classify those that are the most common and provide some examples to see the characteristics of the situations and shootings.

Emergent Arguments. The type of drive-by that occurs more or less accidentally or spontaneously emerges out of arguments. Typically, some gang members in a car with a gun will say something to a person in a rival's neighborhood. Often the statement will be a gang challenge. For example, the following driving-shooting occurred when three Little Africa Pirus encountered four Eastside Pirus. Since usually Pirus fight Crips, this incident stands as an exception to the unstated alliance, but the example clearly illustrates the type of situation where cars and guns are used in emergent arguments:

> Three Little Africa Pirus were at a stoplight at an intersection when a car with four Eastside Pirus pulled up next to them. One of the Little Africa Pirus said, "What's up, blood?" to the boys in the other car. After some further verbal exchanges, one of the Eastside Piru members pulled out a

handgun and shot several bullets into the Little Africa Pirus' car. Two of the occupants were wounded, and jumped out of the car and ran to a nearby gas station. The Eastside Pirus drove off.

It is possible that the shooter thought the boys in the Little Africa Pirus' car were Crips, since the statement, "What's up, blood?" often prefaces a shooting by the Crips. (The Pirus preface their attacks of Crips with "What's up, cuz?")

Sometimes the targets may actually initiate the violence. These are cases where the target says or does something to intentionally antagonize the shooters in the car. For example, the following cases illustrate interchanges that resulted in a shooting from a passing car:

> Three East Side Pirus were in front of their house lifting weights when a car with West Coast Crips drove by and one of the occupants shouted, "Fuck the Pirus!" The Pirus left the yard and walked down the street, where the car passed them again. The second time it passed, a shotgun was pointed at them from the rear window. One of the Pirus, who apparently did not see the shotgun, threw a rock at the car. The car continued down the street, made a U-turn, and came back toward the Pirus. As it passed the third time, two shots were fired from the car, hitting one of the Pirus in the back.

A third type of emergent argument occurs when there is an immediate attack on the drivers and counterattack by the shooters in the car. This type of emergent argument typically occurs when a car with known rival gang members appears in another gang's home territory and is recognized. The target gang mobilizes and attacks the drivers. The following incident, described by non–gang and gang witnesses, involved the West Coast Crips and Lincoln Park Pirus:

> Two West Coast Crips drove into a parking lot in front of a fried chicken franchise and record store that was the home territory of the Lincoln Park Pirus. When they drove into the lot, they were recognized by the Lincoln Park Pirus, who began attacking them. A non–gang witness said, "I pulled into the lot and everybody was throwing rocks and bottles at each other. These dudes got out of this green Chevy that was parked in front of Dr. J's lot and started shooting. There were two people in the car. The driver got out of the car and fired six shots. There was one other guy in the car. Then they both jumped in the car and tried to run over some of the people that were throwing rocks at them."

A Lincoln Park Piru, who was shot and wounded in the drive-by, provided the following account of the same incident:

> I was just standing on Lowe's lot with a couple of my homeboys, and these two dudes in a six-nine Chevy pulled onto the lot. I don't know either one of them by name but I know they were from the Coast [West Coast Crips]. I

had seen them around a couple of times before. There was an "18 and over" party at the record shop. A couple of my homeboys and them got into an argument and my homeboys said something like, "fuck the Coast." Then the dude that was driving pulled out a gun. It looked like he really meant to shoot me 'cause he pointed the gun right at me. I hear a couple of shots, and then I knew I was hit, but I kept on running. I got dizzy and fell down. The next thing I remember the paramedics were there.

Such encounters provide members of both gangs with enough evidence that they showed heart, demonstrated character, and were generally tried-and-true gangbangers. The shooters in the car could claim they took on a numerically superior group and wounded one. The target gang could claim they faced a gun with mere rocks and bottles. Furthermore, the situation grounded the beliefs of both gangs in empirical experience, giving them substance. It showed the necessity of fighting back, the nefarious nature of each other's opponents, and the reality of establishing character. All of these could further be attributed, *positively* from the gang boys' perspective, to gang affiliation.

Hanging Out.   The situations of the last two examples of emergent argument were also examples of drive-bys occurring where the target gang is hanging out. A distinction is made here between emergent arguments and hanging out as situations of drive-by shootings on the basis of one generating a situated reason for the shooting. In emergent arguments, the shooter can always point to something that the target did or said on the shooting occasion that resulted in the shooting. In the preceding example, something was said or some action was taken by the target gang before the shooting gang began firing.

The difference between a hanging-out situation and one of emergent argument is that in a hanging-out situation, the target has little time to say or do anything before the shooting starts. We can review emergent-argument situations and say that were it not for the fact that the target gang *did* say or do something to antagonize the shooter, the shooting may not have occurred. In other words, we can argue that emergent-argument situations are in part *situationally victim precipitated*. That means that something the target group did *in the situation* of the drive-by shooting helped justify the shooting.

By contrast, hanging-out situations, while they may be victim precipitated, are not situationally victim precipitated. For example, suppose a gang crosses out another gang's *placaso* (gang signature.) The gang whose *placaso* has been defaced justifies a drive-by shooting against the offending gang. They execute the drive-by later that day, that week, or even that month. We can say that the gang who crossed out the *placaso* contributed to its being targeted for a drive-by. In that sense, the drive-by is victim precipitated. However, it is not *situationally* precipitated because the offending action occurred in an occasion separate from the drive-by. The following is an example of this type of hanging-out situation that was precipitated by a member of the target gang. The shooter had been beaten up by some Neighborhood Crips. The drive-by was in retaliation for the "jumping" (beating). The following was related by the shooting victim:

> I was talking to a couple of fellow at Gompers Park . . . when we saw this car turn the corner at Hilltop and Carolina. It started moving toward us. They were yelling "Piru" several times, and we all started running. I could hear them yelling "Piru," and I also hear one of them yell, "What are you running for, blood?" While I was running away, I saw the passenger behind the driver point what appeared to be a double barrel shotgun and fire two shots. . . . [T]he first shot hit me in the back, and I continued running toward Forty-seventh Street, through the park. We kept on running until we were somewhere near C Street and Myron helped carry me to a house where he called the police.

As can be seen from the example, there was nothing that the targets did in the situation to precipitate the shooting during the occasion of the shooting. However, it became clear in the investigation that the shooter was involved in the drive-by because of an earlier offense by Neighborhood Crips. Thus, the case is victim-precipitated but not situationally so.

Parties. In most ways there is not a lot of difference between a drive-by targeting a group hanging out and one that targets a party. Parties were selected as targets because they provided an opportunity for a gang to show it would fearlessly attack a massed rival, and party gatherings provided large targets. The shooters may also have considered parties a good target since the party-goers were likely to be intoxicated and not able to quickly respond:

> Some Shelltown homeboys were at a birthday party for one of the boys' grandmother when some VELs drove by. One Shelltown boy was standing on the street when two VELs got out of the car and said, "Where are you from?" He replied, "Shelltown," and they responded, "Encanto, Encanto!" [VEL is an acronym for Varrio Encanto Locos—roughly translated it means, "The crazy guys from the Encanto neighborhood."] The Shelltown boy ducked down when the VELs began shooting at him before they drove off.

The details of the shooting itself are little differentiated from one where shots are fired in a hanging-out situation. In some of the drive-by shootings observed at parties, it was noted that there tended to be a larger grouping, and girls were more likely to be present. In some of the drive-bys at parties, girls in fact were wounded. Since females are not usually targeted in drive-bys, they are considered innocent bystanders, but there does not seem to be remorse or embarrassment when girls or other innocent bystanders are shot. The view is, "They shouldn't party with those guys if they don't want get shot at."

Another reason that gangs target parties is to enhance their reputation. This can occur when there is little or no past conflict between the gangs. By hitting a party, there is an immediate and wide recognition of the event since the party is likely not only to attract most of the gang members, but also others who attend the occasion as dates or guests of gang members. In one such event, the Spring Valley Locos attacked a Shelltown party. The Shelltown boy who was gunned down in the drive-by was considered a fringe member and had no record of violence himself. In interviews after the incident, the party-goers all said that there was no rivalry between the two gangs. Since the gangs were separated by about twelve miles, they did not attend the same schools, and they had no common territorial boundary, it was unclear why the attack occurred. Eventually, some Shelltown boys pointed out that the Spring Valley Locos wanted to enhance their reputation. The attack and killing would get around and the Spring Valley Locos would be seen as a gang of heart.

Since two weeks prior to the drive-by, a Shelltown boy had been killed in the Spring Valley Locos territory, it would seem that the Spring Valley Locos had already made their reputation as a dangerous gang. An alternative accounting would be that the Spring Valley Locos attack was to thwart a *payback* (revenge attack) by Shelltown. Jankowski (1991:164) cited fear of being attacked by a rival as a reason to strike first. The first strike is supposed to generate fear that attempts at revenge will call on more retaliation. From this research, it appears that fear is not so much a *factor* as Jankowski used the term, but rather it is a gang *account*. That is, in the vocabulary of motives for engaging in a drive-by shooting, *fear* is an acceptable account if presented correctly. None of the gang members want to appear cowardly in front of their fellow gang members, and so fear must be presented as a rationally grounded reason instead of a gut reaction. In citing Jankowski's own example, we can see the rational account more so than the fear:

"That's it man, we attack the [rival gang's name] and leveled some impressive destruction. . . . No, I don't know if they were planning to attack us or not. If they weren't thinking of it now, they would have had to think of it in the future, so it was best we got them now." (Jankowski 1991:164)

The account may have implied fear, but it also implied an empirically grounded account for making an attack based on what other gangs honor. Whether it is running from fear or leaping into a situation bringing on honor and the identity associated with it is not so important as was the fact that the reasoning is considered a valid accounting of the events by gang members. Thus, it is not context-free rationality, but rather a rationality grounded in the gang culture, which itself is reflexively grounded in the gang situations.

Business Competition.   In the early 1980s, business competition did not appear to be a reason for gang violence at all in San Diego. However, by 1988, many of the gang-related drive-by shootings, especially among African-American gang members, did appear to be connected to the sale and distribution of crack cocaine.

The profits from the sale of crack cocaine were so great that the African-American gangs were all engaging in it to some extent. With wider distribution, sales and profits would increase. In an attempt to expand their business, Los Angeles gangs attempted to take over some of the San Diego areas serviced by local African-American gangs. When this occurred, the rivalry between the local Crips and Pirus was suspended while both gangs fought off the challenge from Los Angeles. However, the Los Angeles gangs were not going to be run off easily. The following attack was made by a Los Angeles gang on West Coast Crips:

> Two West Coast Crips and a non–gang member were walking along the sidewalk when a car drove by and shot at them with an automatic rifle (machine gun). The non–gang member was suspected in a shooting a few days previously.

The non–gang member with the two Crips may have been involved in drug deals, and the gang violence thus may have been a reflection of violence among drug dealers for customers. The increase in drive-by shootings in 1988 makes it clear that *something* occurred that year to make the number increase so dramatically. Since crack cocaine was introduced to the neighborhoods primarily through African-American gangs at that time, sales competition is hypothesized to be a primary cause.

Nonperson Targets.   In addition to shooting at people who could be seen, targets in drive-by shootings also were physical objects that belonged to targets. Most common were automobiles and houses. In the case of targeting automobiles, it was fairly clear whether or not someone was in the car. However, houses were sometimes occupied and sometimes not.

Shooting at a gang member's house or car can cause damage to the physical target, breaking windows, and putting holes in the stucco walls and metal car panels. In addition, such attacks threaten the victim, and the shooters can claim they have caused a loss of face for the rival gang.

The most problematic issue that arises in examining drive-by shootings at houses is the nature of norms in the context of strategic interaction. While gang members are definitely the desired target if anyone happens to be at home, there is a good chance that others in the house may be wounded or killed. Do norms exist that protect innocent family members? They do not seem to, for drive-by shootings include shooting at houses when parents and siblings of gang members are at home. A former gang member recalled when his family at dinner had to dive for the floor as a rival gang sprayed the house with bullets. He was the only gang member in the family even though he had several brothers and sisters.

CONCLUSION

Drive-by shootings have become synonymous with gang violence. As a strategy in the context of rival gangs armed with manufactured firearms, it is far superior to other forms of gang warfare. A gang can hit a target miles away from its home territory, and then speed away unscathed. In these situations, gang members can build an identity as having "heart" and live to tell about it. While risky in terms of counterstrikes by the rival gang and police apprehension, a drive-by can be conducted by virtually anyone who can ride in a car and shoot a gun. As such, this type of violence is the most deadly and is likely to be a continuing source of gang power.

5

Gangbangs

INTRODUCTION

A second major form of gang violence is called the *gangbang*. This chapter explains exactly what a gangbang is and its place in the context of gang warfare. Unlike the drive-by, however, a gangbang is more emergent in its development and is far more interactive. Therefore, it is necessary to analyze the situational construction of a gangbang as it develops between antagonists. Again, Erving Goffman's analytical framework is employed to examine the interactional moves that lead to gangbangs. They are examined in terms of different types of situations where they develop and in different behavioral settings.

GANGBANGS IN THE CONTEXT OF GANG WARFARE

The term *gangbang* as used by San Diego gang members is very much bound to the context of its usage. In general, a gangbang refers to some type of fighting, especially between rival gangs, but it is differentiated from drive by shootings. In talking with one *chola*, I inadvertently used the terms *gangbang* and *drive-by* interchangeably. She corrected me saying, "Drive-bys ain't gangbanging. You know, jumping [assaulting] somebody, that's gangbanging."

Gangbanging was also used to refer to doing *anything* with other gang members. Hanging around together, going out and stealing things, fighting, and other activities with the gang have been described by gang members as gangbanging. However, the most common use of the term by gang members was in reference to fighting rival gang members.

The term *gangbanging* is not new in gang lore. In the 1960s, in his study of the Vice Lord gang in Chicago, R. Lincoln Keiser (1969:29) noted that the term was used to refer to a gang fight. The term *humbugging* referred to fighting in general, and *gangbanging* was used when gangs fought one another (p. 50). However, if two gang members as individuals fought, the term *humbugging* was used but understood in a wholly different context (ibid.). A strong-armed robbery was called *hustling,* but if the main purpose was to beat up a person and incidentally take his money, then the Vice Lords called it *wolf packing* (ibid.). The primary purpose of wolf packing was to build one's reputation, while the main goal of hustling was to get money. African-American gang members in San Diego referred to street robberies as *jacking.*

In San Diego, the term *gangbangers* was commonly used to self-describe gang members. Both Mexican-American and African-American gang members would use the term in their graffiti. For example, the Lomita Village gang 70s had a large mural on the side of a public restroom in its home territory park. There was a drawing of a *cholo* logo—an abstract of a man with a brimmed hat, dark glasses, and goatee—captioned with the word *gangbangers.* Likewise, even though African-American gangs are more likely to use the term *gangsters,* or *original gangsters* (or *OG*) in their graffiti, they will refer to others in their own or rival gang as gangbangers.

For the purposes of clarity, the term *gangbanging* will be used here to refer to any fighting between gangs other than drive-by shootings. Also, since group rape has been referenced by the term *gangbang,* discussions of gang rape will use standard English. Since there were few reports of gang-related rape for which data were gathered, this will not be much of a problem.

In order to get a sense of gangbang situations, the following excerpts from the data on gangbangs serve as illustrations:

> At a party, a fight broke out. During the fight, a Logan gang member was shot in the stomach and taken to the hospital by his friends. He refused to cooperate with police.
>
> Some Logan boys started throwing beer bottles at Del Sol members who were at Chicano Park, in Logan territory.
>
> A Piru was standing at a bus stop when a Neighborhood Crip arrived and said, "Hood rules." The Piru replied, "Hood ain't shit." At this time the Crip pulled a knife and stabbed the Piru member.
>
> A 5/9 Brim was leaving a church carnival when some Neighborhood Crips challenged him to a fight. He accepted the challenge, but before he could begin fighting, one of the Crips sneaked up behind him and shot him in the back.
>
> A VEL was at the park when he was challenged to a fight, which he accepted. During the fight he was stabbed.
>
> A West Coast Crip was leaving a liquor store when an East San Diego gang member approached him and said, "Your homeboys sold me some bunk [bad narcotics]. You owe me. I'll have to take it out on you." The ESD

member began pushing the Crip, and when he noticed the ESD boy had a knife in his hand, the Crip ran away. He was caught and stabbed in the side. [This case is unique only insofar as it involved Hispanic and black gang members.]

Two hard-core East San Diego members were outside a restaurant when approached by a Logan member who said "I'm from 3000 Logan," and threw a beer bottle at them. The two ESD members began fighting the Logan boy and an Imperiale member who was with the Logan member. The Logan boy pulled a knife and hit one of the ESD members in the head with his fist. Both fell to the ground and the knife with dropped. A third person with the Logan and Imperiale boys, a Hispanic female, picked up the knife and stabbed the ESD boy in the side abdomen. All three fled after the stabbing.

Some Sidro boys drove up to the recreation center and got out of their car. When asked where they were from, they said, "Sidro." At this point several Del Sol members attacked them with rocks, hitting the boys and their car, causing one of the Sidro boys to be hospitalized.

Fights and Assaults

In order to provide some general guidelines for examining gangbangs, we have divided them into two categories: fights and assaults. *Fights* are defined as involving parties who more or less initiate action against one another. An *assault* is where a victim is attacked without wanting confrontation. We have also divided the participants into gang and nongang categories. In the next chapter we will discuss nongang victims of gang activities, but here we will only deal with gang versus gang actions.

In examining the patterns of nonrobbery violent crimes we can see in Table 5.1 that gangbangs make up the majority of gang versus gang violence. In 1981, most of the assault victims were nongang, but by 1988, the majority of the victims were gang members (Table 5.2).

It is interesting to note that bulk of the drive-bys are consistently against other gang members, while until 1988 the bulk of the assaults were against non–gang members. The change in the pattern may have been due to the emergence of a greater number of hit-and-run attacks

Table 5.1. Type of Violence 1981 and 1988

Type of violence	1981 (N = 86)	1988 (N = 133)
Drive-by	23.3	42.9
Fight	15.1	9.8
Assault	61.6	47.4

Table 5.2.   Victim Status by Type of Assault, 1981 and 1988

	1981			1988		
	Drive-by (N = 20)	Fight (N = 13)	Assault (N = 53)	Drive-by (N = 57)	Fight (N = 13)	Assault (N = 63)
Gang	70	62	28	77	85	59
Nongang	30	38	72	23	15	41

against other gang members. Since assaults were defined as attacks without mutual consent, they were the kinds of situations where a larger group of gang members would find an individual or smaller group from a rival gang and attack them. For example, the following assault has many of the characteristics of a drive-by, but it does not involve shooting:

> A Logan member was walking down the street when two Shelltown boys jumped out of a car and pushed him into a doorway of a closed business. One hit the Logan boy in the face with a bottle, and the other stabbed him. They then got back into the car and left the area.

By 1988 when crack cocaine competition was active between African-American gang members, these assaults also may have represented running competition off one's home territory or incursion on a rival's territory. However, why hit-and-run tactics would be employed instead of drive-by shooting is unknown. The reason may be nothing more than the fact that a gun was not in the car when a rival gang member was spotted. From interviews with gang members, it is clear that most gang-bangs are unplanned, and so these mobile assaults probably reflect opportunities where a quick assault was feasible.

Building the Gangbang Situation

We can usefully study gangbang situations by examining *unfocused* and *focused* gatherings (Goffman 1963a:24). Unfocused interaction is the type that occurs in public places such as shopping malls, school corridors, and sidewalks. The participants monitor one another enough to communicate who and what they are in general terms and glean information from others by momentary glances. Such interaction is used in managing copresence. It is a way that people keep from bumping into one another, recognize friends, and avoid (or confront) enemies.

When people come together to sustain a single focus of attention, they move from unfocused to focused interaction. The focus of attention can be a topic of conversation, attention to a lecture, work cooperation, or a gang fight. The contemporary gangbang situation appears to emerge from a situation of unfocused interaction to one of focused interaction. We will examine the dynamics of this transformation in both generic and specific forms.

Interviews with gang members indicate that the sense they have for gangbangs is one of opportunistic meetings. Members from different types of gangs all claimed that in unfocused gatherings they would accidentally encounter a rival and attack him. They said that if they were specifically after someone, they would employ a drive-by shooting. But typical gangbangs occurred where rival gang members occupied the same area by happenstance. The following interview excerpts illustrate how the gang bang developed:

> We just go cruisin' till we feel like doing something. It is never planned.
>
> Beating up someone is not planned. It's just, "Let's go do it." We just saw someone at the wrong place at the wrong time.
>
> At the mall we rushed someone that was from another set. He was in our territory. It wasn't planned. He just got beat up.

In talking about planned attacks, usually drive-by shootings, the gang members had different replies. They would intentionally mobilize to go after an individual or a gang. Such gatherings are *initially focused* to get someone, while the typical gangbang emerges from unfocused gatherings. The following two interview excerpts illustrate the focal point:

> We only plan it when something happens to your hood. Like when someone gets hurt.
> One time one of my homegirls got hurt by some Bloods, and we went to Long Beach to get guns. But we never saw those Bloods again, so they never got hurt.

From the victim's perspective, the situation can be just as unfocused initially. What he sees is the same chance-unfocused interaction that comes to be focused in a way he had hoped to avoid. The following excerpt narrated by a Neighborhood Crip illustrates the transformation of the situation from an unfocused to a focused one:

> I was with my buddy, Lil Boo Yow [street name of fellow gang member]. We had been walking from my house. Lil Boo Yow was walking in front of me. When we reached the store over there on forty-seventh, he walked into the store. As he walked into the store I heard footsteps approaching

me. I turned to see what it was, and there were these two guys running towards me. I turned around, and I recognized both of them. I had seen them once before. One of the guys had shot at me once before and when he shot at me last time he was wearing a green jacket [color of rival gang]. The guy shot at me and said, "What's up, cuz?", then I turned around and said, "What that neighborhood like, cuz?" He then reached around into his right pocket and busted on [shot] me with his right hand. I tried to run, and then he let off and caught me in the leg. I don't know how many shots he fired. I was just trying to save my life so I ran into the store. I ran into the back of the store, and I fell down on the floor, and I stayed on the floor until the police came and the ambulance came.

Change of Focus

Another type of gangbang occurs when there is a change of focus. The initial gathering is focused, and then the focus changes from a sociable one to a combative one. There is a transformation, not from unfocused to focused, but instead, it changes form in the content of the focus. There may or may not be some type of negotiations, requests, or demands to mend interactional transgression and keep the focus the same and avoid combat. The following excerpts show the transformation from one focal concern to another in a situation involving Skyline Pirus and a Linda Vista Crip:

The phone rang, and it was [girlfriend]. She asked me to come to her house.. . . So I walked up there. When I got there she answered the door, and I walked in. It was kind of strange because instead of the normal greeting that she gives me, which is a hug and a kiss, she just opened the door, and I walked in and looked around. There were these three guys sitting in there. I walked in and spoke to them. I said, "Hey, what's up, Charles?" I hadn't seen him in a long time. We used to go to school together in high school, but I hadn't seen him in a long time because he went into the navy, and I got locked up. So I sat down and started talking to him for a while, just kickin' it with them. Then [girlfriend] went into the bedroom and Charles got up and went in the bedroom behind her, so I was kind of trippin', because he went in the bedroom and she went in, then he would come out, go back in, and he would come out, go back in. He did this a few times. So I was really trippin' off of all this because me and her have been messin' around for a long time.

[At this point an argument about a car accident begins.] So that night when I got stabbed I could see he was just trying to front me off about it. Trying to make it look like I was the one that had messed up the dude's car. So, after he ran the mess about, "Yeah, you fucked up my uncle's homeboy's car." I just said, "Fuck you, fuck your uncle, fuck all you guys." Then Anthony got up and punched me in the nose. [Then the four of them went outside where they fought. The Linda Vista Crip was stabbed twice, once in the leg with a knife and once critically in the back with a screwdriver.]

The change of focus from sociability to combat was accomplished by an assault on the *face* of the gang member who was stabbed. Goffman describes an interactional *incident* as an occasion where "events whose effective symbolic implications threaten face" (1967:12). In standard interaction, members of the occasion work to reduce loss of face and embarrassment through *face work*—the process of restoring lost face and counteracting incidents. However, when a fight or assault is the goal of at least some participants in the situation, the opposite of face work occurs.

When members of one gang want to force an incident, one way of doing so is by accusing the other gang of an offense against them. In other words, to generate an offense against face, they allege an offense against face. In so doing, they claim, "You have broken the rules of civilized conduct by making us lose face; therefore, you deserve to lose face." In the above example, a member of one gang was accused of wrecking the car of the relative of another gang member. This led to an outburst of name-calling by the accused, which led to his being struck in the nose. Once the blow was thrown, the victim of the blow accepted the tacit challenge to a fight. At that point the focus was transformed to one of combat.

In the context of gang life, one of the most important elements is face or reputation. Defined more precisely, *face* is the positive social value a person effectively claims for him- or herself in the context of a given situation (Goffman 1967:5). In situations of play or joking, or among clique members, face may be treated lightly with insults being treated as evidence of camaraderie. However, in situations where rival gang members are present, keeping face is a matter of maintaining one's reputation along with that of the gang's. So even in situations where he is outnumbered and may have to run a gang boy's exit must not repudiate his gang membership or his own face. Shouting *"Setentas, y que!"* or "Hood rules!" while beating a hasty retreat from unfavorable odds is no loss of face. It is an exit with an insult thrown in the face of the attacker, which is as good as sticking around to suffer the certain consequences of the opponent.

On more even terms, where running away even with a well-placed insult is the cowardly option, a loss of face must be enjoined with an attack. In the last example above, three-to-one odds may seem to be a bit extreme to face off, but since the single gang member was promised a fair fight against only one opponent at a time by the other three, he would have lost face by running off. He stayed and fought quite well until he was knifed and jumped by all three Pirus.

So the main ingredients of this type of gangbang are the gang-generated strong desire to maintain a reputation and the use of face-losing incidents in focused interaction. In cases where only one side desires a fight, that side uses insults to back the opponent into an inter-actional corner where he is left with the choice of losing face and reputa-tion or striking back. Where both sides want combat, they throw the insults at one another until they have generated enough anger and/or courage to force an actual attack. As we continue to examine gangbangs, we will see the many ways in which this ritual is accomplished.

SITUATIONS OF THE GANGBANG

This section examines the behavior settings and occasions of gang-bangs. The focus is on the actual occasion and the dynamics that lead gangs to assault and fight one another in a face-to-face gathering. With drive-bys, the occasion of the drive-by itself immediately and unequivo-cally transforms any prior occasions to that special aftermath following drive-by shootings. It may or may not involve the police, but whatever occasion was there is now gone.

With gangbangs, there can be a more gradual transformation of the situation as it is changed from an unfocused to focused interaction or there is a change in the focus itself. In order for there to be any kind of combat, more than one gang must be present and create an incident that brings about the combat. By examining those mutual gatherings, we can predict where to find gangbangs.

Mutual Gatherings

Virtually any place that gangs may go, either in or out of their own territory, they can encounter rival gangs or gang members. From time to time, a gang member will have to transgress the territory of another gang, whether it is a shopping mall, park, or city street. On one occa-sion, a Piru, bedecked in his identifying red outfit, had to disembark from a trolley that ended before the Piru territory began. He tried to make it out of the Crips' set (a gang term for territory) and into Piru area without getting spotted. Even a casual observer will notice that the African-American residents of Crips territory do not wear red. They are afraid of accidentally being mistaken for a Blood and shot before their true identity is known. (The lack of blue in Blood territory is equally notable.) In this particular incident, the Piru was spotted and was beaten and stabbed.

Even out-of-town gang members are subject to attack when they visit friends or relatives. The following narrative by a member of the Los Angeles gang 9/2 Bishops UBN (United Blood Nation) illustrates rivalries across city boundaries (Los Angeles is about one hundred miles north of San Diego):

> Me and my brother went to take a walk. We had been drinking a few beers. When we got down there where those guys hand out, this guy came off the porch and said, "What up, cuzz?" [Calling a Piru/Blood a cuz (or cuzz) is an insult since Crips refer to one another as cuz while Pirus call one another Blood.] We kept walking and a homeboy threw a bottle at us and then the one that came off the porch, he started talking that "What up, cuzz?" shit. He said, "What up, cuzz? What up, cuzz?" Then all the rest of them came off the porch and then a dude said, "You can't be walking down through here with all that red on." And as he was saying that he was taking off his jacket. As soon as he took off his jacket he threw up his hands. I was waiting to see if he was going to talk it out or not. Then we just started fighting. He was just a little bit bigger than me, so he tried to muscle me, you know, trying to slam me down on the ground. While he was holding me, one of his homeboys started socking me in the head.
>
> Then my brother hit the other dude, who was punching me and they started to fight too. Then I head someone say, "He's got a knife, he's got a knife." The next thing I knew my brother came and grabbed me from the back by my jacket and said, "Come on, let's go." I had already jacked the homeboy and had him laying across the top of his truck and I was punching him out. Then, as I said my brother came and grabbed me. We just took off and ran. We ran down the street then over to my mother's house. We were at home for thirty-five to forty-five minutes before the police came. [The reason the police came was that the narrator's brother was the one who had the knife and had stabbed one of the attackers.]

The interesting aspect of the above incident is that the Los Angeles Bloods had attempted to avoid a confrontation. They had even allowed loss of face by not responding to the jibe, "What up, cuzz?" His claims were further backed up by the nongang brother of one of the Crips who had attacked the Los Angeles Bloods. He told the police,

> Those two dudes were walking by minding their own business. They weren't bothering nobody. Somebody said, "What up, cuzz?" and they kept walking without saying anything. The fellas said, "Hey cuzz." The dudes said they wasn't into that gang stuff and they didn't claim anything. . . . [T]hem guys (Crips) started throwing bottles at them. Jeffrey rushed one of those dudes and they started fighting.

> To be honest with you my brother and them guys fucked up because those dudes was just minding their business and they got jammed for nothing.

The territory was doubly alien to the Los Angeles Bloods since they were from out of town and in a Crips neighborhood, and so avoiding a fight did not have the same stigma as it would have in their home territory. One of the Los Angeles Bloods made the following remarks to the police:

> If I had know that was Crip territory, I would have never been walking around down there with that red jacket on in the first place. And I told those guys we didn't want any trouble when they first jammed me up. I told them we were just walking through and we were down here trying to visit family, because we had just really came down here from L.A. the day before that just to visit my mother. . . . If I knew that's what it was like in San Diego, I would have never came down here. I came down here just wanting to cool out a little bit and get away from all this shit, but now, I see what it's going to be like, and I don't want anything to happen to mom's house so I'm just going to get out of here. As a matter of fact, I'm getting out of here as soon as you guys let me go.

The police let the Bloods go even though they had knifed one of the Crips. They characterized the incident as one of self-defense. Usually in a situation where one side uses weapons and the other does not, it is the side with the weapons that initiates the conflict. However, in the above case, even the police recognized the interactional moves made by the Los Angeles Bloods to avoid the fight. The police did not take the wearing of the red jacket by the Bloods as a challenge but rather as an honest mistake.

BEHAVIORAL SETTINGS AND OCCASIONS OF GANGBANGS

For the most part gangbangs occur in the expected behavioral settings of the streets, but not as often as drive-bys. (Virtually by definition, drive-bys occur in the streets.) In 1981, about 57 percent of the fights and 54 percent of the assaults by gangs occurred in the streets. By 1988, the figures were pretty much the same, with 53 percent of the fights and about 43 percent of the assaults occurring in the streets.

Several gangbangs occur in transit occasions, that is, when gang members go from one place to another, such as the store or the park. As we have seen in other examples in this chapter, several incidents occurred while gang members were going to or from a location. Contact in transit situations is more readily available than in more focused gatherings. For example, the following case illustrates the mutual availability and vulnerability of gang members in such situations:

> A Shelltown boy was walking along the street when a group of six Logan Lucky members approached him and asked his name. He replied with his street name, "Candyman." When asked what he claimed, he said he did not claim anywhere. At this point the Shelltown gang member was hit in the eye with a club, and then he was beaten and stabbed. When the Shelltown boy passed out, the Logan Lucky gang left the area.

The openness to approach makes the transit situation a risky one for gangbangers and non–gang members alike. In rape cases, it was found that the transit situation was the most likely one for a woman to be initially contacted by rapists (Sanders 1980). The situation of transit has an open character to it in that people place themselves in a position of contact, but it does not have the same normative orderliness of other open occasions, such as the horse races (Scott 1968). In the looser occasion of transit, nonparticipants typically elect not to get involved, and other than calling the police or increasing the distance between themselves and the trouble in a public place, gang members can expect noninterference. By *looking the other way* the non–gang members communicate their disinvolvement in the incident, and even to shout "Stop it!" they would admit to some participation in the gathering they are trying to avoid. Thus, any social control that others in public have that tacitly oversees transit places is voided.

The transit occasion is also the occasion for the initiating gang. Gang members, like young people following legitimate pursuits, spend time looking for something to do. They too spend time looking around to see what opportunities may arise. The following is from an interview with a Neighborhood Crip who used the street name Babydracc. It illustrates an interesting twist on the assault form of gangbangs with a rival gang member who displayed the incredibly bad judgment of using an Automatic Teller Machine (ATM) in a hostile set:

> Me and my homeboys were drinking and getting messed up. We had nothing better to do. We started walking around looking for some bitches, but all of the sudden we've seen a *slob nigga*. [*Slob* is the term Crips had for Blood members. *Slug* was used by Bloods to describe Crips.] He was not from our gang.
>
> I walked up to him and said, "What are you doing?" meaning "Dude you about to get jacked" at an ATM. When he went to respond I bombed on him to his mouth. He fell down. My homeboys started to kick him, then we stood him up—put him up against the wall. My homeboy put a

gun [on him]. We checked him for goods. He had three hundred dollars. He kept on talking shit, so my homeboy shot him in the toe. We kept hitting him. We put him in the trunk of his own car. We drove around for six hours, getting drunk, showing him off in the set. Late at night we dropped him off at the naval base. We kept the car and later crashed into a pole. We ran to our homeboy's pad. My homeboy went to the hospital [for injuries sustained in the car crash].

Babydracc explained that in a gangbang situation it is best to make a move first so as gain tactical advantage and avoid getting shot or hit yourself and be unable to retaliate. Even in situations where the rival obviously is at a huge disadvantage and shows no indication of wanting any trouble, there is a strike-first mentality.

In San Diego, as in all of Southern California, transit situations occur most often in automobiles. However, the automobile in gang warfare is typically used for drive-by shootings, and so is not considered in this chapter. Nevertheless, there are situations that have the character of gangbangs when automobiles are used. The primary feature of gangbangs involving automobiles is that the participants come into some type of eye-to-eye encounter and communicate mutual hostility. It goes from an unfocused to a focused encounter, which generates the hostile incident. For example, the following account of a gangbang involving cars illustrates this. The interview subject belonged to an Oceanside gang, Krook City Blood. [Oceanside is a community in an area called North County in the San Diego area.]

We were drunk and budded out on a Friday night, and we decided to go to the Center Street Locals neighborhood. We had nothing better to do and someone brought up the idea. There were four of us. I brought my gun because all youngsters get guns . . . ya know for protection. Everyone has them—anything might happen. We were there and we were about to leave when a car came up slowly towards us. We knew from the way they looked that they were from another gang—"mad-dogging" [mad-dogging is a tough stare] us until we met up with them. We stopped ten feet from each other. I got out and shot at their car. We drove off yelling "What that Krook City like, Blood." This is what happens if you mess with us. I made my move first before I got smoked.

Dances

Most of the gangs did not venture into rival territory unless they had some type of special attraction there or they were hunting for rival members to attack. One type of special attraction was dances sponsored by recreation centers or church groups. Typically, if a dance were going to occur in one gang's home territory, members of a rival gang would only go if they were "carrying" (weapons) and expecting to cause trouble or defend themselves against it.

In one instance, a charitable group of Jesuit brothers had an antigang crusade. They attempted to put on programs they felt would wean gang members from violent activities. They were certain their program would be successful and were openly disdainful of the police's efforts, claiming the police did not understand the gang members' needs or problems. (This was especially galling to the police since the majority of the gang detail members were of the same minority groups as the gang members and the good brothers were all white.) At the brothers' first church-sponsored dance for the homeboys, there was a stabbing after members of rival gangs mad-dogged each other and "threw" their signs (made their gang's hand signs) until shoving and hitting ensued. Eventually someone pulled out a knife and stabbed a rival gang member. Undeterred by the incident, the next year the brothers put on another dance. There was another stabbing, and the police began calling the event the "Our Lady of Angels Annual Stabbing Dance."

The most interesting aspect of the gangbangs that occurred at dances is that dances are relatively controlled occasions. The dances examined occurred in sponsored settings with conventional adults present, and so it would seem that the situation would be an unlikely one to generate gang conflict. This would seem to be especially true when a religious organization was actively promoting intergang harmony.

However, like all such events, the sponsors' intentions may have little to do with the social realities of those gang members who are invited to the occasion. For a gang member, the event is a situation where a rival gang member may attack him or his homeboys. Bringing weapons to such gatherings is justified as being realistic about the situation by the gang members. In effect, the background of the dance provides the reason the weapons are present. Everyone knows the occasion will attract members from rival gangs. In the social reality of the gang members, such an occasion virtually demands bringing weapons.

By examining how the events at dances lead up to gangbangs, we can reverse the tenets of smooth interaction. The first ill-mannered gesture that contributes to gangbangs at the dances examined is mad-dogging, which can be done up to any distance where eye gestures are visible, including opposite sides of a room. Goffman notes the following in discussing intrusions on the territories of the self:

> Eye behavior is an example [of an incursion]. In lower-class Mexican-American youth gangs, for example, the notion of a "bad look" seems fairly well-established, involving an infraction of the rule that subordi-

nates are supposed to avert their gaze having returned the superordinate's
for a brief time. Turf and the dominance hierarchy can be at issue. (1971:45)

At the dances, the failure to glance away is not a matter of respecting a
superordinate, but rather it is the issue of dominance that Goffman
notes. The stare, when it is not averted, becomes an intrusion upon
one's self. In effect, it is a manner of symbolically elbowing one's way
into another's domain. Pushing back is accomplished by returning the
same "bad look" in the form of mad-dogging.

In addition to intruding upon one's personal space with a stare, a
different kind of stare can intrude on one's possessions. A girl who is at
the dance with one gang can be the target of an admiring stare from rival
gang members. This has the same effect as intruding on one's territory
of self as Goffman points out in dance occasions: "Further at dances, a
youth may find it necessary to defend the integrity of his relationship to
a girl whom another boys has looked at overlong from across the hall"
(1971:46).

So in addition to provoking a rival by not averting a challenging stare,
a gang member can use a flirting stare at a rival's girl to insult him as
well. According to one former gang member, the girls often not only
invited the attention of rival gang members on such occasions, but they
would use the occasions to demand that something be done to preserve
their honor. They would go up to their homeboys and say, "Those guys
are looking at me. What are you going to do about it?" At the same time,
though, they may encourage the attention by smiling shyly or failing to engage in the other signals that women use to discourage male
attention.

Given at least two ways in which staring can offend—intruding on
one's own territory and upon one's property—we can see how offensive
behavior sets the stage for combat. At the same time, we can see that
none of the remedial interchanges are employed by either side. Basically, a remedial interchange is work that is done by an offending party
to convince the offended party that his or her offending communications
were not intentional. For example, a remedial interchange might go
something like the following:

> [Man is staring at woman.]
>
> She: "What the hell are you looking at?"
>
> Him: "I'm terribly sorry, you looked so much like my sister who recently
> died that I could not take my eyes off you."

The remedial interchange acknowledges the offending behavior, offers an apology, and provides an account for the offending behavior.

Whether the account is true or the apology sincere is a moot point. The offended party's face has been restored, and as long as continued offenses do not occur, the incident is dropped.

Goffman (1971:109–15) describes three sorts of such interchanges. First, there are accounts. They represent reasonable explanations for norm violations and assure the offended party the slight was unintentional. Compared to offering placating accounts, gang members either provide no account at all or give accounts that add further insult. The query "Where are you from?" can be answered with the counterchallenge *"Sherman, y que?"* However, the initial offense is the question, "Where are you from?" So the offender is not the one who gave the truculent reply, but rather the original questioner. In a gang context, "Where are you from?" is a challenge, and assuming the person questioned understands the question as such, the *"y que?"* phrase is a rejoinder, not a throwing down of the gauntlet. Were the question not meant to elicit a counterchallenge, the questioner could introduce a remedial interchange by an account explaining that the query was a literal, sociable one and not a challenge. For instance, he might say, "I was just asking since I used to live over there myself." Indeed, such remedial accounting may occur frequently between nonrival gang members, but they would not result in violent confrontations. Instead what is seen in the violent confrontations is the lack of remedial accounts.

Apologies are a second type of remedial interchange and may be harder to swallow than accounts for offending gang members. In the context of machismo, apologies are a sign of capitulation. Indeed, the famous cultural line, "Never apologize—it's a sign of weakness," uttered by John Wayne in one of his movies, is cited as a macho dictum. Accounts are used to change an incorrect interpretation, cite mitigating circumstances, or in some other way free the offending party from blame. Apologies, on the other hand, involve splitting the self in two: a part who accepts responsibility and blame and a part who dissociates from the offense and reaffirms a belief in the rule that is violated (Goffman 1971:113). It is a form of self-castigation, and at the same time accepts the moral nature of the offended party. The part who sides with the offended party shows he should be accepted by the offended side.

For gang members there is a twofold problem with offering apologies to other gang members. First, there is self-blame, which by implication brings shame on the gang. Since rivals are defined, one and all, as lesser forms of life, admitting blame would be equivalent to accepting blame for stepping on a slug. The attitude among gang members is, "If you don't want to be offended, stay away from me. If you don't stay away from me and you are offended, it's your own fault, so why should I apologize?" Given that stance, remedial interchanges using apologies after an initial offense are rare.

Finally, apologies are requests to be accepted back into the fold. Since a gang member is not asking to be taken back into a rival's fold, he has no reason to present himself as siding with the offended party. As a result, gang incidents are rarely defused by apologies.

The last type of remedial interchange is in the form of a request (Goffman 1971:114). Requests take place prior to a potential offense. For example, if members of a gang are entering another gang's territory, they might request entry. A common practice in gang life is dating girls from other territories. (These relationships are not of the Romeo and Juliet variety but rather a strange breach in the walls of mutual distrust and separation existing between gangs.) A common courtesy might be to explain one's intentions to a gathering of the local gang members to avoid interpretations of invasion. Usually, though, there is a good communication net that would inform the gang members of any intruder's intentions involving the homegirls. Usually the other girls who dated homeboys would spread the word effectively. However, such information would not restrict the home territory gang from asking the outsider's business if he did not make a request. As was seen in another example in this chapter, when the Bloods visited their mother in another city but in the middle of a Crips neighborhood, failure to request the use of the area even for a family visit led to a violent confrontation.

The discussion of what leads to gangbangs at dances carried into a more general analysis of offending behavior and lack of remedial work. We will see that other settings for gangbangs have the same possibility of contact, offense, and lack of remedial interchanges. Instead of acting to remedy offense, gang members act to intensify it to the point of physical violence. Therefore, by examining what gang members do in gangbangs, we can examine not only the structure of violence, but also its opposite, the necessary forms of behavior that reduce offense and loss of face.

Parties

Unlike dances, which are relatively controlled and structured, parties are less formal, looser, and less controlled occasions. The settings for parties are typically private houses or apartments instead of recreation centers or other more public places. Parties are less likely to be planned far in advance, and they are often spontaneous gatherings on the spur of the moment. However, they account for only a small portion of the situations of gang violence. In 1981, 8.6 percent of the gangbangs were at parties, and only 2.3 percent in 1988.

Since partying is a very large part of gang life, one would expect more incidents at parties. Not only are inhibitions likely to be low during party occasions, but a large portion of the gang is in one place, enabling quick mobilization. With escalating violence in gang encounters, it may be that gangs are avoiding parties in rival territories since the likelihood of a shooting or stabbing is almost certain. Unlike events that intentionally attempt to bring rival gangs together, parties initiated by gang members do not extend invitations to rivals. Moreover, given the private settings of parties, not just anyone can come.

Incidents occurring at parties often take place when the party spills over outside the house. The individuals outside can come into contact with rival gang members who walk by the party location. (This would be an occasion where a rival was not attacking the gang in a drive-by shooting.) For example, the following occurred at such a party:

> A Logan boy was in the front yard at a party when some Lomas boys approached him. They asked him where he was from, and he said, "Logan Heights." At that point, the Lomas gang members pushed him to the ground, fired a shot into the air and then shot the victim in the shoulder.

Like the drive-by shooting, such an assault targets a situation where there is a good likelihood that rivals will be present. However, such attacks at parties can be risky since the attackers cannot quickly flee if the rest of the assembled gang decides to counterattack. Moreover, since parties usually occur in the party-giver's home territory, an attacking gang is isolated from the protection of its own neighborhood. As a result, we do not see too many nonmobile attackings (i.e., attack and fleeing on foot) unless the incident occurs when gangs are in close proximity.

If a gang has a party in the home territory of a rival, there is almost certain to be some kind of confrontation. The gang that has the party, though, is very likely to be prepared since it recognizes the risks of going outside its own domain for such a gathering. Sometimes at such events, it is the home territory gang that ends up second-best, as the following incident illustrates:

> Some Varrio Chula Vista boys with their dates were having a New Year's Eve party at the house of an uncle of one of the Chula Vista boys who happened to live in the Del Sol gang's territory. Some Del Sol boys drove up to the party and asked to talk to the uncle. The Chula Vista boys said, "Puro CV" [pure Chula Vista], and the Del Sol boys said Chula Vista should not be in their territory. The Del Sol boys got back in their car and began driving away when twenty to thirty Chula Vista boys started throwing bottles and rocks at the vehicle and shots were fired. Three Del Sol boys were hit by gunfire. All of the shooting victims tried to run away, but two collapsed and died.

For the Chula Vista gang, the attack was likely to have been a preemptive strike against the Del Sol boys before they could gather more gang members and return. The Del Sol members may not have realized how many Varrio Chula Vista members were there and ready to fight. Since Del Sol and Chula Vista did not have a history of animosity, the Del Sol boys may have expected to be invited to the party themselves as a form of apology for not having been given a prior request to have the party. Whatever the case, the Del Sol boys wholly underestimated the reaction their visit caused.

As far as gang norms are concerned, the Chula Vista gang had challenged Del Sol tacitly by having a party in its area. Had Del Sol done nothing, it would have lost face. Instead of mounting an all-out attack or a drive-by shooting, it sent what turned out to be an undermanned delegation to demand some face-saving solution, such as an apology or invitation to the party. Since enough Chula Vista homeboys were armed, they felt they did not have to back down, and instead of backing down from their encroachment and reducing tension, they escalated it to the point of a double homicide.

Parties, as loose occasions, do not seem to generate gang violence due to the nature of the occasion per se. Instead, parties come to be occasions where several gang members are in the same place at the same time. As such, they become targets of opportunity for rival gangs.

Park Activities

Parks in low-income areas are gathering places for people who have relatively little or undesirable personal space. San Diego is a city dotted with parks, and every neighborhood has close access to parks. Gangs, especially the Mexican-American gangs, identify with and use the parks as their main gathering places. However, over the years, the park is less and less likely to be a point of gang violence. In 1981, 7.3 percent of the gangbangs were in parks, and by 1988, the proportion had fallen to 6.6 percent.

Three different types of parks can be identified: large public parks, special-use parks, and neighborhood parks. Large public parks, while the scene of criminal violence, especially against the homeless, are not a typical setting for gang violence. San Diego is famous for its zoo in Balboa Park, located adjacent to several gang territories. However, Balboa Park is not the setting for gang violence. Because it is a tourist attraction, having several museums and a replica of a Shakespearean theater in addition to the zoo, any gang activity there would be subject to more scrutiny than the gang members would want.

Special-use parks have some unique theme but are not large public parks. The best known of these in San Diego is one called Chicano Park. The park is decorated with murals depicting Mexican themes and activities in the United States and Mexico and is the site for Mexican-American celebrations, such as Cinco de Mayo. It is located in the Logan Heights area not far from several gangs territories, and it is used as a home territory park by a gang called the Red Steps.

One of the ideas behind dedicating this park to Mexican-American activities and heritage was to attempt to reduce the gang graffiti that defaced the area. Colorful and elaborate murals were painted by Chicano artists on the freeway pillars and supports, showing the plight and achievements of Mexican Americans. This had the initial effect of reducing the graffiti, but in a short time after the initial murals were painted, gang graffiti began appearing again, even though they did not deface the bulk of the murals.

A number of instances of gang violence have occurred in Chicano Park, involving both nongang victims and rival gangs. Since the park is in the home territory of the Red Steps, whenever a rival gang wants to attack them, it will go to the park. Also, during certain Mexican-American events held in the park, members of rival gangs will come for the festivities but end up fighting one another after contact has been made. Since for the out-of-area gang members it is common sense to bring weapons to a rival's territory, all such gatherings have the potential for violence between gangs.

Finally, the neighborhood parks are the kinds of parks where gangbangs are most likely. Since the parks are relatively small, spotting a rival gang in one is fairly easy. For example, the following case typifies the kind of gangbangs occurring in small parks used by one gang as a gathering place:

> Members of the Shelltown gang were having a party and hanging out in Southcrest Park, located in the middle of the Shelltown territory. Some boys from Calexico but claiming Varrio Spring Valley started a fight with the Shelltown gang and killed one of the Shelltown members. [Calexico is a border town about one hundred miles to the east of San Diego. On occasion, young men from Calexico come to San Diego, claim a San Diego gang, and then fight one of the claimed gang's rivals. In 1981, two gang-related homicides involved attacks by Calexico boys who linked up with San Diego gangs.]

In the parks that lie between the gang territories and are not the primary hangout of any single gang, occasions arise where two gangs will be at a party or picnic at the same time. Sometimes they keep separate, neither wanting to recognize the other's presence, thereby avoiding a fight. On the other hand, when there is acknowledged contact, each side may egg the other on to start a fight. For example, the following incident occurred when two gangs met during mutually independent outings:

> Del Sol and Sidro gangs were at one of the larger parks in the South Bay area where the residents of the area often went for picnics. When the gangs saw one another, they began exchanging jibes and mad-dogging one another. One of the Del Sol boys had his hand inside his coat as the gangs approached each other, calling one another names. A number of the Del Sol boys said to their member who had his hand inside his coat, "You going to take that? You going to let them talk to you that way?" He pulled a gun out of his coat and shot one of the Sidro boys point blank in the face. At that point, he started shooting at the rest of the Sidro gang, who ran down a hill away from him. He chased them, continuing to fire his gun. The other Del Sol boys held back. When he reached the bottom of the hill, the shooter ran out of bullets. When the Sidro gang realized this, they attacked and killed him. The other Del Sol members escaped in their vehicles.

The nature of the above incident is such that we again see a breakdown in face work. An incident is created by a word or gesture that creates loss of face by the other. Verbal and gestural retaliation follows without any attempt to defuse the incident.

Beach Activities

Other than the gangs in nearby towns, none of the gangs in San Diego are beach gangs per se. The only near-gang in the beach area is the PB Rats (also known as the PB Vermin), and while they generate problems, they are not considered a gang. (Residents in the Pacific Beach area requested that the police department send the gang detail to deal with the PB Rats, describing them as a menace to the area, but given the peskiness but nonlethal orientation of the Rats, the police left them to be handled by the beach patrol.) Most of the gang activity at the beaches occurs when a gang travels to the beach.

There have been robberies by gang members in beach areas and even a few gangbangs and drive-bys, but not many. The most notable feature of the beaches is that they serve as mutual meeting places where gangs can come together. This occurs during both nighttime and daytime. Since the beaches change their character from night to day, we will examine them as two different social entities during the different times.

Sun Beaches. The San Diego area sun beaches run along the coast from Oceanside to the Mexican Border and, given San Diego's climate and orientation, are popular gathering spots. During the day, there have been incidents involving gang members, but they are rare. The large number of nongang, nonneighborhood participants at the daytime beach gatherings limits the security of the gangs. Also, the beaches are heavily patrolled by the police to prevent making this major tourist attraction less desirable.

Some gangs, notably the Southeast Asian gangs, have partitioned one section of beach into Cambodian and Lao domains. In one confrontation between the Oriental Boy Soldiers and a Lao gang, one of the gangs left the area and returned with guns, firing on its rival. The event was considered remarkable in that bullets were fired into such a large gathering with the only death being a girl who was running away from the shooting when she was struck and killed. For the shooters, it simply added to the growing gang lore developing around Southeast Asian gangs.

Leisure Lagoon.   One of the areas near the beach that is frequented by gang members at night is called Leisure Lagoon. It is a best described as a family park area, which has tracts of grass, barbecue pits, and walkways along the water.

The gangs that go there do so not to fight, but rather for evening recreation. They will bring beer, wine, something to barbecue, and their girlfriends. On the several occasions on which I saw them while I was observing with the gang detail, they acted and looked like the others at the lagoon. However, when different gangs arrived there, they often would fight, and several stabbings and shootings occurred. For example, the following illustrates the very minimum requirements for gangbangs:

> A number of Red Step gang members were at the lagoon, when a single member of Calle Trienta arrived. Generally, the two Logan Heights gangs are compatible, sharing common foes in the Sherman and Shelltown gangs. Indeed, in the Logan Heights area, a number of *placas* have the sign for Logan Heights without mentioning the specific gangs. The Calle Trienta member went up to the Red Steps engaging in friendly conversation. After a while, though, the Red Steps started pointing out that the Calle Trienta gang members came from the poor part of Logan Heights. [The Thirtieth Street area of Logan Heights is more typically the area where newer immigrants settle and it does have a generally lower income.]
>
> The Calle Trienta member attempted to retaliate by hitting his tormentors, but he was outnumbered. The Red Steps roughed him up and told the Calle Trienta boy to go away. Returning to his car, the Calle Trienta gang member opened the trunk and pulled out a rifle. He shot one of the Red Steps in the head, and then left the area.

Like the other gangbangs discussed in this chapter, the incident began with the loss of face by one of the gang members. There was no face-saving in the form of remedial interchanges, and a shooting took place. The mutual resolution of violence, roughing up the Calle Trienta member and shooting the Red Step, was typical of the way in which these incidents are resolved.

Family Activities

One other type of event that draws gang members from rival sides are family activities. Weddings and baptismal parties draw in family members from all over the city and even from out of town. When these events occur, the setting is provided for fights between gang members. We will discuss Mexican-American baptismal parties since they seem to have the largest share of such conflicts.

Baptismal Parties

In Mexican-American culture, baptismal parties are large gatherings of family and friends. They reinforce the family and serve as an opportunity for solidarity between families in a particular church and by extension the community. However, since the occasions can bring rival gang members together, they are settings for gangbangs. The following is a typical gangbang at a baptismal party:

> A baptismal party attended by Sherman gang members and a gang from Chula Vista called Primera Flats had its origins in an insult a year before in a youth detention camp. One of the Primera Flats boys had X'ed out a Sherman gang member's *placa* on his tennis shoe. The incident was brought up. First, the gang members mad-dogged each other, and some punches were thrown. One of the Primera Flats boys left the party after he was punched, and was chased down by Sherman boys and stabbed.
>
> After the stabbing, the Sherman boys returned to the party, leaving the Primera Flats boy seriously wounded. Later at the party, a second fight broke out, and another Primera Flats boys was stabbed. When the police arrived, they arrested a Primera Flats member who was swinging a baseball bat at the Shermans.

The interesting aspect of the above incident is that what sparked the stabbings was an event that occurred in neutral territory (juvenile detention) over a year before the party. Since the two gangs were not rivals otherwise, some minor occurrence was dredged up to use as a reason to fight. The ritual of mad-dogging led to a punch being thrown and eventually a stabbing. Since the Primera Flats boy left the party after being punched, it was clear that he was doing the only thing he knew would decrease the violence. However, the move was not accepted by the Shermans and he was stabbed.

SUMMARY AND CONCLUSION

Gangbangs can occur whenever members of rival gangs come into contact. They do not seem to be planned, but the gang members often carry weapons to plan for the eventuality of a gangbang. Ironically, the defensive planning provides all of the tools that make gangbangs violent.

What typically occurs is a breakdown in remedial interchanges after one side has suffered a loss of face and wants redress. However, because the gang members either desire to escalate the violence or lack the interactional skills to avoid it, gang fights and assaults occur.

The settings and occasions are important primarily because they constitute a point where the gangs come together. There is nothing inherent in the settings or occasions that generates the violence other than that they tend to be of a looser nature. Instead there are blatant or implied gang challenges when the rivals occupy the same time and space. These occasions further ground the beliefs that weapons should be carried and that rival gangs only respect coercive power. Any insult that is tolerated is considered a sign of weakness, and the offender cannot engage in remedial interchanges either because of lack of skills or because such interchanges are considered signs of weakness. The gangs believe that signs of weakness will result in further attack, and as we have seen from several examples, attempts to avoid confrontation are indeed taken as signs of weakness and result in attacks.

CHAPTER

6

Other Types of Gang Violence

INTRODUCTION

While the bulk of gang violence studied was directed at rival gang members, a good deal of gang violence targets victims who have no gang affiliation or identification. There are two basic types of such violence. First, there are attacks and threats for financial gain, including robbery and extortion. Virtually all of the victims are nongang. Second, gangs assault non–gang members and so are involved in other than gangbang activities. Unlike gang vs. gang assaults where each side may be involved in the escalation of violence, many of the gang vs. nongang assaults include a reluctant participant. These acts are instructive in examining the elements of interaction where one party to the interaction attempts to avoid a violent confrontation.

GANG VIOLENCE AND NON–GANG MEMBERS

While the interchanges in gangbangs and drive-bys involve members of groups that use violence themselves, this chapter examines incidents where the targets of violence are nonviolent. In these situations we can see two things. First, we can examine certain other forms of gang behavior as gang-generated occasions. This helps complete the mosaic of gang life in terms of the occasions that one can expect to find in the day-to-day rounds of gang life. Second, we can use some of the occasions to examine the interaction between those who may wish to minimize violence and those who wish to maximize it. These occasions provide a resource for seeing how the *lack* of remedial interchanges serves to escalate violence.

In examining the police data on gang violence, we find that a large proportion of victims are not affiliated with gangs. However, it is almost impossible to tell with any assurance whether the information received by the gang detail is an accurate representation of actual gang incidents against nongang victims. In 1981, the vast majority of reported gang cases (71.4 percent) involved non–gang members, and by 1988, only about a third (34.4 percent) of the cases listed nongang victims. The variation may involve some changes in gang patterns, but most likely they reflect a problem in accurately cataloging the cases as gang-related. As we noted in Chapter 1, the problem of categorizing a crime as gang-related is extremely problematic when dealing with non–gang members.

For example, jacking (strong-arm robbery) by gang members is a routine way of getting money. Whether the proceeds from jacking go into a general fund, to a clique, or to the person who did the robbery is almost impossible to determine. The contention that mere participation in a crime by a gang member does not mean the crime is gang related assumes a certain organized vision of the gang that may be inaccurate. Other than age and gender groupings, the only common structural characteristic of gangs in San Diego was the cliques. Since jacking was usually done by cliques, the money was shared by those in the robbery, and not the entire clique and certainly not the entire gang. Even in highly organized gangs such as Chicago's *Vice Lords*, the cliques and individual members had money based on their own initiative and not the gang's. Often the younger members would have money that they did not share with the older, less active members (Keiser 1969:63).

In a case where one gang member does something on his own, such as beating up a nongang youth over lack of respect shown, it still may be gang related. If membership in a gang leads to expectations of certain types of behavior from non–gang member (e.g., deference), and a gang member assaults another person because those expectations are not met, then the action is gang-related. Likewise, if a boy in a gang assaults an individual on his own initiative but knows that retaliation is unlikely because of the protection the gang gives him, the assault can be construed as gang-related. In fact, patterns of criminal behavior, including both criminal actions and motives, can be attributed to gangs, for it can be argued that without gang association, such behavior would never have been learned and used. Therefore, Spergel and Chance's (1991:23) notion of *gang motivation* can be interpreted widely or narrowly, depending on how a gang is structured and the effect gang participation has on the independent actions of its members. (See Chapter 1 for a full discussion of Spergel and Chance's conceptualization.)

For methodological purposes, the Spergel and Chance definition was unusable. The idea of separating gang crime and nongang crime by gang members has a certain useful conceptual purpose for delineating crimes that are instigated by gang membership and those that would happen if there were no gang. However, since that separation is virtually a practical impossibility in research, gang-related crimes involving nongang targets are defined as those incidents involving gang members. Since any violence by a gang member can be attributed to the gang in this definition, it allows discretion to delete any cases or instances that seem to be clearly independent of gang affiliation. In the research and the examples discussed herein, all cases that appeared not to be gang-related in any way have been culled.

In addition to the problem of defining an incident as gang-related or not, there is the problem the police had in getting the information that a case was gang-related. Often a gang-related case that did not obviously involve two gangs fighting each other was not sent to the gang detail, but rather went to the robbery or major-crimes unit. Later, when the detectives in these other units defined the case as gang-related they sent it over to the gang detail. Once in the gang detail, it was logged as a gang-related case. Usually the other units were not certain a case was gang-related, and so there is no way of knowing to what extent cases involving gang members ever reached the gang detail. A more elaborate system attempted to advise the gang detail of all cases involving a gang victim also, but this system was in its infancy when I left the field; so it was not clear if this system worked as expected and/or if it gave the gang detail better information.

Finally, the drop in reported gang robberies from the early 1980s to the later part of the decade may be due to an actual drop in robberies. When crack cocaine sales expanded around 1988, the recorded gang-related robberies dropped. Since there was more money selling crack cocaine than in armed robberies, as the robbery rate went down, so too would the number of nongang victims of violent gang crimes.

Knowing the limitations on the data of the incidents not involving conflicts between rival gangs, we will examine various types of violent crimes by gang members on non–gang members. These crimes have been divided into robbery, assault, extortion, rape, and violence associated with drug dealing.

ROBBERIES

Robberies involve taking property by force or threat of force. The most common type of robberies by gang members is jackings, street robberies against persons. According to some gang members interviewed, jackings are not planned, but are rather crimes of opportunity. However, it does seem clear that even though a single robbery may not be planned, gang members will go to areas where they are looking for robbery victims.

Jacking

Most of the robberies gang members call jacking are against individuals. There is nothing necessarily gang-unique about jackings since non-gang groups exhibit similar patterns in street robberies. There is a difference in terms of interethnic contact, however. African-American and Mexican-American gang members involved in robberies victimize members of different ethnic groups even though there are not inter-ethnic gang rivalries between blacks and Chicanos. For example, the following robbery occurred in Chicano Park:

> A black male was sitting on a bench in Chicano Park when a Red Step pointed a knife at his throat and took his cassette recorder. The victim chased the Red Step member and got his recorder back. Then two more Red Steps attacked the victim, took his recorder, and beat him.

The only unusual aspect of the above case is that the victim pursued an armed gang member in the middle of a Hispanic area and recovered his property, even temporarily. Since Chicano Park is a major hangout for Red Step gang members, the setting of the robbery was fairly typical.

By and large, the gangs do not go outside their area to rob people. Robbery victims were found to be victimized in gang territories in all different types of situations. The following are some examples of such robberies in gang neighborhoods:

> A white male was walking down the street when a West Coast Crip approached and asked if he were new to the area. After the initial contact, he started pushing him toward a vacant lot. A second gang member then helped the first one get the victim into the lot where seven other Crips joined in beating and robbing the victim.

> Two Mexican-American sailors were at Chicano park talking with some Logan gang members. The gang grabbed the sailors and dragged them into the bathroom, holding one at knifepoint and the other at gunpoint and robbed them. One of the victims escaped, and the other was shot in the leg with a shotgun, almost severing the leg. After the shooting, the gang members drove off.

> A transvestite was at a bus stop when four Sherman members approached him and demanded cigarettes and money. The victim refused, and they tried to grab his purse. When the victim resisted, he was stabbed in the lip and thigh.

> In the public rest room in Encanto, five VELs confronted the victim and one said, "Give me your money, or I will hit you with this bat." The victim

refused and was hit in the head with the bat. Another VEL picked up a bottle and threatened to cut the victim, and then they knocked him down, kicking and hitting him. Eventually, they got twenty-four dollars from him. (Later the victim refused to cooperate with the police.)

An Oriental male was returning home from college classes when a group of six Insane Family Gang members approached and demanded money. The victim said he had none, and they started hitting him. The man ran and was shot in the back with a handgun and shotgun.

These examples of robberies are typical of gang jackings. Compared to nongang street robberies, about the only difference would be in the number of robbers involved. A typical street robbery involves one or two robbers, while a typical gang street robbery involves more than two robbers.

Sometimes the targets are more specific. In the following, somewhat rambling interview excerpt, a member of a Southeast Asian (Lao) gang, Oriental Killer Boys, explains how he robs drug users and homosexuals:

Me and another dude deal crystal [methamphetamine], not the gang. I sell a pound a day. I had been up for a week. When you're tweekin' [under the influence of methamphetamines] you don't give a fuck, and me and my homeboy, we were going around the beach selling to stoners. We just go up to them and ask them if they want some. I was really paranoid. I think everyone is undercover. I always have a gun so that's how you jack people. If they have a lot of money, we take it. You know University [Avenue] where there are a lot of gay dudes and that gay bar? They like know the dealer. They all call him for some crystal, you know they like crystal, and they're scared; so we jack them. But sometimes those faggots have a gun too.

The interesting aspect of the interview that may not be gang-typical is the combined activities of selling drugs and robbing drug customers. Given the volume of drugs they were selling, it would seem to be defeating their purpose to rob some of their customers.

On the other hand, it is not uncommon for gangs to rob drug dealers. According to John Allen's autobiography, in the late 1960s and early 1970s, robbing drug dealers of money and/or drugs was a common practice (1977:177). As the gangs became more involved in selling drugs in the 1980s, the drug dealers had more protection from robbery. However, independent drug dealers *may have been* targets. The gang detail received several cases involving victims who had large amounts of cash on them when they were robbed. For example, the following may have involved a drug dealer victim:

At 10:30 P.M. on a Sunday night, a man was robbed of his two gold necklaces, his watch, ring, and two hundred dollars in cash. He said he was going to the park because he had heard it was a good place to lift weights. When he first went to the park, a group of Sherman gang members had told him to leave, grabbing the two gold necklaces he was wearing. One told him, "Get out of here or I'll kill you."

Fifteen minutes later the man returned to the park, and a Sherman gang member threw a rock through his car window. The man stopped to see who had thrown the rock when he was assaulted, pistol-whipped, and had his money and jewelry taken. He told police he would not aid in prosecution of the suspects since he feared retaliation.

The case may have involved an honest citizen who was doing exactly what he claimed. However, the police wondered why the victim had returned to the park after being warned off by gang members, and why he would want to lift weights in a known gang territory late at night with so much cash on his person. Furthermore, since the victim lived in National City, it was unclear why he would want to come to San Diego just to lift weights in a park.

Mexican Aliens. A special type of gang-related robberies is against Mexicans who illegally enter the United States. After dark each night, hundreds of illegal Mexican aliens attempt to enter the country in the San Ysidro area on the border. An eastern suburb of Tijuana called Colina Libertad is the staging area where men, women, and even children gather to cross the border. The area is selected due to the canyon terrain and the difficulty the U.S. Border Patrol has in spotting illegal aliens. Gangs from both the U.S. and Mexican side of the border rob the illegal aliens in the canyons where they too cannot be seen by the Border Patrol.

In the late 1970s, the United States set up a special Border Task Force whose goal was to protect the illegal aliens from robbers. The task force met with some success in arresting and shooting some of the robbers, but they were accused of entering Mexican territory and even shooting some Mexican police, who were believed to be in league with the robbers (Wambaugh 1985). Due to the political tensions created by the task force, it was disbanded, with some of its members becoming the core of San Diego Police Department's gang detail.

At the beginning of my research in 1980, the Border Task Force was gone, and the robbery rate against illegal aliens was up again. The following two cases illustrate typical robberies of Mexican aliens:

Three illegal aliens were robbed by two Sidro gang members with knives. They took the money from their victims and told them to drop their pants. One victim tried to run and was stabbed.

Two Mexican aliens were crossing the border when they were attacked by two Libertad gang members and beaten with clubs. One victim went to the

Border Patrol for help, and the police arrested two other illegal aliens (the Libertad gang members) for the robbery. [Libertad is a Tijuana gang that was illegally on the U.S. side of the border.]

Sometimes the illegal aliens are not robbed until they are away from the border crossing area and out of the canyons. The Sidro gang robs the aliens once they feel they have safely made it past the Border Patrol. In this situation, the victims are unlikely to report the case to the police.

Business Robberies

Business robberies by gang members seem to have about the same lack of planning as their street robberies, and they share common patterns with nongang robberies. Other than choosing an area and looking for targets of opportunity, the robberies are unplanned. The following cases show typical gang robberies:

An member of the East San Diego gang approached the gas station attendant to buy gas in a milk container. As he approached the attendant, another East San Diego member came from behind the attendant and side, "Give me all the money or we'll blow you away. Open the cash register. Give me all the money." The victim could not open the cash drawer, so the gang members took the money on top of the counter and fled.

Three gang members went into a store. One held a knife to the cashier's throat and took the money from the cash register and the other two walked out with beer.

A Sidro gang member robbed and assaulted a cab driver with a broken beer bottle and a flashlight. He took the cab and the cab driver's money and fled.

About the only gang-unique form of robbery by gang members involves what might be called shoplifting with threat of force. A typical shoplifting is a crime of stealth where the goal is to take goods from the store without being seen. The problem for gang members is their visibility as gang members and the scrutiny of store clerks they attract. Since they are often seen taking goods from stores, they are challenged by the clerk or store owner. When this occurs, they threaten the clerk and transform a petty theft misdemeanor into a felony crime. The following cases illustrate this:

Some Sidro gang members entered the store and took beer and cigarettes. When the clerk told them to pay for the beer and cigarettes, they said, "Stick it in your ass, and if you call the cops, I'll kill you." After the suspects fled, they were seen by a police officer throwing bottles of beer over a fence. He stopped and questioned them, but he did not make an arrest since he apparently did not know about the robbery. About an hour after the first robbery, the same group of Sidro boys returned to the store and robbed more beer telling the clerk, "Motherfucker, if you call the cops, I'll kill you."

Several Del Sol gang members entered a convenience store and took beer from the case in the rear of the store. A woman running the store told them to put the beer back, and they threatened her. She then sprayed liquid mace on the gang, and they fled.

Sidro gang members went into a convenience store and demanded beer. The female clerk refused and one member pulled out a chain and further demanded the beer. Two other Sidro boys tried to stop him, and he threw the chain at the clerk, hitting her in the face. They picked up the chain and pulled the third member out of the store.

EXTORTION

Essentially two types of gang extortion were encountered in the research. First, there was extortion of schoolchildren by gang members themselves still in school. Gang members would extort lunch money from students, or from other youths outside school. In interviews with a former gang member, I was able to learn that gang members routinely took money from students in school, on the way to school, and after school. In one sense these cases represent nothing more than robbery, but the students were paying for "protection," and in that sense it represents gang extortion. The fact that the police received few if any reports of this extortion does not mean it was not a common practice. Rather, the extortion existed in the environment of fear that the gangs hoped to generate. The following case was reported to a school police officer, and the victim clearly indicated his fear of reprisal:

> Oriental Boy Soldiers drove by the victim in his car and shot at him with a shotgun and other unidentified guns. The victim explained to a police officer assigned to the school that he had been intimidated by the Black Jacket clique of the Oriental Boy Soldiers for some time, and they had attempted to extort money from him. The victim explained that the shooting incident was part of the extortion intimidation pattern he had experienced.

The second type of extortion case, against businesses, was also rarely reported. The only case found was one where the proprietor refused to be extorted any more and was murdered:

> Two East San Diego gang members went into a taco shop and demanded free food as they had successfully done in the past. When they were refused and told to leave the shop, they attacked the proprietor with a club and knife, beating and stabbing him to death.

How typical business extortion is carried out is unknown from this study. However, Jankowski (1991:122–23) argues that protection is one of the primary services that gangs provide businesses. Moreover, Jankowski claims that the vast majority of store owners who pay protection money to the gangs do not need coercion to convince them. Since the businesses offered protection are typically in a high crime area, they are more than glad to get the protection they feel is not otherwise provided. Likewise, Chin (1990:139) noted that Chinese gangs extorted protection money in Chinese-American communities. Since illegal gambling establishments in Chinatown could not ask for police protection, the gangs filled this function. In Miller's (1969) study of white gangs, the Bandits felt obliged to protect their home territory candy shops and would take it as a personal affront if it were the target of theft or robbery. To what extent gang protection is an extortion racket or a desired service depends on how the business really views the practice.

About the only sustained reports of business extortion in San Diego by gangs are in the Southeast Asian communities, where Vietnamese gangs are rumored to extort money from Asian-American businesses in the area. The accuracy of such reports and rumors has not been verified. If the Cambodian and Lao gangs begin offering protection to Southeast Asian businesses, they may do so on the basis of protecting them from African-American and Mexican-American gangs. Given the violence visited on black and Hispanic gangs by Southeast Asian gangs in the early 1990s, there is every reason to believe the Oriental gangs could successfully dissuade these other gangs from bothering protected Southeast Asian businesses.

ASSAULTS

The high proportion of violent acts against non–gang members is not limited to robberies. Many of the assaults and fights have involved gang members attacking non–gang members. While most of the cases involve clear instances of gang members initiating the violence, some cases do no involve gang initiation. For example, in the following case, the victim may have begun escalating the violence:

> A group of West Coast Crips was creating a disturbance in front of a small church. One of the church members came out and told them to be quiet, and they attacked him. The church member stabbed one of the Crips with a knife, and then he ran. When the other Crips caught up with him, he was stabbed and beaten to death.

As was seen with gangbangs, an *incident* occurs when one party intrudes upon another, causing loss of face. The presence of weapons sets the stage for escalation of the violence when one party confronts the other. When both parties feel they are within their rights to stand their ground or demand some type of remedial work, regardless of an outside, objective rendering of the situation, there is violence. In the last example, both the man from the church and the gang members had weapons and both felt the other was in the wrong.

Typically, non–gang members go to great lengths to avoid direct confrontation with gangs. However, at some point, the gang pushes the non–gang members into a position where there is open conflict. The following case, from a nongang victim's perspective, nicely illustrates this:

[The statements are being made about shootings and fighting at a party where uninvited members of Calle Trienta showed up. In order to avoid a confrontation, they were not initially asked to leave.] At about one in the morning, this guy . . . came up and told me that this guy had been writing on the side of my house. I walked over to the side of the house with my older brother and my father following behind me. When I got there, I saw this guy they call Cougar wearing a brown and beige checkered Pendleton with dark khakis standing by the wall which had the writing on it. When I had walked up to him I asked him if he had wrote on our wall and he said that he did, and then he asked me, "Why?" I then told him, "What do you mean why? Because it's my house and you're being disrespectful." That when he told me, "So, what's up?" I then told him to leave which was when he started walking towards the front of the house while I followed behind him. Four other guys from Logan 30th Street [Calle Trienta gang] followed me, which was when my older brother and father trailed behind him.

    Once out in front of the house, the guy went at me, which was when we both got into the fight outside in front of the house. [The fight was eventually broken up, and the party resumed.]

    When I got back to my party, I heard and saw this other guy from Calle Trienta challenging a friend, but they didn't fight. As I stood there telling the Calle Trienta guys to leave . . . two girls, one which was from Logan Red Steps and the other from Logan 30th Street, started fighting. That's when my father came up to me and told me to shut down the party because he didn't want any more problems. [As they attempted to shut down the party several Calle Trienta members returned to the house, starting another fight. During the fistfights, one of the Calle Trienta members started firing a gun, wounding three people.]

The incident that sparked violence was the gang member writing on the wall. The interchange between the gang member and the non–gang member illustrates how each pursued a course of action that resulted in violence. The following sequence shows the track taken:

1. Painting on house: Original offense
2. Confrontation: Demanding explanation
3. Response: No remedial work
4. Retaliation: Demanded gang member leave party
5. Counterretaliation: Fight

Once the fight broke out, other fights followed. The attempt to end the violence by stopping the party did not work since the gang members refused to be satisfied by any kind of truce. They engaged in negative rather than positive remedial work. The nature of remedial work is such that both sides must engage in it for it to be effective. If one side refuses to cooperate in face-saving behavior, the other side must passively take abuse, physical and/or verbal, attempt to leave the situation, or fight back. After attempting to defuse the situation by ending the occasion of the gathering, the non–gang members were physically attacked.

The sequence of a face-saving encounter has five parts (Goffman 1967:23):

1. Offense
2. Challenge
3. Offering
4. Acceptance
5. Sign of gratitude

In the above example, we saw the offense (writing on the side of the house), and the challenge (demanding an explanation). Had a different set of responses been used after the challenge, the violence could have been averted. For example, the following sequence is an example of remedial work that the challenged party could use to avert violence and restore face:

> *Offering:* "I guess I had too much to drink and wasn't thinking. Let me clean off the wall for you."
> *Acceptance:* "Ok, I'd appreciate that. Everyone's been drinking a lot, so don't worry about it. See you back inside when you get the wall cleaned up."
> *Sign of gratitude:* "Thanks. See you in few minutes."

In bar arguments and near-fights, it is not uncommon to see an argument end with one party buying the other one a drink, either as a sign of acceptance or one of gratitude. However, when remedial work is seen as a sign of weakness, and an offense a sign of manliness, there is little likelihood that the necessary interactional repair work can be accomplished, even if one side is willing to do so. In Luckenbill's (1977) study of homicides, the escalation of violence continued since remedial interchanges were taken as a sign of backing down. In situations where remedial work was successful, however, homicides did not occur.

The original offense is subject to contextual interpretive work. The behavior that is offensive may not have been intended to offend, and the challenge to the unintended offense is viewed as the initial offense. For example, the following situation has such an equivocal offense matrix:

> Some members of Oriental Boy Soldiers were standing near a man's van, and he told them to get away from it. The man left to eat lunch, and while eating, heard some shots being fired from the area where he had left the van. He returned to his van and found it had several bullet holes in it.

In this case, the original offense could either be the gang members hanging around the man's van or his telling them to stay away from it. In one context, a nongang one, an adult telling kids to stay away from a vehicle is not considered especially offensive. Likewise, kids hanging around a vehicle is not especially offensive. However, in the context of gangs, the man telling the group to leave was an order and one that offended them. They retaliated by shooting the vehicle.

In another case, the interaction between the nongang victim and the gang was nonverbal, and whether offense or play was behind the incident is unclear:

> A man and his wife were in their car on the freeway when some Vietnamese-American youths fired three shots at them. The victim followed the shooters, and notified the police on his car phone.

The case is unusual in that there did not seem to be any offense by the driver of the target car, and the boys who did the shooting seemed to do so for fun—to scare the driver of the target car. The car was in a nongang area, and since the victims were white, there did not seem to be any connection to the family of gang members. Further, while freeway shootings are not unknown in Southern California, gangs shooting at each other or at nongang victims are very rare on the freeways.

Other gang assaults appeared to be relatively nonutilitarian, even in terms of an offense to face. A speaker at Chicano Park was urging the Mexican-Americans to strengthen their solidarity and "unionize" to better their collective lot. After his speech, he was attacked and beaten by a Logan gang. His speech may have implied that the gangs were undesirable side effects of minority discrimination. And so while we can analyze gang assaults in terms of face work, it is important to understand that a gang looking for an offense to challenge can find it in virtually any actions.

RAPE

As a reported crime, rape by gang members was rare. There were some cases of rape, but not enough to justify a statistical category. Of the rapes that were reported, one involved illegal Mexican aliens who were abducted and taken to a motel by members of Sidro gang and raped. From what the police found out, this was a typical Sidro activity, but the other rapes were not reported. Another sexual assault that was reported involving the Sidro gang occurred with a male victim as detailed in the following case:

> The victim was walking along the sidewalk when he went up to a Sidro gang member and asked for a cigarette. The Sidro members said he had a carton in his apartment and invited the victim up. When they arrived in the apartment, three more Sidro gang members were there. They demanded money from the victim, and when he told them he had none, they began beating and kicking him. Then they told him to take his clothes off and have sex with one of the four gang members. They took him in a back room where he agreed to orally copulate one of the gang members. The gang member began beating him and stabbed him, but the victim was able to get away by breaking a window and jumping out.

A single case was also reported from Juvenile Hall where two West Coast Crips sodomized one of the nongang white inmates, but outside detention there were no other reported cases of gang sexual assaults against males.

The few other sexual assaults by gangs that were reported are typified by the following two cases:

> Four Neighborhood Crips who were in the West Coast Crips' set jumped two females who were walking in the area. They raped them both and made them orally copulate them in an empty lot behind some bushes. They threatened the victims with a switchblade knife and hit one of the girls. One of the Crips said, "I'll cut your throat if you don't shut up" when the victim began to cry.

> A thirteen-year-old girl and her friends were walking down the street when they approached a group of 5/9 Brims in the Skyline area. One of the gang members grabbed the thirteen-year-old and said, "I like you" and tried to fondle her breasts. She resisted, and he struck her several times, knocking her down. She got up and left with her friends.

The important thing about both of the above cases is that they are few in number. Over the entire period of research, less than a dozen cases were reported involving sexual assaults of any kind against males or females. Other studies of gangs also seem to indicate by the lack of discussion of rape cases that rape is not something that is a routine type of violence.

In interviewing gang members concerning rape, they all said that rape absolutely was not something their gang did. Since the same cohort of subjects openly discussed all types of other crimes, it is noteworthy they denied involvement with sexual assault. However, their understanding of rape may not match the conventional definitions of rape.

One former gang member said that the girls who went to their parties were available for sex after the party reached a certain point. He said the *nice girls* left when the party reached a certain stage, were not invited, or did not come at all, and the ones who stayed were sexually available for the gang. When queried what would happen if one of them refused, he said they had "better not refuse or they'd get slapped around."

In an interview, a girl who affiliates with a gang had a somewhat different version of the same theme. She explained that at parties, at some point in time, gang boys would ask if anyone wanted to go "cruisin'" with them. If a couple of girls volunteered or were talked into going in the car with several of the boys, she said that they made themselves available for sex with those in the car.

She also pointed out that the girls were usually intoxicated and/or high on drugs on these occasions, and so probably they wouldn't know what was happening to them. Thus, they were portrayed by the girl as either unintentionally or intentionally helpless. The ones who were unintentionally helpless were characterized as those who naively drank, smoked, or ingested too many intoxicants. On the other hand, those who were intentionally helpless were characterized as girls who either had or appeared to have had too much so that they could have sex without sanction.

Jankowski (1991:300–301) noted that the media portrayed gangs as attracting females who were slutty women from the "dark" side of the racial continuum. He noted that such characterizations were both sexist and racist. While sex in gang life does not live down to the media's portrayal, gangs and the girls with whom they associate do not appear to be celibate. One gang informant explained the Mexican-American dichotomy of women in the context of *Mariaisima*, the counterpart to *machismo*. This view of the sexes divided women into two groups: those who were like the virgin Mary until they married, and those who were not. This is a division of the world into "nice girls" and "bad girls." Such a characterization is not limited to gangs, but is a belief in a subcultural sense and reflects the double standards regarding sexual activity in society at large. Thus, bad girls with gangs are no better or worse than girls with a similar label in any other part of society. The difference is that the bad girls connected with gangs are used sexually without consent in certain situations.

SUMMARY

While the most noted part of gang violence has been warfare between gangs, a substantial amount of gang violence is against non–gang members. Robberies are a way of getting money, and while rival gang members may be targets, they typically are not. Targets of gang robberies are typically non–gang members from gang areas. Gangs have ventured out of their areas to hit rival or richer targets, but by and large they target people in their own communities.

Assaults against non–gang members have the same interaction dynamics as do gangbangs with the exception that non–gang members typically are open to some kind of remedial work and rarely start fights. Gang members, as in situations of gangbangs, do little to remedy loss of face with non–gang members, and they will take otherwise insignificant incidents and use them as a call to use violence.

Rape cases are rarely reported to the police, and there is a clearly expressed posture against rape in gangs. The reported rapes that occur appear to be similar to most other reported rapes with the exception that it is done by gangs as groups rather than individually. There is also some evidence that a gang may expect sexual intercourse with girls on demand in certain situations, and such encounters may be considered rape as well. However, the situations described by gang members may not be all that different from similar situations involving non–gang members. Nevertheless, to the extent to which gang members do make women submit to them sexually without consent, they constitute another set of nongang victims.

7

Mexican-American Gang Styles

INTRODUCTION

This chapter and the next two examine different styles of gangs. In understanding and applying the concept of grounded culture developed in this book, the cultural side of the equation implies a shared symbolic reality. This reality is made up of the language, beliefs, and values displayed in the culture or subculture. It is passed on from one generation to the next, and so it is possible to see certain subcultural styles in gangs and gang behavior over time.

The Mexican-American gang in San Diego pivots around a *cholo* lifestyle. This style and the attending behaviors help provide a clearer picture of how the situations that come to create and define the *cholo* are constructed and maintained. The primacy of territory is centered around a network of family and friends in the barrio or neighborhood, and the gangs protect their area from real and imagined threats. There is a reflexive connection between the ideal of the *cholo* protector and the reality of gang violence in that one justifies and elaborates the other. To be violent shows not only heart, but it demonstrates that the homeboy puts his barrio above his own personal safety, further sustaining the *cholo* ideal and violent reality.

SE TÉ VA A CAER EL CANTON
(Your House is Going to Fall Down)

The oldest gangs in San Diego are the Mexican-American ones. The earliest definitive date found on their establishment in the San Diego area goes back only to the early 1970s, but they probably were active before that time. The border areas of San Ysidro, Otay Mesa, Palm City, and Imperial Beach all had gangs early on in the formation of gangs in the San Diego area. Their orientation was toward Mexico, and their parties were often held in Tijuana. The other major center for Mexican-American gangs was in the Logan Heights area, with gang development to the south and east of Logan. Their orientation was more toward the United States with their Mexican ties being looser cultural ones compared with the gangs nearer to the border. In 1980, the police identified about a dozen active Mexican-American gangs and about half as many African-American gangs. By 1988, there were about the same number of active Mexican-American gangs, but they were no longer the majority of gangs or identified as responsible for the majority of gang violence. The African-American gangs by that time took up most of the police gang unit's attention, and the Filipino gangs had become active. By 1991, the Mexican-American gangs were one of four major gang groups along with the Filipino-American, African-American, and Southeast Asian–American gangs. Moreover, by 1991, the neighborhood patterns had changed so that a number of whites and blacks were joining previously all-Chicano gangs.

By examining the general style of Mexican-American gangs, we can see certain patterns emerge. They have a number of characteristics in common with other gangs, and in this chapter we will examine both the uniquely Mexican-American-style gang and typical elements of the Mexican-American gangs.

PRIMACY OF THE TERRITORY AND HOMEBOYS

The center of life for the Mexican-American gang is the *barrio* (or *varrio*). Roughly translated, barrio means something like neighborhood, but barrio implies a stronger attachment to those in the neighborhood (Vigil 1993:98). Joan Moore (1978:35) describes the territoriality of a gang as very deep, and the phrase *mi barrio* and can equally refer to "my gang" or "my neighborhood." John Quicker provides a Mexican-American sense of the gang and barrio in the following interview excerpt: "Well, [name], that's the name of our barrio—our gang. It's just a name, but to us it's not. We're like one family" (1983:6–7).

For most of the Mexican-American gangs in San Diego, their barrio or some feature of the barrio is part of their gang name, as Table 7.1 shows. Sometimes gangs will refer to themselves and other gangs by the location in which they live instead of the gang name that is used in the *placaso*. For example, the VELs might refer to themselves as Encanto, the name of the district in which they live. Likewise, the Setentas will refer to themselves as Lomita or Lomita Village instead of Setentas or 70s (which they pronounce as "seven-ohs").

Table 7.1. Gang Names and Locations

Gang	Territory
VELs (Varrio Encanto Locos)	Encanto
Red Steps	Part of Logan Heights area identified at one time by a red stairway
Calle Trienta	Near Thirtieth Street in Logan Heights (*Trienta* is Spanish for thirty)
Setentas, 70s	Seventieth Street is the dividing line between Lomita Village and Encanto
Sidro	San Ysidro
Sherman	Name of elementary school in the neighborhood
Shelltown	Area between Logan Heights and National City, called Shelltown

The Mexican-American gangs do not have territorial intergang violence per se, but rather adjacent territories give rise to intergang encounters that develop into incidents. These incidents can lead to fights or assaults on isolated gang members. Such encounters require a *payback* to even the score, which in turn requires retaliation, ad infinitum. Certain Mexican-American gangs have been enemies for years, and as each new generation of homeboys enters the gang, they learn who the enemy is. The original incident that brought the gangs into conflict is part of gang lore, and even if the matter is trivial, it is passed on in an oral history. The Setentas and VELs recount a baseball game where disagreement over the score led to multidecade animosity. Other gangs, if they do not have a specific incident in gang lore, will cite a recent problem caused by their rival gang.

In San Diego, there are occasions when nonadjacent Mexican-American gangs will fight. The best example of this was between the Spring Valley Locos and Shelltown, separated by twelve miles and several other territories. The conflict seems to have begun when a Shelltown boy went to a party in Spring Valley. He was challenged, attacked, and murdered by Spring Valley Locos. A couple of weeks after the murder, the Spring Valley Locos drove by and killed another Shelltown boy. This type of violence is characterized as a preemptive strike out of fear. Jankowski (1991:164) points out that "first strike" is based on the assumption that the other gang is going to attack anyway, and so it is better to get in the first hit. In this particular case, the Spring Valley Locos feared that Shelltown was going to attack them for the killing of their homeboy. So in order to scare them out of attacking, they attacked first.

There were few other instances of nonadjacent Mexican-American gangs fighting, and most Mexican-American gang conflict is between gangs in adjacent territory. However, it is not over territory, and there are no cases that were found where Mexican-American gangs took and held territory out of their own barrio from a rival gang.

Mexican-American gangs can split into clear-cut nonrival factions in the same barrio. The area of Logan Heights—Barrio Logan—has had a number of different gangs that all claim Logan but are separate gangs. By 1991, there were only two Logan gangs—Calle Trienta and Red Steps. However, throughout the decade of the 1980s there were up to four gangs in Logan at one time—Logan Luckys, Calle Trienta, Red Steps, and Calle Trienta Tres. The gangs in Logan were targeted as a group by rival gangs, but they operated independently of one another.

There is a constantly shifting cohort in gangs, and rivalries between Mexican-American gangs seem to have come and gone. Through the decade of the 1980s, and for as long as anyone there could remember, the VELs and the Setentas were enemies. By the early 1990s, though, the major concern of the Setentas was the Paradise Hills Locos (P-H Locos). The VELs were not seen to be allied with the P-H Locos, and the VELs never ceased their enmity with the Setentas, but the P-H Locos were a definite enemy of the Setentas. During the early 1980s, all of the gangs feared the Logan gangs, but by the end of the decade, the Logan gangs were being attacked by several other gangs simultaneously. Since the Mexican-American gangs were not involved in drug sales on a major scale, the conflict was not over customer territory. More likely, the Logan gangs had generated enough concern by their bellicose actions and size that the other gangs were taking a first-strike tactic.

From about 1989 to 1991, there emerged an intergang, interethnic conflict between one Mexican-American gang and a Southeast Asian gang. Unlike most of the Mexican-American gangs, which had a compact well-defined area within a fairly homogeneous ethnic boundary, ESD's was a sprawling territory in the East San Diego and City Heights area that included many different ethnic groups. The ESD gang bullied the Southeast Asian refugee children in the area for years. When a Cambodian gang called the Oriental Boy Soldiers was formed it was a target of ridicule and attacks by ESD. However, the attacks by ESD ended abruptly, as the Oriental Boy Soldiers turned the tables and terrorized ESD and any other groups that had bullied them in the past. In 1990, ESD was a target of at least six drive-by shootings by Oriental Boy Soldiers, and there were no reported cases of ESD retaliating. The police referred to ESD as "professional victims," with little sympathy for what ESD had brought on itself even though they were concerned by the new upsurge in Southeast Asian gangs. (The police later learned that the

Southeast Asian gangs had been attacked by ESD, but they did not report the attacks.) By 1991, the common wisdom among the city's several Mexican-American gangs was "Don't mess with the Orientals."

THE *CHOLO* STYLE

The concept of a *cholo* for the Mexican-American community is variously a tough punk, a party-loving but irresponsible youth, a guardian of the barrio, and a general neighborhood style (Vigil 1993:96). A uniform consisting of a Pendleton shirt, buttoned at the top over a white T-shirt, a hair net over short hair combed straight back, a bandanna tied around the head pulled down just above the eyes, dark sun glasses, a hat, and baggy khaki pants makes up the outward *cholo* style. Stylized tattoos with various themes around *la vida loca* (the crazy life), gang names, and street names are also part of the *cholo* style. There are many variations that change over time and in different neighborhoods, but even so the *cholo* is an option of life-style that has been recognized for decades in the Mexican-American community. The following two interview excerpts, one female and one male, describe the *cholo* style:

> [Female] A person with neatly groomed hair with three-flour grease [a type of hair cream], their clothes are ironed and the shirts and pants have creases. Their pants are saggy [hang low]. Sometimes they wear bandannas on their head. If they wear a hat, it is also creased in the front. They usually have shaved their head to train their hair to go back or to look "crazy." They could have a goatee. They are smooth-talkers and they usually get what they want. They can sweet-talk their way into anything. When a bunch of *cholos* get together, they get crazy ideas and they [do crazy things] like, "Let's go get Logan." They get hyper when they think of their enemies. *Cholos* are sweet to girls, but around the guy friends, they act all crazy and hostile.

> [Male] *Cholo* means a certain way that a gangbanger dresses. They wear baggy pants. . . . They are very particular about dressing neat. They wear hairnets with their hair greased and bandannas. Most Mexicans dress as *cholos*. The *cholos* get the girls because they dress good, and they are down for the set [stick up for their neighborhood].

Both excerpts express the point of view of committed gang members, and can be taken as such. In the larger Chicano community, the *cholo* is variously viewed as anything from a transitory youthful style to a "low life." Given their high drop-out rate from school, they tend not to go beyond low-income options available for dropouts.

Cholo Routines.   While the focus of this book has been on gang violence, the day-to-day routines of Mexican-American gang members are not necessarily or even typically violent. Part of the *cholo* life-style includes a willingness to do violence and violent activities as we will discuss in the next section, but the normal day does not include a stabbing, shooting, or serious fight. Rather, the kicked-back and entertaining aspect of *cholo* life makes up the routine of being a *cholo*. The following two interview excerpts detail the simplicity of the routine day:

[Male] Most guys [*cholos*] don't go to school, or they may just ditch certain periods of class. In the morning I leave my house as if I was going to school. That way my parents won't hassle me. I would go to a place to meet up with my homeboys—parking lot, somebody's house, the park. Most of the time we just kick it and get high.

[Female] For a *cholo*, they take forever to get ready in the morning. To iron their clothes and to look perfect. They take a lot of showers. Sometimes they go to school and kick it with all their homeboys. Cliques are very strong at school. A new kid could get rushed or pushed around. He will go to school to be with his friends and that he has to attend classes. At lunchtime, they sit and look at people and look to start fights. At lunch there are usually a lot of fights. Sometimes gangs from other schools come to their school at lunch just to start some trouble. Or maybe after school a gang will be waiting for them in the parking lot. Cops wait all around the school because they know that there is a lot of trouble. After school, they go to a member's house and drink and smoke. Then they go home a little later to take a shower and get ready to go out. When they meet up again, they either go cruising or go gangbanging—whatever comes up at the moment. If they see someone that they don't like, they will rush them— kind of like there is a power in the group. One thing they like to do is spray paint gang signs all over the place—especially on other gang's areas. This is a lot of fun for them. Some members don't even go to school. They wake up around noon and then later they go out and sell drugs. They just kick it while some of the others are at school.

While the idea of "kicking it" and enjoying the camaraderie of fellow *cholos* is a key and important part of understanding the *cholo* life-style, the other aspect of the life-style is the violent component. The violence shows the other gang members one has heart or courage to stand up for his barrio. It is also an exciting adventure, shared with the other homeboys.

Routine Violence.   The sense of the *cholo* life-style, especially the violence and combative nature of it, can be seen in excerpts grounding it in action. The following is from a written narrative of a boy who was asked to write about his gang:

Casa Blanca is a old neighborhood very old. In English it is called "white house." My nick name is niteowl [*sic*]. They call me that because I walk out at nite and because my dad's name is niteowl. My dad is from Corona. The reason we are from different neighborhoods is because I lived with my grandma and he was in prison. If you been rised there you are from there. I am in The Devilwolves gang. Everyone heard of us because we do alot [*sic*] of shooting at our enemies. We hardly get along with anyone.

I started getting into a gang when I was 8 or 9. Every time, when we had a meeting we had to go to the park and meet. I was the person that holds the guns and the weapons. One day when we were coming back from school our worst enemies drove by our neighborhood. They were looking for guys to shoot. They saw us and said "Big bad East Side," so we told them, "Fuck East Side. It's all about big bad Casa Blanca Los Devilwolves gang." So they took out there guns and started shooting at us. So all of us ran and jumps the wall but they shoot my homeboy and killed him. My homeboy was real close to me.

So we had another meeting at the park. We all went to East Side to look for the guy that shoot my homeboy. I got off the car and walked down the street with one of my other homeboys, saw some guys kicking back. So we went up to them and asked them "Where are you from?" They said, "East Side." So I told them, "Who is your leader?" Some guy said, "Me. Why?" I told them, "Fuck East Side. It's all about big bad Casa Blanca Los Devil-wolves gang." I took out my gun and shoot at the guy. So we started running down the street with the gun. My homeboys picked us up in the car.

We took off back to our neighborhood. We saw road blocks so my home-boy stopped the car and some of us took the guns, started running and jumped over some houses and back to our neighborhood and meet the other guys. So the guys from East Side would come back to our neighbor-hood and shoot. We could go back and start shooting at them. This has been happening for a long, long time.

The protection of one's neighborhood is a key element in understand-ing the *cholo* life-style. The family and barrio are centers of focus for the Mexican culture, and the rivalry between gangs in the different barrios is the key element in Mexican-American gang violence. The problem is answering the question of why.

According to Jankowski (1991:142–3) in the Chicano community *honor* is a dignity that is automatically endowed in all people. It is not earned, yet it must be preserved. The concept of Chicano honor contrasts with that of *respect*. Respect is defined by Jankowski as an active concept that must be earned—achieved deference. Honor, on the other hand, is granted as an assumed right of all people, and gang members enter the gang with honor.

The problem area arises in explaining the preservation of honor. If honor is a granted condition in Chicano culture, it is difficult to explain why a person's honor would be attacked. There is no indication that attack on another's honor brings the attacker honor unless it is to preserve one's own. Jankowski (p. 142) points out that most aggression was directed at those who were perceived as showing lack of respect or challenged their honor. At the same time, though, Jankowski (1991:342) notes that honor, along with respect and reputation, are used by gang members to manage emotions of frustration, fear, and ambition to *avoid violence*.

If the Mexican-American community values honor, and the *cholo* gang life-style is willing to use violence to avenge questioned honor, what is the element that motivates offending a person's honor? In other words, why would a Chicano gang or gang member want to be attacked by offending another's honor. From the narrative of the gang member who called himself Niteowl, it is clear that part of the ritual of violence is to insult the rival gang—to question its honor. Such challenges are uttered as cause for revenge and as cause to provoke violence.

We could argue that gang violence in the *cholo* world is a matter of one long unresolved feud. That is, at one time a gang's honor was offended, which led to an attack of revenge. The revenge led to an offense to the honor of the other gang, and all gang warfare since then has been a vendetta with no end. Since honor is defined in the Chicano community as including one's family, and presumably one's gang, new members in a gang are introduced to the unresolved honor conflict, thereby preserving the conflict from one generation to the next.

The problem with such an analysis is that it is not consistent with what the gangs in fact do. First, the long-term gang violence between Mexican-American gangs was between gangs who lived in adjacent barrios. After an attack by nonadjacent Varrio Market Street, the VELs did not counterattack. Likewise, after two of its members were murdered by Spring Valley Locos, the Shelltown gang did not attack the nonadjacent gang.

Second, other gangs and individuals were a threat to Chicano honor beyond the other Mexican-Americans but did not become targets of *cholo* revenge. Whites in general had long been accused of taking honor away from the Mexican-Americans, but they were not a favored target of gang violence. Likewise, the much-feared Oriental gangs repeatedly attacked ESD. Instead of taking care of it themselves, the ESD gang members called the police, and it was the Southeast Asian gangs who thought calling the police was dishonorable. Such actions hardly seem to be those of preserving honor.

One way of explaining the *cholo* gang's action on the basis of Jankowski's concept of Chicano honor is to look at the issue from the point of view of the *cholo* gangs. From the perspective of the *cholo* gang member, and even perhaps the Mexican-American community, the whites, blacks, and Orientals may be viewed as not understanding their concept of honor, and so they cannot be held accountable for breaching honor in the same way as can other Mexican-Americans. That is, they view the other groups as having no sense of honor, and so they are not worth attacking for a breach of honor. Moreover, since they have their hands full fighting other Mexican-American gangs, the *cholo* gangs do not need to fight the blacks, whites, and Orientals. Furthermore, given the stereotypes that they have of the Southeast Asians, and Orientals in general, there is a huge risk of offending them. They are viewed as treacherous, dangerous, crazy, and experienced with all sorts of automatic weapons. (Even some police officers shared this stereotype.) The repeated attacks by the Oriental Boy Soldiers ground such stereotypes in their reality.

An alternative way of examining honor is to treat it as an *account*. In the Mexican-American community, honor is used to explain a number of different actions. It is a gloss for a wide variety of behaviors. Since all actions can be seen as inherently vague in specific meaning outside some interpretive work and scheme, talk of honor is a means of clarifying situations (Garfinkel 1967). An act can be explained as breaching honor and as such, a reason for attacking a rival gang. Likewise, a group can be discussed as having no sense of honor, and so it is a target not of attack but of scorn. Individuals and groups who attack them for no apparent reason are accounted for as being either insane, which is a cause for alarm, or trying to prove something, which is cause for cautious ridicule.

In looking at honor as an account or interpretive scheme for understanding one's own and other's actions, instead of an objective reality, we can better understand the variance in Mexican-American gang actions. Even a gang being attacked by another gang can be seen as giving the target gang honor. For example, when Spring Valley Locos killed a Shelltown member, one explanation by Shelltown was that they were chosen because of their honor and reputation. By attacking them, the Spring Valley Locos were trying to enhance their own reputation, and only by choosing a worthy opponent could Spring Valley Locos hope to gain status. Therefore, Spring Valley Locos did an honor to Shelltown by attacking them. Of course, the same action could be accounted for in terms of dishonoring Shelltown, and so it could be formulated as a cause for retaliation. In either interpretation, honor is used as an account, not an objective reality.

What is important about honor in the *cholo* world is that it is an often-used interpretive scheme. The more a group uses honor as a way of viewing and interpreting the world, the more likely it is to find an offense to honor and cause for violence. Furthermore, with few etiquette skills and lacking the accounting practices associated with remedial interchanges, the *cholo* worldview is one fraught with reasons to fight.

The barrio perspective can be taken as another way of accounting for one's own and other's actions. Everyone in the neighborhood is accounted for in terms of being "in" the barrio, and all others are either legitimately related to those in, or somehow "out." Those who are out are either other Mexican-Americans who live in other barrios or simply *others* (African-Americans, whites, Orientals, etc.). The other barrios, especially adjacent ones, serve as the potential enemies. With this scheme of understanding self and others, the barrio, as an explanatory concept, sets up potential rivals.

Two more gang members' narratives show how this conception of "us" and "others" works in talking about their gangs and explaining the structure of gangs in general. In both narratives, the speaker is explaining the structure of the gang:

> [Female member of East Side Brown Angels] There is what you call veterans—the ones that started it in San Diego. And then there are OGs—which are original gangsters, family members of the gang members. Affiliation in gangs is passed through generations. Then [there are] the new people called new bodies, the ones that have been in less than one year. People join to feel like they are part of something. Like the way someone joins a football team. There is no real pressure to join. But when you have problems with our family, you get our of your depression by acting out and doing bad things. The violence is a thrill to release the pressure. It's just a thrill—a way to get back at your parents. Sometimes you are just born with it [being in a gang]. My dad is in a gang and he never stopped me. I saw him beat up people when I was young. He was just a bad influence. Plus your friends are a bad influence. It is interesting to see what exactly you can get away with.
>
> A raker or buster or hood-hopper is when a person hangs with one gang and then switches to another gang. I personally don't do that, but it has been known to happen. If you are known as being in one gang then you risk being killed for doing that. For girls, once you are pregnant, you are out automatically. It is too dangerous. Then later you will be considered a veteran and your child will follow in your footsteps.
>
> [Female from the Sherman gang] The highest level are the veterans. Usually by the early twenties they are still from there but they don't fight any more. They get all of the respect because they have been through all of it. Most of them have been locked up before. My mom and dad are both from Sherman gangs. Since I was also raised in Sherman, then I became part of it all. The next step down from the veterans are the youngsters. They can be as young as nine and they stay as youngsters till their twenties. The real young (just jumped in) are called the new bodies. As you get older, you get more and more respect. I get a lot of respect because my whole family

is a part of the Sherman gang. The Mexican gangs don't fight for colors. The Mexican gangs only fight between each other—not with Black or Oriental gangs. When I got jumped in, I really got beat up. They want to see if you can take it or if you'll run away.

A Mexican gang is a lot of people that are just from the neighborhood. Not all members are bad. The only ones that sell drugs are usually just supporting their own habit or their family. A lot of them have been kicked out of school and have a hard time finding a job. So they may sell drugs— just a way to support his family. They usually have a lot of kids and it is hard to work when someone has to stay home to take care of the children.

My gang is very neighborhood oriented. My father was involved and even spent time in prison. He did try to keep me out of the gang stuff. But, as a teenager, I never listened. My friends' influence was much greater. Now my dad tells me to finish up my time and get it over with. He comes to visit me every Sunday.

Both narratives emphasize the role of the barrio/family and the to-getherness of the gang. The first girl's account is peppered with some counseling jargon and psychological accounts, but at the core of her narrative is the theme of barrio/family. Likewise, the Sherman gang member provides an account of the problems gang members have since they are kicked out of school and cannot find jobs. There is no sense that the gang activity itself may be related to school expulsion, but rather it is listed as a reason why some of the gang members cannot find jobs and "need" to sell drugs. The barrio/family is accounted as an all-forgiving, understanding unit that justifies and supports gang activity.

The *cholo* life-style is surrounded by the barrio/family theme. Cholos self-characterize what they do in a romanticized version of protecting the barrio/family. This serves to justify violence against other Mexican-Americans, especially rival barrio gangs. The pattern occurs in the context of relative depravation, antiwhite/antiestablishment sentiment, and cultural themes depicting the glory of the ancient Mexican Indios, *la raza* (race and spirit of the Mexican people), and other tragic/heroic elements of Mexican culture and Mexican-Americans. These together provide further grounding for gang behavior.

MEXICAN-AMERICAN GANG STRUCTURE

Sociologists tend to promote an *overstructured* view of gangs. The various roles that go to make up legitimate public and private organizations are often sought out in gangs, and somehow are found by sociologists. In defining gangs, Miller (1975) found that gang experts believed that identifiable leadership and developed role division (division of labor) were a necessary criteria for a group to be identified as a gang. However, in examining the typical Mexican-American gang, there seems to be little vertical differentiation, and what differentiation can be found is based on age and gender. Specialized roles are informal, such as the Devil-wolves member who described his role as being in charge of weapons.

The Mexican-American gangs were organized around cliques and barrios. Within a barrio, there can be different gangs or only a single gang. Most San Diego barrios had a single gang associated with them. Larger barrios, such as Barrio Logan (Logan Heights) had from two to four gangs over the period of this study. However, since the Logan gangs identified closely with their barrio and felt mutually threatened by non-Logan gangs, there were infrequent clashes between the Logan gangs. At the same time, though, there did not seem to be coordinated activities between the Logan gangs either against other gangs or of mutual social interest.

Each gang was made up of age groups and cliques or *klikas*. Each clique had one or more informal leaders. The girls had an auxiliary role and formed their own clique. So the structure was very loose in the sense that it was not made up of a hierarchy, and there was little role differentiation. Other than the veterans, the youngsters and the new bodies, there was hardly any hierarchy to speak of.

However, the lack of differentiation and hierarchy did not in any way take away from the strength of the gang as a social organization or group. Each gang and clique within the gang is held together by a strong mechanical solidarity centered around the idea of the barrio. Transgenerational ties and family ties gave the gang a very strong and lasting life. *Gemeinschaft* relationships characterize the organization and give it a strength in loyalty and identity. The loyalty and identity with the barrio/gang concept were reflective, and provided the members with the status of being part of something. For example, each member could feel "I am Red Step" or "I am Del Sol." At the same time, the identity with the barrio/gang reflected one's loyalty.

Jankowski (1991:70) said that Chicano gangs in Los Angeles often used what he described as a *horizontal/commission* model of organization and leadership. Under this form or organization there were several officers who shared power equally. A less organized form of gang, according to Jankowski (p. 66), is based on what he called the *influential* model. Under this model, there were no officers, but there were clearly influential leaders who were followed by clique members or the gang as a whole. Of these two models, the San Diego Mexican-American gangs appeared to have more of the influential model of organization.

In order to understand the Chicano gang, it is more important to understand it in terms of the level of commitment to the gang, the willingness to do violence, and the character and number of hard-core members at any one time. As explained in our discussion of gang structure, a gang is made up of hard-core, affiliate, and fringe members. Given the age cohorts that make up the gang, the leadership, and number of hard-core members, the gang is in flux. The stability of the gang lies in the constancy of the barrio, but the gang as an active entity depends on the hard-core members who are willing to fight for the gang. As long as a gang is not attacked by a rival, the fringe members can keep the gang alive by nothing more than assuming a *cholo* attitude, hanging out together, and claiming the gang. While the barrio exists as a coherent unit, and the families of the barrio do not move out to other areas, then even an inactive gang can exist as a social reality in neighborhood. In San Diego, the Del Sol gang became relatively inactive after 1981 when three of its members were killed. However, it continues to exist since the barrio still exists as a coherent neighborhood.

When the hard-core element of the gang grows in size, or an age cohort with a large hard-core membership moves into a central position, it becomes more violently active. It challenges more rival gangs and in turn is challenged. If a number of hard-core members are arrested, killed, or grow out of the primary active age, then the activity recedes. So while Jankowski provides an excellent structural explanation of the leadership organization in the Chicano gang, either as influential or horizontal/commission, it is important to understand that these structures are superimposed on cohorts that are more or less willing to engage in violence. If the hard core is large, then the gang will be violently active, but if the hard core is small, then the gang will be violently inactive, regardless of the static structure.

GANG ORIENTATION

The orientation of Mexican-American gangs is one of action, status, and kicking back. The action is achieved through risk-taking activities such as gangbanging and drive-bys. Not only is there a thrill in taking chances, one can establish character by chancing fate (Goffman 1967:214–8). Status is achieved by belonging to a gang that is feared and/or respected by others in the community. Within the gang, status can be further enhanced by participating in gang activities that demonstrate the attributes of character valued by the gang. Finally, kicking back is a gloss for hanging out with the other gang members, partying, drinking, and ingestion of drugs. Of all of the gang activities, kicking back is the most frequent and typical of the Chicano gang.

Unlike the African-American gangs whose orientation is more toward business, with drug sales as a major means of raising funds, the Mexican-American gangs are not too often involved in drug sales. However, they are heavy drug users. When selling drugs, they usually do so to support their own drug needs or to provide their homeboys with drugs. On occasions when they need something, they will steal or rob victims in the community, but they typically do not have any ongoing money-generating enterprise.

SUMMARY

The essence of the Mexican-American gang is best understood in terms of the barrio/family concept. The barrio/family is used as an interpretive scheme to provide the sense of and justification for the Chicano gang. The gang members have a highly romanticized view of themselves in terms of the barrio, which they protect, and the Mexican-American culture and history of which they see themselves an integral part.

The Mexican-American gang as an organization displays features of *Gemeinschaft* relationships reflected in the close ties of gang members and their fierce loyalty to the gang. The ties are an extension of the barrio/family ideal of caring for those in the same neighborhood. The gang organization is fairly flat, reflecting the egalitarian nature of the barrio/family idea with age groupings making up the gang's only hierarchical order.

The gang's primary orientation is one of sociability. However, the sociability does not detract from its violent activities. The violence in the gang is determined largely by the hard core element in a central age group at any one time. The presence or absence of a hard-core is measured by the relative amount of violence the gang is engaged in as an initiating side.

8

African-American Gang Styles

INTRODUCTION

Many of the characteristics displayed by Mexican-American gangs are also displayed by African-American gangs. These common characteristics are general *gang characteristics* that are seen in the use of drive-by shootings, gang names, and similar gang-generic phenomenon. However, there are also several other features of their culture and structure that provide a different grounded culture as a base for the gang experience. There are a number of style differences between African-American and Mexican-American gangs that reflect both subcultural differences and gang style differences. This chapter attempts to show what the unique features of the African-American gangs are, primarily in contrast to the Mexican-American gangs.

CRIPS AND BLOODS

African-American gangs in San Diego are divided into two major groups: the Crips and Pirus (Bloods.) Largely, the gang style of African-American gangs was imported from Los Angeles in the late 1970s and early 1980s as youth returning from California Youth Authority began using the names, colors, and rivalry of the Crips and Bloods. Before that time, there were some ganglike groups in the Skyline and Logan Heights area of San Diego. The Skyliners were one of the original African-American gangs that later took on the Piru name, and were in opposition to the West Coast Crips, located in the Logan Heights area.

The African-American gangs coexist in the same territory with many of the Mexican-American gangs. The West Coast Crips territory overlaps with the Mexican-American Shermans, Red Steps, and Calle 30 gangs, and borders the Lomas area. Piru gangs share territory with the Setentas, VELs, Varrio Market Street, and ESD gangs. However, as noted elsewhere, the gangs do not fight across ethnic boundaries. There have been incidents with some of the Southeast Asian gangs, but these are isolated clashes and have not congealed into an ongoing rivalry.

By and large, the reason that the Mexican-American gangs occupy the same areas as the African-Americans is due to the low-income housing patterns. There are some ethnic groupings in these areas, but not enough to keep gang territories all African-American or all Mexican-American. Thus, while the economic situation of African-Americans and Mexican-Americans is similar, their social groupings are separate. There are a few African-Americans and whites in Mexican-American gangs, but there are no Mexican-Americans, whites, or Orientals in African-American gangs. At the time of this writing, African-American gangs were all black. One gang, the Linda Vista Crips was a mixed bag of African-Americans, whites, Mexican-Americans, and possibly some Orientals and Pacific Islanders, but they were not considered to be an African-American gang since they took on a mixed style and not a typically African- American one. The only African-American gang characteristic of the Linda Vista Crips was being shot at by some Bloods. African-Americans in Mexican-American gangs took on a decidedly *cholo* style including dress, street names, speech, and barrio affinity.

PRIMACY OF MAKING MONEY

While the Mexican-American gangs are primarily focused on the barrio, the African-American gangs are primarily focused on making money. There is a strong loyalty to the *set*, the neighborhood, but not so much so as the Mexican-Americans. The police said that if they wanted to find a Mexican-American who belonged to a gang, they could find him at the location where his gang typically hung out, even if the boy knew he was being pursued by the police. With African-American gang members, there is not the same type of tie. The African-American gang territories are larger than the Mexican-American ones, and each territory is made up of sets where the gang members comfortably hang out. However, there is another dimension to the territory that looms large in the African-American gang: the area that belongs to the gang for marketing illegal goods and services.

In Jankowski's (1991:40–41, 80–81) business-recreation continuum of gangs, the African-American gangs fall solidly into the business category. A major motivation for joining the gang is that it provides a means of making money and having nice things. This does not mean, however, that the gang is held together by organic solidarity or that the relationships are primarily *Gesellschaft*. The ties among African-American gang members are very strong, characterized as *Gemeinschaft,* and their animosity against their rivals—Crips or Bloods—is very emotional.

Compared to Mexican-American gangs, though, African-American gangs have a number of features that suggest some ties based on organic solidarity and *Gesellschaft* relationships. While the Mexican-American gang members take all types of drugs, including heroin and crack cocaine, the African-American gang members generally do not. The norms of the gangs are such that taking certain heavy drugs is considered an impediment to selling drugs for profit. Gang members who are known to take drugs other than marijuana are sanctioned by beatings and/or taking away the privilege of selling drugs in the set. According to interviews, taking heavy drugs would result in an "ass kicking" by the older members in African-American gangs.

Money is made in other illegal modes by African-American gangs as well, but the gang detail's information ties gangs primarily to robberies and drug sales. However, the following interview excerpts show that while drug sales are the main source of income, prostitution is another means the African-American gangs have of getting money:

> I was getting my money selling drugs—large amounts—drugs like sherm [PCP-laced marijuana], crystal [methamphetamine], weed [marijuana], and the main killer cocaine. We deal through Cubans and Mexicans in big events, then eventually to the Mafia. [There is no evidence that the person being interviewed had any direct connection with the Mafia. She was most likely speculating or bragging about such connections.]

> Gangs are all about money now. Selling drugs is like taking chances with the police and getting stuck with bad dope. [On] average [I] make nine hundred dollars a day. A lot of people do have jobs such as construction or driving a bus. They still hang with the set.

> Pimping girls is also a popular way to make money. They [girls] volunteer to participate. They are young—twelve or thirteen. They don't consider themselves prostitutes—just a "hoe." Sometimes they take them to Las Vegas.

> The way they get their money besides selling drugs . . . they have hookers to get money for the OGs [original gangsters]. The hookers are not in the gang. They are just drug addicts. All gangs are known for this.

> Drug dealers go days without sleep. Weed is the only drug that drug dealers use. Most [drug dealers] don't go to school, but the ones that do will go to school, and then sell drugs after school till sometimes 3 A.M. Then he will wake up the next day and start all over again.

At one time robberies were a major money-making activity. In 1981, the African-American gangs were identified as being involved in twenty-four robberies, but by 1988, only three robberies were listed as

African-American gang-related. The police believe that by 1988, there was so much money to be made in selling drugs that robberies were considered too risky and the profits too low to be worth it.

The violence associated with the sale of cocaine, especially rock or crack cocaine, was most pronounced in 1988 with the escalation of the so-called crack cocaine wars in San Diego. On the one hand, African-American gangs from Los Angeles had come to San Diego to begin selling drugs. The profits to be made in the business were too good and business conditions in Los Angeles had become too crowded. At the time, cocaine was available wholesale in Los Angeles for about $300 per ounce and could be resold on the streets for between $800 and $1,500 per ounce. By coming to San Diego, they hoped to cash in on an unoccupied market. However, the Los Angeles gang members collided with the interests of the San Diego Crips and Bloods, who were busily making money selling rock cocaine.

A number of gang-related shootings ensued: Over half of the victims of gang-related homicides were African-American gang victims and a number of victims were from Los Angeles–based gangs. Not all of the homicides involving African-American gangs were related to the sale of drugs, but most of them seemed to be. It also appeared that the locally based Crips and Bloods were fighting against the Los Angeles–based Crips. It did not appear so much to be an alliance as it was that both major San Diego gangs would shoot any outsider who attempted to encroach upon their territory.

GANG ORGANIZATION

The gang connection with more organized crime elements may presume some kind of more formal gang organization in African-American gangs. However, while gangs must necessarily have connections with organized crime to obtain the quantity of drugs that they do, it does not mean that the gangs themselves have to be organized beyond having at least some of their members having connections with organized crime syndicates. The gangs are not training grounds for organized crime syndicates, but instead they serve as a wholesale distribution point for organized crime. Jankowski notes, in relation to the idea that gangs are part of organized crime syndicates, "it would be more accurate to view today's gangs as independent components of the broad structure by which contemporary crime has been organized" (1991:132).

It seems that African-American gangs have very little organization. According to their published accounts, the police see the gangs as having a fairly flat organizational hierarchy based on reputation and age. For example, one San Diego Sheriff's Office investigator characterized black gangs as follows:

> In the black street gang, there is no one member in charge of everyone or formal rank or structure. There are members with more influence than others, but the term leader is seldom used. A person's age, physical stature, arrest record, and behavioral background are the main factors involved in weighting an individual's influence upon a gang. Gang members demonstrate their nerve in order to gain respect, influence and power within a particular gang. (San Diego County Deputy Sheriffs' Association 1990:35)

Likewise, in a Los Angeles police publication, African-American gang structure was characterized as follows:

> Black streets gangs are non-traditional in nature and contain no formal structure. The older members in the gang (late 20's to early 30's), especially those with access to drugs and money or who have developed a reputation for violence, are the influential members or "shot callers," as they are often times called. These older members have influence over the younger members and use them to sell drugs and commit violent acts upon other gangs. (Los Angeles Police Department, n.d.)

This view is in contrast with what Jankowski and Keiser found in African-American gang structure. Jankowski (1991:68–70) argued that the gangs that had the vertical/hierarchical organizational model were most likely to adopt the model for effectively and efficiently maximizing profits. In order to obtain a larger customer base, it was necessary to take over more territory. Not only would this allow the gang to have more potential customers, it would also add to the recruitment pool for the gang. In order to coordinate such a widening domain of sales, a strong centralized leadership with a clear hierarchy was required. Otherwise the gang could be chipped away at the edges as other, more coordinated gangs sought to take over the various uncoordinated cliques. Jankowski (pp. 69–70) notes that in part the gangs in New York were impressed by the success of organized crime, primarily the Mafia. Also, they were impressed by rival gangs that were highly organized, and survival was seen to be dependent on being well-organized. *Well-organized* was defined as adopting the vertical/hierarchical structure.

In Chicago, Keiser (1969:12–19) found the Vice Lords to have a highly organized gang. The Vice Lords were divided into branches variously called Albany Lords, California Lords, 5th Avenue Lords, and Lake Street Lords. Within each branch, there were age groupings, and most of the age cohorts had a hierarchy of officers. Within each grouping there were cliques or "running partners" that were informal but influential in the gang structure.

Under an older system of organization, each branch's president or war counselor would decide if the branch would fight. For a fight involving all of the branches, the president of the City Lords branch would decide. After a reorganization of the Vice Lords, a board made up of members from the various branches plus some older members made decisions affecting the Vice Lords as a whole. This board was backed up by a council of twenty members who would fill in if a board member were arrested or killed. The board was advisory in nature, and the various branches were fairly autonomous.

The interesting aspect of this new organization is that it diffused the responsibility for ordering an action that would legally endanger a single leader. That is, with a board, it was difficult to pinpoint a single leader to charge with giving the order to attack a rival gang or individual. Since people were often killed in such attacks, a homicide charge could be brought against the person who ordered the attack. However, a board decision diffused the responsibility, and any single leader could deny ordering an attack (Keiser 1969:19).

What's more, the way in which the board operated further diffused responsibility. If an issue was raised by a member regarding an attack on another gang, the board would not vote and announce its intentions *to attack*. Instead, it would make a decision and announce "Well, we with the fellows" if it wanted to attack a rival (Keiser 1969:19). Using such wording further diffused responsibility for an attack throughout the entire gang, and not just the board.

Given the vertical/hierarchical order of the African-American gangs in New York and Chicago and the lucrative drug business the San Diego gangs operated, it seems that the San Diego gangs would have had a similar structure as New York and Chicago. However, from observations and interviews with gang members, it appears that African-American gangs in San Diego have the influential model of organization. One Blood member described the structure as follows: "[I]t's just a bunch of members. The older people are the leaders. The young ones have to respect the older members. There is no *leader* to speak of."

For running a lucrative drug business, such an organizational model may appear to be too weak or unstructured. However, as long as there is a link between at least some members of the gang and a wholesale suppler of drugs, the influential model of organization can be a very powerful one and one that is difficult for the police to counter.

One major problem in characterizing gangs in terms of influential, horizontal/commission, or vertical/hierarchical is that it tends to presume that the model is the main organizational structure around which the gang is formed. On the contrary, the gangs in San Diego appear to have the bedrock of their solidarity and structure in the barrio, set, or neighborhood. The very term *homeboy*, used by all of the gangs, refers to the neighborhood. Jankowski (1991:71–72) implies that the barrio egalitarianism of the Chicano gangs was a barrier to their forming a more structured organization. Yet at the same time, the strengths of neighborhood gang solidarity and loyalty may outweigh and overshadow any form of organization superimposed on the basic neighborhood structure. The same is true with the African-American gangs. The strong feelings that gang members have for their homeboys is very real and functions in ways that other organizational structures may not affect. Moreover, within the gang, even structured ones, the clique is often more powerful than the hierarchy. Keiser (1969:16, 18) notes that some of the cliques in the gang were more powerful than either the older cliques that were supposedly higher in the hierarchy or the ruling board. Since such cliques are based on *Gemeinschaft* relationships, there tend to be stronger sentimental ties and greater loyalty than those based on *Gesellschaft* relations emanating from organizational structures. The organizational structures appear only to work as long as they are in tune with the informal structures centered around the neighborhood ties.

The way the organization worked as a drug-dealing and profit-making gang rested very much on the neighborhood ties and common background of the gang members. According to interviews with gang members, if someone wanted to make money dealing drugs, they would be given drugs to sell by established dealing members. They would go through an apprenticeship during which they would receive no money. If they brought all of the money back and proved to be honest and reliable, they would be given a percentage of the profits and be in business.

The ultimate test would come when a gang member was arrested. If the lower-level dealers refused to turn in their homeboys from whom they obtained their supply—out of loyalty, fear of group ostracism, or fear of group retaliation—the organization as a profitably functioning one would be very strong. Since there is no kingpin who runs the organization, there is no single person for law enforcement to target, and given the strong neighborhood gang ties, members are less likely to inform. As a result, the structure of the gang, while not a vertical/hierarchical one, is still a very strong organization for profit-making.

As far as fending off attacks by other gangs with an influential model of organization, the African-American gangs in San Diego effectively ran off the encroachment of the Los Angeles gangs who tried to move in on their drug-selling businesses. Their success could have been due to the fact that the Los Angeles drug-dealing gangs are organized along the same lines as those in San Diego. If the Los Angeles gangs are organized in a vertical/hierarchical fashion, whoever was at the top decided to back off since they failed to take over any of San Diego African-American gangs' drug-dealing territory.

GANG ROUTINES

Like the Mexican-American gangs, African-American gangs do not spend the majority of their time gangbanging. The routine of "kicking it" with their homeboys seems to be the major thing they do. The following description by a gang member from Los Angeles describes their routine:

> We wake up around noon since most of my homeboys don't go to school even though some do attend. Once I've gotten dressed and I go outside to look for the homeboys at their house or at the spots where they kick it. Then we just kick it for a while. Someone will decide to get some beer or some weed. We only drink and [use] a little dope—no heavy stuff. Some guys use, but the OGs [older members] will tell them to stop.
> On like a weekend, we will get drunk and kick it till someone say "Let's do a drive-by." We get in the car and take care of business, meaning to look for the other set and blast them out. After all of this we go back to the hood and celebrate. Most of the time we just hang out, kick it, to strap it, smoke bud with the homegirls. We have certain houses we will kick it at.

Like the Mexican-American gangs discussed in Chapter 7, the main activity of African-American gang members is hanging around with their homeboys. The violent aspects of gang life are always there—either defensively or as an offensive option. However, according to members' accounts of daily routines, the main gang activity is relaxing in the company of friends. As such, juvenile gang behavior reflects what is likely the main pastime of nongang, nondelinquent youths. The routine use of alcohol and some drugs, along with a higher school dropout rate, sets them apart from wholly nondelinquent youths. Take away the willingness to use deadly violence, and the pattern is that of a street group or "hanging" group. However, it is the defining element of deadly force that makes a gang a unique delinquent entity.

Another part of African-American gang routines is selling drugs. This is done on the set, often in the open, but also from rock or crack houses. The various locations in the gang's set are reserved for different cliques or individual dealers, and the overall set is under the protection of the gang. Sometimes selling drugs is done actively by standing in a certain location and going up to buyers in their automobiles, and at other times it is done along with "kicking it"—the buyers know where the gang hangs out and will go to them without any effort on the gang's part.

Violent Routines. Since the possibility of deadly violence is always with the gangs, it affects their routines. The use of a house to "kick back" is safer than the streets, a cul de sac is safer than a corner, and being ever alert becomes a way of looking at the world. Gang members are not paranoid since paranoia assumes a *delusion* of persecution. Gang members are hunted down and attacked by rival gang members, and this can occur in all different types of situations. Therefore, a stance of distrust of others, especially other African-American males who are not immediately identified as members of one's own gang, is part of the routine of being a "gangster." The following interview excerpt with an East Dago Mob Crip illustrates this view:

> When you are walking on your side of town and you see someone with different colors—you know that they are just looking for trouble. If you are at a neutral area such as a shopping mall, you wear or sport your own colors so everybody else knows where you are from. The rag hanging out of your back pocket signifies who you are and where you are from.
>
> For instance, you are at the mall and someone comes at you—like gets in your face. Then you tell each other what set that you are from. Usually this is a time that gang signals would be flashed. If they seem real aggressive then you might want to fight. But, in these days, people carry guns so you can't be looking at too many people "crazy." For example, if he were to pull a gun on you but didn't shoot you. The next time you see him you feel like its mandatory to pull a gun on him for putting your life in jeopardy. Whether you shoot or not depends on the situation. If you feel like you are going to get caught you just lay low. Later you go look for him. Fighting is not a big thing because it's too easy to get shot. You get a gun for ten dollars on the streets. A fight will almost always end up with gunshots sooner or later. The one thing that will set off a fight, regardless of guns, is when someone says, "Fuck his set," because this is total disrespect. It is a known fact that this will start a fight and that you really want to get into it. Another instance would be when someone drives into your set and lights your color rag [a piece of cloth of the gang's color—usually red or blue] on fire and throws it on the ground. Retaliation is usually what starts a fight. If your homeboy gets hurt from a gang it's a known fact that you have to fight back.

Most gang members use retaliation as an account for violence, but as we have seen in previous chapters, there are too many instances of gangs instigating violence. For example, driving into a rival's set and setting his colors on fire is an example of provocation. It can be part of a drive-by shooting, and the cases where color-burning or flaunting has occurred, there is usually a gun in the vehicle. It seems that gang violence in this context is "something to do." Besides being exciting, as are all events where one's life is at risk, gang members can embellish their reputations. This aspect of violent routines is little different from the Mexican-American gangs, except that the Mexican-Americans usually do not have colors. (Defacing a Mexican-American placaso [gang name on the wall] has the same effect as burning colors.)

However, the ritual of mad-dogging rivals in neutral or nongang territories is riskier as more and more gang members carry guns. What used to be a simple fight can quickly turn into a shooting. Thus, while taking risks can build a reputation, the more knowledge of the risks gang members have, the more they are likely to temper bravado with prudence. One can always save face by noting the inopportune nature of the situation and claim retaliation at a later date when the situation lends itself better to retaliation. Furthermore, since even a showing of gang signs can be used as reason for future action, there is always some incident available that can be used to account for the need for retaliation.

SUMMARY

The primary difference between African-American and Mexican-American gangs lies in the use and sale of drugs, the size of the gangs and alliances, business dealings, and linkage to territory. The African-American gangs are less likely to use heavy drugs but more likely to sell them than are the Mexican-American gangs. Use of drugs such as heroin, crack cocaine, and PCP is considered bad for business by the African-American gangs, while they are a recreational drug for Mexican-American gangs.

African-American gangs tend to be larger and cover more territory than Mexican-American gangs. The African-American gangs are divided into two supergangs with many nonconnected but allied branches of the Crips and Bloods. Mexican-American gangs are centered around the barrio, with smaller groups, and they do not have an allegiance outside the barrio to a general gang such as the Crips or Bloods.

Finally, while African-American gangs are more business oriented, Mexican-American gangs are more barrio-oriented. The business orientation of African-American gangs has led to stricter sanctions against the use of heavy drugs and gang warfare over contested sales territories. Mexican-American gangs have a set barrio territory and do not attempt to usurp more territory. However, underlying the strength of the

African-American gangs is a strong attachment to the set and the homeboys. This underlying structure is its strength, and given the longevity
of the African-American gangs in San Diego and their ability to fight off
interlopers, they apparently have not had to adopt a vertical/hierarchical
or even a horizontal/commission structure to succeed.

9

Other Youth Gangs

INTRODUCTION

This book has argued that culture or structure alone cannot generate gang violence and gangs as groupings. A belief system (culture) not grounded in some kind of reference point in action is insufficient to generate gangs. Likewise, even a structure filled with poverty and discrimination is not enough to generate gangs and their accompanying violence unless there is a belief system to justify and support the concept of gang violence.

This chapter examines the cases of newly emerging gangs and groups that did not form gangs. In this examination, we find how the structure and the culture meld or fail to meld into a grounded culture fostering gang violence. Since the research period spanned over a decade, it was possible to see new gangs emerge and how they developed. This allowed insight into how the cultural and structural elements came together. Some, such as the Filipino gangs, surprised just about everyone involved in gang research as well as in the community. Others, such as the Southeast Asian gangs, took longer to develop than expected and did not develop in certain groups at all. Finally, some comparative data gathered in Great Britain and information about the lack of white gangs provide further understandings about the process that led to gang development and violence.

WHO'S INVOLVED?

While at Cambridge University in 1984, I attempted to find American-style youth gangs in Great Britain outside of Northern Ireland. At the time, I could find none in London and in an interview with Jimmy Boyle was told that the gangs in Glasgow, Scotland, about whom Boyle (1977) had written, had degenerated into heroin users. Even the skinheads had greatly reduced their racists attacks against Pakistani and West Indian populations. About the only ganglike violence at the time was a persistent pattern of hooliganism at the soccer games. Hooliganism involved working-class youth starting riots and brawls at soccer matches, some of which had fatal consequences.

From a structural point of view, one would have expected that youths in the lower or lower-working classes would have formed some kind of gangs, as was the case in Glasgow in the 1950s and 1960s. Combining the low-income and minority status of the West Indians and Pakistani populations with discrimination against those groups, which matched the Mexican-American and African-American populations in San Diego, at least there should have been some expectation of ganglike behavior. But like the white British youth, the British minority groups did not have violent gangs in 1984.

In San Diego, the same questions were asked. Low-income whites did not form gangs even though they lived in the same neighborhoods as the Mexican-American and African-American gangs. Even more remarkable was a large population of former "boat people" made up of Southeast Asian refugees who were poor, had minimum English language skills, and suffered minority discrimination. The discrimination was not only or even predominantly from the majority whites, but from established American minority groups—African-Americans and Mexican-Americans. They felt the Southeast Asians were encroaching on them and the scarce resources and services they had been able to obtain. Besides, they dressed, looked, and talked differently from "real Americans." However, the Southeast Asians were not forming gangs to an extent documented by the police in the late 1980s, and other than isolated incidents, the refugees were considered to be law-abiding citizens, like most Asian-Americans.

By 1990, though, there were Southeast Asian gangs with all of the violence characteristic of the established American gangs. The same forces behind the African-American and Mexican-American gangs served to generate Southeast Asian gangs. It was necessary to reenter the field in 1991 to gather more data for the completion of this work.

It was not the Southeast Asian gangs that were the next group to develop, however. In 1988, when the second extended period of fieldwork was done, the Filipino gangs had become active. This is the first group we will discuss, and more than any of the other groups who formed gangs, the Filipinos are the most surprising, given their background in San Diego.

FILIPINO GANGS

The Filipino population in San Diego is connected to the military establishment and the nursing profession. A large contingent of Filipinos who served in the U.S. military, especially during the Vietnam War, was allowed to immigrate to the United States during the 1970s. Likewise, a large number of Filipino nurses immigrated to the United States during the 1970s when a nursing shortage generated a more liberal immigration policy for nurses. Thus, a typical Filipino household in San Diego contained a husband who was employed in some way by the military and a wife who was a nurse. This allowed many Filipino families to enjoy a middle-class way of life shortly after migration with their combined incomes and various fringe benefits the military provided for families, such as commissary and post exchange privileges. In the elementary and secondary schools, the Filipino children were good students, and it was common to see them winning awards for good scholarship and citizenship.

In the middle-class areas where Filipinos resided, they felt some discrimination by the predominantly white population, but on the whole, whites and Filipinos got along very well. The parents of whites and Filipinos intermingled in the various neighborhood, school, and youth sports functions that bring all suburban families together. Economically, there was equality, and they shared the same problems and goals in getting the kinds of schools, parks, and other services the suburban dwellers expected and demanded. Furthermore, the Filipinos were socially and politically conservative like much of the rest of suburbia. So, while there may have been some discrimination, it was more in style than substance, and since the Filipinos posed no threat to the non-Filipinos in suburbia, there were generally good relations between them and the other groups in suburban San Diego.

Throughout most of the 1980s the Filipinos were not only low in crime statistics, but no Filipino gangs were recognized by the police. However, by 1988, about 14 percent of all gang-related incidents recorded by the police department's gang detail involved Filipino youths, and by 1991, 18 percent of the drive-by shootings were by Filipino gangs. There was enough activity among the Filipino gangs that a full-time investigator was assigned to handling their cases exclusively.

The gangs began in lower-income areas, where a high percentage of military families lived, and then the Filipino gang development moved north and south. The Paradise Hills area of San Diego is located directly east of National City and north of National City and Chula Vista. It is a mix of families of noncommissioned officers and working- and middle-class families.

The first Filipino gang in the area was called the Be Down Boys. They and a much smaller group, called Da Boys were in conflict. The Da Boys gang allied themselves with a Mexican-American gang called the Paradise Hills Locos (PH Locos). The alliance led to the shooting death of one of the Be Down Boys by members of the PH Locos. There was retaliation against the PH Locos, and the feud seemed to end there. (By 1991 the PH Locos were in an ongoing fight with the Setentas in Lomita Village, another Mexican-American gang.) Later, a larger rival Filipino gang call Bahala Na-Barkada formed in Paradise Hills. It identified with the African-American gang color blue and was considered a Crip faction of the Filipino gangs even though there was no connection between the Filipino and African-American gangs. The Be Down Boys chose red and identified as a Blood faction.

Two other Filipino gangs active in 1988 were in the South Bay areas of Nestor and Del Sol. The Southside Blood operated in the Del Sol area in the eastern part of South Bay, and the Southside Posse operated in the Nestor area between Imperial Beach and Del Sol. The socioeconomic makeup of these areas was similar to Paradise Hills, and each gang took on an identification with the Blood and Crip names and colors. However, like all other Filipino gangs that adopted the African-American gang names and colors, there was no connection between Filipinos and blacks.

The final two groups that came to be Filipino gang rivals were the Northside Blood and the Ruthless Possee Crips. The Northside Blood was in the relatively affluent middle-class suburb of Rancho Peñasquitos, and the Ruthless Possee Crips resided in an adjacent suburb to the south called Mira Mesa. Mira Mesa was a mixed middle-class area adjacent to the Miramar Naval Air Station in the north part of the city. Because of the large Filipino population, the subdivision was sometimes referred to as Manila Mesa. However, the Filipinos were a minority there and had the same general acceptance as elsewhere in San Diego. Many of the Filipino families moved from Mira Mesa north to Rancho Peñaquitos as they became more affluent. As a result there were many family connections among Filipinos between the two suburban areas.

Most of the information on the Filipino gangs indicates that while they took on the names and colors of the African-American gangs, they tended to take on the general behavioral patterns of the Mexican-American gangs. Their major criminal activity seemed to be gangbanging and drive-by shootings. They were not known to be involved in drug sales or robberies, and there did not appear to be a major interest in car theft as was the case with Southeast Asian gangs that developed later.

In interviewing Filipino gang members, we found the same general patterns of behavior characteristic of Mexican-American and African-American gangs. The following interview excepts with a member of Bahala Na-Barkada illustrate this similarity:

> Our rivals are Be Down Boys [Bloods]. We fight against them [gangbang]. The only time we fight is when we run into each other. Or we may look for revenge against them. We are not mainly known for selling drugs. Only some of us use drugs. Most members just drink. There are about three hundred guys in our gang. A lot of our members have normal jobs or we get money from our parents. About a quarter of us dropped out of school. The rest of us attend school on a regular basis. I was known for not attending school.
>
> On an average day I would leave my house as if I was going to school, but I would end up at a friend's house instead. Back then, my friends were more important. We would kick it, or go to a girl's house—someone that also ditched or had already graduated—and do whatever. Sometimes we would drink or smoke weed. We would drive around, not necessarily looking for trouble, but sometimes we would run into guys from other gangs. Most of the time we had guns in the car. If they outnumbered us, we would shoot at them. If they shot at us first, we would duck and hide and try to shoot back if we had a gun. Our gang is known for having a lot of guns, yet we don't like to carry them in the car because we get pulled over a lot for looking suspicious—having a lot of kids in the car. We most keep our guns at home. On special occasions we do carry guns—like when we know something is going to go down. [Note the contradiction in the statement.]
>
> They consider us like the Crips. We fight Bloods, yet, we dress more like a Mexican gang [member], similar to the *cholo* style. Some dress like a black gang member. We dress however we feel like. There is no absolute certain way to dress.
>
> The hierarchy is make up of OGs [original gangsters], the older heads [ages in twenties] and then the juniors, the new kids.

About the only *possible* difference between Filipino gangs and the other gangs is the percentage estimated by the interviewee to have dropped out of school. Without exact figures, it is difficult to say, but the other gangs seem to have a higher dropout rate among the hard-core members. Otherwise, the routines of the Filipino gangs mirror those of the other gangs in San Diego.

SOUTHEAST ASIAN GANGS

Southeast Asians gangs had their origins in the waves of refugees that came from Vietnam, Cambodia, and Laos after the Communist forces came into power. An important distinction between refugees and migrants is that migrants have a choice of leaving their home countries or staying there, albeit in poverty. The typical Mexican-American immigrant comes to the United States on his or her own accord to find work. Immigrants can plan their move and take resources with them. Refugees are usually persecuted to the point of having to leave or are simply made to leave their country of origin. As a result, they tend to be poorer and less prepared to move than migrants. This was the case with the Southeast Asian refugees who came to San Diego.

A total of approximately fifty thousand of the nine hundred thousand Southeast Asian refugees who fled their home countries settled in San Diego (Ima 1991:19). The rough breakdown is shown in Table 9.1. The refugees came in three waves. The first wave occurred between 1975 and 1979, and was made up principally of the Vietnamese who had either worked with the Americans or were fleeing Communism. The refugees tended to have greater resources, be better adjusted to urban living, and be more educated than those in the next two waves.

The second wave of refugees, from 1979 to 1982, consisted of a combination of Chinese-Vietnamese, Cambodians, Hmong, and Lao, better known as "boat people" (Vigil and Yun 1990:149). This group suffered terribly, with estimates of up to half of their original number dying in the attempt to escape. The Cambodians fled the persecution of the Pol Pot regime and the infamous "killing fields," where over a million Khmer people died. The Chinese-Vietnamese were driven from their country when the border war between Vietnam and China led to persecution of Vietnamese of Chinese background. Likewise the Hmong and Lao fled from persecution in Laos when their country fell to the Communists. These people tended to be less educated, more rural in background (farmers and fishermen), and less likely to speak or read English than those in the first refugee wave (Ima 1991:18).

The third wave began in 1982 and continues today. The migration of those in this wave is facilitated by an agreement between the Vietnamese and United States governments permitting orderly immigration

Table 9.1. Southeast Asian Refugees in San Diego

Group	Number
Vietnamese, Chinese-Vietnamese	25,000
Lao	12,000
Khmer	10,000
Hmong	3,000

of Vietnamese to this country. There are still boat people coming from various countries of Southeast Asia, and they are poorer, less urban, and less educated than the second wave. Also there are Amerasians, who were fathered by American soldiers during the Vietnam war. In their home countries, Amerasians have been denied access to even the most elementary education and opportunities that would help them succeed in the United States (Ima 1991:18). Since they were rejected as mixed-race by the Southeast Asians in their countries of origin, many of them find themselves in the United States with virtually no reference group and without the strong family ties that have helped the other refugees making the transition to living in a new homeland.

The first group of Southeast Asian refugees moved into the Linda Vista area of San Diego in 1975. Linda Vista had been an area where there were "wannabe" gangs for a number of years, but only sporadic gang violence occurred there throughout most of the 1980s. When gangs did begin appearing in Linda Vista, they had the distinction of being interethnic, made up of Mexican-Americans, Filipinos, Anglo-Americans, and African-Americans. The Morely Street Boys, a street group more than a gang, and the Linda Vista Crips were the two major gangs there in the 1980s. However, as an offshoot of the Linda Vista Crips, the Tiny Oriental Crips (TOC) developed sometime in 1990–1991. In September 1991, the median selling price for a single-family house in San Diego was $179,000 and $165,000 in Linda Vista. By no means could one describe Linda Vista as all low income; however, there were three thousand low-cost government housing units built in World War II. They are still occupied by working families (Pryde 1984:223).

The second and third waves of refugees settled in the area known as East San Diego, located south of Interstate 8, east of Interstate 805, and north of Route 94. The area is characterized by a range of low- to moderate-income housing and a rich mixture of ethnic groups and gangs as well. The Eastside Piru, ESD, 5/9 Brims, Syndo Mob, Varrio Market Street, and Setentas all have gang territory in East San Diego.

Other refugees have come to Southeast San Diego in similar low- to moderate-income areas of mixed ethnic neighborhoods. Southeast San Diego is one of the lowest-income areas in the city, with median single family homes selling for about half of the city median.

Unlike most Asian-Americans whose income level is above the norm, Southeast Asian refugees have high poverty rates. Table 9.2 shows the percentage of families of Southeast Asian refugees living in San Diego below the poverty level.

Other than the Vietnamese and Chinese-Vietnamese, whose wealth is not abundant, the Southeast Asian refugee groups have a poverty level well in excess of more established American minority groups. This con-

Table 9.2. Southeast Asian Families below Poverty
Level

Group	Percentage
Vietnamese, Chinese-Vietnamese	Over 50
Lao	80
Khmer	80
Hmong	90

dition may have improved some since the figures were tabulated in the early and mid-1980s, when the population was still in the trauma of being resettled in the United States, but they are still much poorer than suggested by the stereotypes of the Vietnam war era profiteers that many imagine them to be.

WHO'S WHO?

Determining the ethnic makeup of Southeast Asian gangs has been difficult. Rival gangs will refer to the Southeast Asians as "a bunch of Chinese-looking guys," and the documentation process does not always guarantee that what a youth tells the police about his or her gang affiliation will be accurate. The distinctions between the Khmer, Vietnamese, Chinese-Vietnamese, Lao, and Hmong are at least as significant as the differences between the French, Germans, and English. And even though they are grouped into an Asian or Oriental category by social and bureaucratic classification systems, they see themselves as distinct. Nevertheless, most Southeast Asian gangs use the label *Oriental* in their names. The Tiny Oriental Crips, Oriental Boy Soldiers, and Oriental Killer Boys make up the three major San Diego gangs composed primarily of Southeast Asian youth. While the names make overly general reference to ethnicity, the gang members are primarily from a single group. The Oriental Boy Soldiers are essentially Khmer, and the Tiny Oriental Crips and Oriental Killer Boys are mainly Lao. The Tiny Oriental Crips were reported to have some Hmong and Vietnamese youths, and the Oriental Boy Soldiers may have had one or two Vietnamese and white youths, but for the most part, the gangs are ethnically homogeneous. A number of Vietnamese were identified with these gangs in probation records, but any affiliation between Vietnamese, Khmer, or Lao identified by the probation officials was most likely an ad hoc association that was a pragmatic necessity. Some incidents in the police records indicate

Table 9.3. Southeast Asian Gang Membership

Group	Number of known members[a]		
	TOC	OBS	OKB
Cambodian	0	14	1
Hmong	9	0	1
Lao	10	2	8
Vietnamese	5	8	1

[a]TOC: Tiny Oriental Crips, OBS: Oriental Boy Soldiers, OKB: Oriental Killer Boys.

association between Lao, Hmong, and Vietnamese in gang incidents. Table 9.3 data were culled from probation records in 1990 showing the ethnic makeup of the main Southeast Asian gangs.

Southeast Asian gang members have the same problem with stereotyping as do the Mexican-Americans and African-Americans. In 1991, some Southeast Asian gang members drove up to two boys standing on a corner in East San Diego and shot one of them to death. The boy who was shot and killed had only been in the United States a few weeks, and it is unlikely he was a gang member or even spoke English. However, he was lumped together with the Mexican-American gang members in the area.

Another interesting group that developed with the Oriental Killer Boys is a female Lao group calling themselves the West Coast Ladies. The name West Coast was most likely borrowed from the African-American West Coast Crips. Given the possible association of the Oriental Killer Boys with the African-American gang Neighborhood Crips, it is interesting that this title was chosen. The girls affiliated with other gangs usually take on the name of the male group with whom they are an adjunct.

The West Coast Ladies had the distinction of being on record in San Diego as the only known all-female group involved in a drive-by shooting. The following case describes the drive-by:

Two Lao girls arranged to meet in a parking lot of an apartment complex to discuss an argument over some "prank phone calls" one had been receiving. One of the girls was affiliated with the West Coast Ladies gang, an exclusively Lao female gang. She was currently dating the former boyfriend of the girl she came to meet. The West Coast Ladies girl brought seven of her fellow gang members with her.

When the two girls met in the parking lot, rather than settling the argument, they began fighting, with the eight gang girls jumping on the other girl. Two males broke up the fight, and the gang girls left. As they left, the girl who had been assaulted threw a rock at the car containing the West Coast Ladies. The gang girl who had initially been in conflict with the other girl told the driver of the car to go back to the parking lot. When the car returned to the parking lot, the gang girl fired two shots from a pistol at the girl standing next to her car. One bullet missed and the other hit the car.

The conflict was a personal one that involved a gang member, but the gang member brought her homegirls with her so that the incident became a gang one.

THE YELLOW PERIL

One of the most interesting features of the Southeast Asian gangs is that they are subject to stereotyping, which heightens their reputation as gangbangers. Since most non-Oriental gangs get their information about Orientals from such diverse sources as kung fu movies, school, and the stereotypes of their communities, they tend to believe that the Southeast Asian gangs are expert fighters (know kung fu, karate, and other Oriental martial arts), are knowledgeable about automatic weapons, are unconcerned about dying, have combat experience from the Vietnam war, and are especially vicious.

These stereotypes are grounded in three incidents. First, in January and February 1989, there were ten home invasion robberies by a gang of Vietnamese. Family members were herded together and threatened or tortured until they disclosed the location of their household valuables. One person died in these robberies. The attacks on family units were used to document the viciousness of the Southeast Asians. The home-invasion robbery is very traumatic for victims since the home is considered a safe sanctuary. Second, two Southeast Asian gang members were killed execution-style by rival gang members. Each of the two was shot in the back of the head. Third, in an altercation at the beach between Oriental Killer Boys and a Long Beach group of Cambodians (Long Beach is about one hundred miles north of San Diego) the Oriental Killer Boys used several guns to shoot into a large group at the beach. One of the girls in the Long Beach group was killed.

Looking closely at these events, we can see that while these groups are violent, they are not necessarily more so than the traditional gangs. The violence in the home invasion robberies was committed by Vietnamese who did not develop into a street gang. They were no more violent than the East San Diego gang members who stabbed the proprietor of a taco shop to death for not giving them free food. As for execution-style killings by gangs, both African-American and Mexican-American gangs have done the same things. In 1981 two African-Americans were found executed next to the freeway, and a Shelltown member made a man beg for his life before executing him. Neither case caused comment about the ethnic background of the killers. The much publicized Enrique Camereña case in Mexico, where a Drug Enforcement Agency undercover agent was tortured and murdered, was not used to document the cold-bloodedness of Mexicans in general. With regard to the drive-by shooting at the beach where a girl was killed, several children have been shot by Mexican-American and African-American gangs, but none of these shootings was used to document the ethnic viciousness of the attacks. This is not to say that the Southeast Asian gangs are not callous and vicious. They are, but no more so than the Filipino-American, African-American, or Mexican-American gangs in the same city.

The drive-by shootings and other assaults by Southeast Asian gangs were similar to those committed by the gangs from other ethnic groups. They usually used a single pistol in drive-by shootings, shot at rival gangs, yelled their gang name, and then drove away. They typically did not use automatic weapons, did not usually kill anyone, and in fact, generally missed when they did shoot. The absurd stereotype that they are familiar with all types of automatic weapons and are trained in using them is belied by their performances.

Another point that contradicts the alleged unique viciousness of Southeast Asian gangs is that they did not usually stop and attempt to finish off wounded victims. Gangs often did make every attempt to kill their victims, even in drive-by shootings. For example, when the Spring Valley Locos drove by and shot a Shelltown boy, they pumped nine shots into the body with a rifle. They stopped their car after the boy had been wounded, and using a rifle finished him off. Likewise, in describing another incident a Mexican-American gang member said:

> We went into Sherman to gangbang. We knew the risk of something happening. We had a shotgun and a forty-five. There were four of us. Once we got to the area, we got out of the car and yelled, "Logan." They started to run, but we caught one and started to beat him up. I put the forty-five to his head—just to make him jump. Then my homeboy got crazy and put the gun to his head. He shot the side of his head where his ear was. It didn't kill him.

While such incidents are vicious, the viciousness is not attributed to being Mexican-American. They are used instead to document the viciousness of gangs and gang members.

Not only is Southeast Asian gang violence characterized as especially vicious, it is also characterized as intentionally planned. The occasions are seen as sober calculations involving highly organized units. However, they are no more calculated, and certainly no more sober, than those of gangs from other ethnic backgrounds. In describing a shooting, a member of the Oriental Killer Boys said to an interviewer,

> They came to our beach and were throwing gang signs. Then they turn on their car stereos and were bumping. My homeboy said, "Let's go get them." We went . . . and got our guns. After that we went to the party where they [rival gang] were at. They had a birthday party for a girl at their beach. We just went in and that's it. That's history. The girl that had her birthday got her head blown off, and seventeen or eighteen people almost got killed. If we planned it, everyone would have died, but we were all drunk and tweekin' [high on crystal methamphetamine].

That account of a drive-by shooting sounds very much like drive-by shootings by gangs from other ethnic groups. There is minimal planning, drug or alcohol use is common, shots are fired into a group, and after the shooting the shooters drive away. The only partially unique aspect of the attack was the use of multiple vehicles and multiple weapons. Usually, a single vehicle and gun are used in a drive-by, not only by Southeast Asian gangs but other gangs as well. Observations by the police department indicate that Mexican-American and African-American gangs have been involved in drive-by shootings using multiple cars and several guns as well as automatic weapons, but these are exceptions rather than the rule. However, the exceptional cases of Mexican-American and African-American gang violence are not used to characterize the viciousness of those ethnic groups.

Interviews with gang members from various ethnic backgrounds show that stereotypes about Asians were clearly held. The following samples illustrate the view of Southeast Asian gangs:

> [African-American Crip] The Orientals are known for having real heavy equipment like nine-millimeter Uzis and stuff. They have the high-powered guns. The Long Beach 20 are really known for it. It's just a known fact that you don't mess with them.
>
> [Mexican-American East Side Brown Angels] The Oriental gangs are more aggressive. They have more guns. My gang thinks they are wannabes, and they are trying to prove themselves.

INTERETHNIC GANG CONFLICT AND THE ORIGINS OF SOUTHEAST ASIAN GANGS

One of the unique features of Southeast Asian gangs is the interethnic conflict they have with other gangs. The great bulk of gang-versus-gang violence in San Diego is between gangs of the same ethnic background. The reason behind the interethnic conflict with Southeast Asian gangs may lie in their origins.

Researchers and police alike speculate that Southeast Asians gangs banned together to protect themselves from the other gangs. The Southeast Asians youths who settled in East San Diego were bullied by both Mexican-American and African-American gangs. Not only did the Mexican-American and African-American gangs serve as a source of persecution, they also served as role models. When they started forming gangs, the Southeast Asians youths did so for protection. Since the other gangs had been bullying them, they were the target for retaliation. There has been a long-standing feud between the Mexican-American ESD gang and the Oriental Boy Soldiers. From police data, it appears that the ESD gang is a recurrent victim of attacks by Oriental Boy Soldiers. But interviews with police investigators showed that the Oriental Boy Soldiers really were not sure how to go about reporting a drive-by shooting to the police. Ironically, while ESD willingly reported attacks by gangs like the Oriental Boy Soldiers, Mexican-American gang members are not as cooperative with the police when battling other Mexican-American gangs. When the Oriental Boy Soldiers gang was a target of an ESD drive-by, their members either were not sure that calling the police was the honorable thing to do (it was "ratting"), or they simply did not know how to go about doing it. When they were questioned by the police, the Southeast Asian youths did complain that the police were not taking action against the Mexican-Americans or African-Americans who had tormented them. When the police told them they would take action if they were notified, the Southeast Asian gang members expressed surprise that they could notify the police about gang versus gang incidents

GANG ROUTINES AND STRUCTURES

The same routines and structures that characterize non–Southeast Asian gangs are also typical of the Southeast Asian gangs. The following interview with a Lao member of the Tiny Oriental Crips shows that his gang is organized like the other gangs in San Diego:

> The organization works this way: First on the top are OGs [original gangsters]. They just kick it. They have been through everything, and they don't want to be involved any more. They usually have families. The get all respect. The next level is the juniors. They are the ones that are out there gangbanging, robbing, and taking parts off cars. They have been in

the gang for a couple of years, but nobody is over the age of eighteen. This is because we are one of the newer gangs. Next, are the new bodies. They are real young—like around age six. Then the juniors, they do a little bit of bang-bang stuff. In a sense the whole gang is together, but everyone does their own thing.

My gang is best known for shooting and stealing cars. They are smart' and they don't get caught much. The big money comes from the OGs' connection with the Mafia. The older, more powerful members can ask a junior to get some money from stealing. The money is given to the older group. It is a trade-off of respect to the older members.

Other than the mention of connections with the Mafia, which may be a fanciful embellishment, the organization sounds virtually identical to that described by every other gang member. Given the role models for gangs, it should not be too surprising that the gang's structure is the same.

Likewise, in describing a typical gang day, the Southeast Asian gangs sound virtually identical to the other gangs. A female member of Oriental Boy Soldiers had the following to say in talking about gang routines:

Our gang don't sell drugs. Some people use, though. They kick back till trouble comes to them. As far as a normal day, few still attend school. I used to skip school a lot. I would go for first period so my parents would think that I went to class. So then me and my gang friends would go to a house to kick it or to a park and meet there. When we got bored, we would either look for trouble or start trouble with black gangs.

Like the other gangs in San Diego, the description of a routine day involves skipping school and "kicking it," possibly with drugs. Their lives are spiced with gangbangs and drive-bys, but otherwise, it is the routine of hanging around together socializing.

AMERICAN STYLE

In general, there is very little that is greatly different in the Southeast Asian gangs than found in the other gangs with the exception of inter-ethnic gang conflict. However, the Southeast Asians do not live up to the stereotypes of viciousness and sophistication that rival gangs attribute to them. There are clear cases of vicious gang activity, but they are no more so than comparable cases involving gangs of other ethnic backgrounds.

It is interesting to note that ethnic stereotypes are not only accepted by members of dominant groups, but other minorities also promote stereotypical thinking within society. Even those who adopt deviant identities tend to view the world from an ethnocentric position. To well-established gang members in the Mexican-American and African-American communities, Southeast Asian gangs are viewed as vicious and in possession of esoteric powers of martial arts. Myths develop and become part of the gang culture. While no one suggests that Southeast Asian gangs are good guys—least of all Southeast Asians who live in gang communities—the point here has been to illustrate that stereotypes have a pervasive quality influencing ethnic groups in a variety of ways.

WHITE KIDS AND GANGS

The lack of white gang documentation by the police is some cause for concern. From a political perspective, it appears as though the police department is discriminatory in its documentation process. The neo-Nazi groups, the Klu Klux Klan, and skinheads are all classified as hate groups, and the police treat them differently than gangs. With the exception of the skinheads, they do not tend to be predominantly youthful, and they are not territorial in the same way as are violent street gangs.

A number of whites have been documented as part of predominantly Mexican-American gangs, with the number increasing. The whites in these gangs, such as the Setentas in Lomita Village, take on the Mexican-American *cholo* gang style, and their actions and outlook are identical to the Mexican-Americans.

The South Bay gang, Four Corners of the World, includes youth from all ethnic groups and appears willing to fight all other ethnic groups. However, its activities are relatively few compared with more established gangs. Street groups, like the Death Wish Kids, may be taking on a more belligerent stance. A mixed ethnic group of Death Wish Kids near San Diego State University (located adjacent to the East San Diego district) challenged one of the university's fraternities to a fight. When they saw they were greatly outnumbered, the group left the fraternity house promising to return later. Likewise, the white group called the Pacific Beach Vermin has been involved in physical assaults to the extent that the people who live in the area have demanded that the police department define them as a gang and do something about them. If the PB Vermin begin fighting other gangs who come to their beach, whether whites from other areas or other ethnic gangs, then they will undoubtedly be classified as a gang.

Other white groups that may be involved in delinquency are surfer groups and doper groups. The surfer groups often are involved with drugs, may claim certain beaches as the own, and may use some violence to discourage "outsiders" from using their beaches. However, the surfers do not employ deadly violence, and they are isolated from most other gangs since surfing beaches are not routinely used by nonsurfers. As a result, surfers do not have a lot of contact with other gangs. The doper groups generally are not violent, and while they use a certain territory, they do not claim territory.

As discussed elsewhere in this book, San Diego does not have clearly demarcated white ethnic groups. That is, there are not neighborhoods that are predominantly Irish-American, German-American, English-American, or Italian-American. In individual neighborhoods, whites may experience a minority group status, when they are a minority to Mexican-Americans, but culturally there is not a minority self-concept. Experiences are not grounded in beliefs of discrimination, and the formation of gangs does not appear to be a viable option. For some white youths in a largely Mexican-American area where gangs exist, there is the gang option. But most white youths see themselves as having other options, and there is no family tradition or acceptance of gangs in San Diego.

As the population shifts from a white majority, white youths in low- and moderate-income areas may feel that all-white gangs are a viable option. However, since most of the long-standing gangs in San Diego have chosen to fight groups from the same ethnic background as themselves, it may take a while for white gangs to develop. Where there are large numbers of low- and/or moderate-income whites, they have not developed gangs, and only a few whites have joined gangs. Where whites have joined gangs they are either mixed-ethnic/cultural groups like Four Corners of the World and the Linda Vista Crips, or Mexican-American gangs with a decidedly *cholo* style. There are a good number of white delinquents and white delinquent groups, but as yet they have not developed into white gangs.

SUMMARY AND CONCLUSION

The expansion of gangs into groups other than Chicanos and blacks has been fairly rapid in the late 1980s and early 1990s. First the Filipino-Americans and then the Southeast Asian–Americans developed gangs. The Filipinos surprised everyone, especially the police, because historically they have had a low crime rate, have gotten high school grades, and have been solid middle-class citizens in San Diego. All the other gangs came from groups with traditionally higher crime rates and lower incomes.

The other major group that formed gangs, the Southeast Asians, better fit into the socioeconomic mold of other gangs. They were poor, recent immigrants, and subject to racism and discrimination. However, the traditional vision of Asian-Americans has been one of law-abiding, hard-working, and honest citizens. Their gangs were believed to be a response to and a model of other gangs in their area. As a group suffering discrimination because of a different culture, language, and ethnic appearance, they did not develop into fully active gangs until the 1990s even though there were isolated incidents before that time. Now they and the Filipino gangs account for a growing number of gang-related incidents of violence.

Finally, whites, while entering mixed- and Mexican-American gangs in growing numbers, still have not formed into all-white gangs in the style of the other gangs. Various delinquent groups of whites do exist, but they have not organized around the routine use of deadly violence in defending territory, especially against other white gangs. There are instead, what Miller (1975) referred to as "street groups," which exist as drug-using crowds and surfer groups in the parks, at the beaches, and at other gathering places. They never developed the cultural prerequisites of interpreting the world in such a way that a gang and gang violence was necessary for them, and the structure of their reality did not include the same kind of violence experienced by the minorities, especially the African-Americans and Mexican-Americans. And since they did not look up to these groups for guidance, they did not adopt or emulate their culture.

10

Police Operations and Gangs

INTRODUCTION

In the study of crime and delinquency, an important element is always the operations of the agencies whose job it is to control crime and delinquency. Such agencies select by policy and contingency who will and will not be the focus of attention. Those who are the focus of attention will be more likely to show up in the official statistics of crime. Unfortunately, there is a tendency to oversimplify the role of these agencies: as labelers, as tools of the powerful, or as empire-building bureaucracies. At some level of analysis, they are all of these, but at other levels they are none. The level of analysis employed here to understand the operations of a police department's gang detail will be at the operational level. That is, we will examine the work of the San Diego Police Department's gang detail from the point of view of middle management—the level of the sergeant and lieutenant. This is the level at which the tactics of dealing with gangs are defined and implemented.

To some extent, we can see many of the gang realities from the examination of police gang operations. The police are required to define gang incidents, and in so doing they define gang members and even gangs themselves. While it is true that the police are not set up to be analysts, what they do is participate in creating a social reality we come to know as gangs and gang occasions.

However, before we begin looking at the gang detail's work, we will briefly look at the issues of labeling, power, and bureaucratic empire-building.

POLICE AS LABELERS

The focus of labeling theory is on the societal reaction to crime. A key contention of labeling theory is that virtually everyone commits some type of crime from cheating on income tax returns to felony drunk driving, but only a few people are labeled as criminals or delinquents. They are so labeled either because their particular crime is a focus of law enforcement policy or due to the contingency that they just happened to get caught. A good example of such labeling is drunk driving. For years, drunk drivers have been the cause of more criminal deaths than any other form of homicide. With the advent of such organizations as Mothers Against Drunk Drivers (MADD), many police departments have allocated more resources to catching drunk drivers. As a result of such policies, more people who drive under the influence of alcohol are arrested and labeled. However, we do not find arguments that the police are responsible for the drunk drivers because they have labeled them as such.

With gangs and gang activity, the labeling theory argument is that the police create the gangs through defining them. Jack Katz notes, "When they [the police] arrest and lock up poor young minority men who are flashing gang symbols but not ready to back them up with violence, law enforcement agents powerfully intensify gang affiliation" (1989:11).

During my research for this book, the police did not lock up anyone for flashing a gang symbol. At worst, they would stop and talk to the youth, document him or her as a gang member, and then call the youth's parents and tell them. Usually, they would ignore them. Those who flashed the police a gang symbol probably were not the ones the police wanted anyway. Only the "wannabes" or fringe members would flash a gang symbol to the police, and the police knew that those who were wanted for drive-by shootings, assaults, or robberies would never do anything that stupid to attract the untender attention of the police.

It is true that the documentation process used by the police labels some youths as gang members. However, those youths are labeled on the basis of identification criteria that would be accepted as reasonable for identification for any group:

1. Admits to gang membership.
2. Wears tattoos, clothing, or has paraphernalia associated with particular gang.
3. Police records or observations confirm close association with known gang members.
4. Arrested with known gang members, participating in gang-related activities.
5. A reliable informant identifies person as a gang member.

Some form of self-labeling occurs before the police apply the label. It would be naive to assume that the police are the only people involved in the labeling process. Members of the community who live in gang areas label gang members, gang members label one another, and the schools are involved in the process of labeling. For example, Mar Vista High School in the South Bay area makes it a point to identify gang members and set up a special program in an attempt to minimize the gang influence in the school. They disallow youths wearing anything that identifies them with a gang. If they have gang tattoos, they must cover them, and they must attend school every day. If they claim they are too poor to buy clothes, there is a special program they have with a local retailer to get them free clothing. The school does label by identifying gang members, but attempts to minimize the gang identification, and thereby the self-labeling of gang members.

Given the official criteria for gang identification, there seems to be a lot of room for mistakenly identifying a youth as a gang member when he or she is not. More likely, a youth identified as a gang member is only a fringe member and has not taken up violence. Table 10.1 shows the total number of youths who have been documented as gang members in each September from 1986 to 1991.

Occasionally, the files were purged to remove invalid documentation and keep newer and more accurate information. However, even though the documentation process did label individuals as gang members, the consequences of such labeling did not appear to be severe. If a youth was picked up for a petty crime such as shoplifting, his label as a gang member might never come to light. If it did, he might have a more severe penalty, but it is unlikely. The police and the juvenile justice system alike allocate their resources on the basis of the seriousness of the offense *and* the offender. A single case of petty theft, such as shoplifting, does not call for resource expenditure, whether or not it is someone who has been identified as a gang member. Under conditions of fewer and less severe cases in the system, gang documentation may play a role in stiffer penalties for those so labeled. But in and of itself, the labeling that the police do is only one part of the labeling process, and its effect does not have the draconian consequences some have predicted.

Table 10.1. Number of Documented Gang Members, September 1986–September 1991

1986	1384
1987	1646
1988	1949
1989	2670
1990	3783
1991	4760

The major way in which gang members come to be known to the police as hard-core members is by involvement in gang-related incidents. In particular, if they are involved in drive-by shootings and assaults, they come to be labeled hard-core, but the mere fact that they are documented as gang members does not put them into the hard-core category. Documented gang members who do not get involved in serious violent gang activity are considered wannabes by the police as well as the gang members themselves.

In addition to involvement in violent crimes, gang members involved in drug sales are targeted both for labeling and punitive actions. The police believe that the money from drug sales is one of the attractions to gang life and provides resources for purchasing weapons. In addition, competition for consumers and sales territories leads to gang violence. As a result, when the police allocate more resources to attacking crack cocaine sales by gang members, there is a resulting increase in arrests, labeling, and punishment of African-American gang members. This is not to say there are any more or less African-American gang members selling drugs, but more have been identified, arrested, and sent to California Youth Authority or prison for involvement in gang-connected drug sales.

As we will see, the gang detail is more reactive than proactive in most of its work. The documentation process is largely proactive, but the documentation is not, for the most part, a creative labeling process. That is, the police do not create the gang label. The gangs and the communities create the label, and the police largely respond to a label that is already there.

POLICE POWER

The power the police have is of two types. First, they have political power in that they can persuade the public to support their efforts to suppress crime in the way defined by the police. Second, the police have contingency power in choosing what crime and criminals on which to expend resources. On a policy level, the police can choose to provide greater or lesser resources in the many different areas of crime. On a unit or individual level, they can decide which groups or individuals to harass or arrest.

The police's political power is limited by the elected political body. When a police budget is submitted, each and every resource must be justified. If there are any that cannot be justified either practically or politically, they can be struck from the budget. However, since the police have the best available information on patterns of crime, they can present a strong argument for pet projects, high-technology equipment, or more personnel. Even in times of limited resources, the police can at least advise where the resources are best spent.

The gang detail, however, did not seem to be a pet project of anyone in power in the police hierarchy. The origins of the gang detail were in 1974 when one officer from the School Task Force was assigned full-time to monitor what appeared to growing gang activity. In the late 1970s, several members of the remnants of the disbanded Border Task Force came to make up the beginning of the gang detail. By 1980 when this research began, the gang detail was a detective unit that was part of Special Investigations. A single sergeant and about six officers made up the detail. Most of the detectives were either African-American or Mexican-American, as were the gangs at that time. Other units in Special Investigations included the pawn shop detail and fencing unit. So the gang detail never was an unusual part of the police organization, but instead simply another part of Special Investigations.

By 1988, the unit had grown, along with the police department, the city, and the amount of gang activity. There were two sergeants, one who handled the African-American gangs and the other who worked the Mexican-American gangs. Each sergeant had seven detectives under him.

The biggest apparent change occurred in 1989 when the gang detail became a part of the Special Enforcement Division, a unit formed to target street gangs. This move was more a reorganization of existing units that had worked together on an ad hoc basis than a reallocation of resources. Moreover, the move seemed to have been prompted by political powers outside the police department to give the appearance that the police were doing something about the gang problem. By 1991, the gang detail itself had three sergeants and nineteen detectives, but as part of the Special Enforcement Division, it appeared as only one of several units. The following units made up the Special Enforcement Division:

- Street Gang Detective Unit (nineteen detectives, three sergeants)
- Special Enforcement Unit (thirty-six uniformed officers, four sergeants)
- Tactical Motorcycle Unit (eight officers, one sergeant)
- Special Response Team (twelve officers, two sergeants)
- Mobile Police Station (six officers, one sergeant)
- School Task Force (fourteen officers, two sergeants)

So instead of having only nineteen detectives, the "gang-fighting" unit had seventy-six officers, thirteen supervisors, plus nineteen detectives. The other units that make up the Special Enforcement Division, besides the gang detail, typically have other activities outside gang-related ones. Thus, while the unit itself appears to be an impressive tool to fight gangs, in reality the Street Gang Detective Unit is still the only dedicated unit used to target street gangs.

POLICE EMPIRE BUILDING

While any bureaucrat worth his or her salt seeks to expand, much of what the police department and gang detail did appeared to be the opposite. Ever since the inception of the gang detail, there has been a tacit agreement with the media, particularly television and newspapers, not to publicize gang-related incidents. If there were a drive-by shooting involving two gangs, the paper would report the shooting but would not mention it was gang related. Only when a special story was done on gangs did the press even mention gangs. Over the period of the research as the gang problems increased, the police and the media, in ignoring gangs, may have appeared almost idiotic from the perspective of the communities where gang activities were prevalent. Nevertheless, the police persisted in the belief that if the media did not publicize gang activities, the gangs would be less active.

Had the officers involved in the gang detail been bent on empire building, it would seem that they would have done everything in their power to let the media know of the growing gang problem. This they did not do. They also resisted external organization's efforts to redefine gangs to include what were essentially radical political groups. Some organizations and activists wanted the police to include groups such as the Ku Klux Klan, Nazis, skinheads, and similar white supremacist groups as gangs and have the gang detail go after them. The gang detail did not encourage such a redefinition, and indicated that those groups were being handled by the intelligence division, which was the most appropriate to deal with them. Had they been bent on expanding the unit, the gang detail supervisor could have generated information to justify such an expansion.

Finally, when the gang detail, now officially called the Street Gang Detective Unit, was merged with the Special Enforcement Division, the move was not at the behest of the gang detail, and very probably not the police department. Instead, there was a political demand that the police enlarge their efforts against gangs. (By the late 1980s gangs were "out of the closet.") Since the police knew of the ebb and flow of gang activity, they knew that any kind of permanent enlargement of the gang unit would be a waste of resources. Therefore, by making the Street Gang

Detective Unit a permanent part of the Special Enforcement Division, politicians and the police could point to a formidable organization component that targeted gangs without any kind of permanent organizational damage to the police department. The other units, which had always cooperated and worked with the gang detectives as they were needed, now had a more solid-looking link in the organization flowchart, but as far as expanding the original gang detail was concerned, its size reflected the growth of gangs and the city more than actual growth in the gang unit.

POLICE STRATEGIES WITH GANGS

The police who first began organizing a response to gang activity were working very much in the dark. There were virtually no guidelines for police working with gangs, and what there was often did not reflect the kinds of gangs and gang activity that characterized those in San Diego. By 1980, the police supervisor in charge of the gang detail had designed a number of general definitions of gangs, gang members, and gang-related activities so the cases pertinent to the gang detail could be recognized. Later, the same supervisor had the department include the category *gang related* on the patrol report form to help in allocating gang cases to the gang detail. Reactive investigative work made up the bulk of the actual case work in the unit, but proactive contacts with gang members by the detail were also instituted. With some refinements and additions those same routines were still in use by 1991.

Proactive Strategies

The primary proactive strategy by the gang detail was intelligence-gathering. The investigators sought to document gang members, make contacts with gang members, and cultivate informants. By gathering this information, the police hoped both to prevent illegal gang activities and to catch those involved in such activities.

As a preventive strategy, the idea was that the police, by having information about gang members, could worry at least some of them into forgoing gang activity. The police also hoped that they might even get information that would allow them to intervene in a gang activity. In once instance, the police had an informant at a gang party in Logan Heights. Shortly before an attack on Sherman, the police were notified and were able to follow the Logan boys as they rode around Sherman

Heights looking for targets. (There were no attacks since the Sherman homeboys kept out of sight that night, and the police took no action since they did not want to risk the possibility of exposing their informant.) Had an assault begun, the police were in a position to intervene and make several arrests before, they dearly hoped, anyone was injured.

A typical police strategy was to go to a place where several gang members were gathered. The gang members would be searched for weapons and/or drugs, and if any illegal weapons or drugs were found, the police made an arrest. If not, they would attempt to determine which in the group met the department criteria for gang membership and document those who did.

Sometimes, if a gang member were caught by a gang detail detective in a less serious offense, such as possession of drugs, the detective would trade leniency for information. If the gang member cooperated in providing information about his own gang or another gang, he could stay out of official trouble. If the gang member had no information or the detective did not need any at that time, the favor was credited to a later time.

A final major proactive strategy used by police was to target gang business. In 1989, the police allocated most of the resources of the Special Enforcement Division to go after crack cocaine dealing by the African-American gangs. This resulted in a large number of arrests of Crips and Pirus and at least a temporary pause in their drug sales. The idea behind the strategy was to hurt the gangs financially, thereby making them less attractive to potential and current members, get the hardcore members in jail, and generally disrupt their operations.

The success of the various police proactive strategies was not measured, but the ebb and flow of gang activity seems to be unrelated to police attention. In 1989 and 1990, the gang-related homicides were down, but they were threatening to reach a new high by September 1991, with a more than 100 percent increase from 1990. Police claim that without their efforts gang activity would be worse, but recorded gang activity goes up and down apparently independent of police efforts. The police claimed that the 1989 crackdown on the Crips and Pirus put a dent in their crack cocaine sales, but since there never was any accurate information on the volume of crack cocaine sales before and after the crackdown, it is almost impossible to tell. (It should be noted that the police are not the only ones who have little or no accurate information on drug sales. Social science researchers, at best, only have estimates based on assumptions of what can be produced and shipped, and the assumptions have only been marginally substantiated.)

Reactive Strategies

The reactive strategies of the police gang detail are virtually identical to those of other investigative units (Sanders 1977). The detectives receive information about a crime from a call to the police dispatcher, a patrol report, the hospital, or some other source. They then conduct a computer check, which includes a background check of the victim, witnesses, and suspects, if they are known. Then they interview witnesses, victims, and finally any suspects. During the time they make the various contacts, they either are or are not able to make a case. If they can make a case, they prepare it for the district attorney's office, or else the case is inactivated until further investigative leads develop.

Beginning in 1980, San Diego had an assistant district attorney specializing in prosecuting gang cases. By 1991, there were six deputy district attorneys and three investigators in the Gang Prosecution Unit in the district attorney's office. Depending on the case, the Gang Prosecution Unit would either rely on the police department's gang detectives, its own investigators, or both to prepare a case.

The connection between the proactive work in gang member documentation and the reactive work in investigating a case was a unique element in the gang detail that is not seen in most other investigative units. The documentation process connected an individual with a name, address, moniker (gang name), automobile, associates, and gang affiliation. This information was used to locate suspects or witnesses if a gang-related incident occurred. For example, if a car in a drive-by shooting had been described as similar to a car of a rival gang member of the target gang, the documented gang member with such a car would be contacted as a possible suspect.

Information Flow. The case information that led to reactive work by gang detail detectives often had difficulty finding its way to the gang detail. Over half of a sample of gang cases reviewed were not marked by patrol as gang related. Furthermore, most of the cases that were not marked for the gang unit were clearly gang cases. For example, the following excerpt, written by the reporting officer, was in a case that the officer *did not* indicate was gang related:

> [Victim] told me that the reason why he and "Huero" fought was because he called the Paradise Hills Gang a bunch of pussies. [Victim] says he belongs to the National City Gang. "Huero" is a Paradise Hills gang member.

As a result of such inattention to form categories, reports to the gang detail are often misfiled and reach the gang detail days after they have been reported, or sometimes not at all. Even with the requirement for the patrol to report all gang-related cases directly to the gang detail, there are often lapses where the information is not passed on. So while the gang detail may have more intelligence information in the form of documented gang members, its reactive work is hampered by the problems in the bureaucracy channeling information to it. Thus, instead of *overlabeling*, the gang detail could probably be more accurately accused of *underlabeling* gang activity since it only receives a fraction of all gang-related incidents.

POLICE, GANGS, INCIDENTS, AND GANG RESEARCH

The police are a unique interface in the sociology of gang research. The police view themselves as practical crime fighters caught in a web of political intrigue, blamed for social injustices that they did not create, and held accountable for labeling citizens as criminals. Social critics view the police as an oppressing force that protects the privileged at the expense of the poor, disadvantaged, and politically disenfranchised. Sociologists and criminologists decry the inadequacy of police data for research purposes, even though the primary mission of the police is not that of data collection. The victim community see the police as ineffective in protecting it against crime but effective in doling out traffic tickets. On top of everything else, the gang as a topic of research is a vague, dynamic phenomenon that is conceptualized as everything from a nurturing group to a collection of violent criminals.

However, in examining gang violence, the police are a necessary and interesting resource. More than any other single agency, they are alerted when gang violence occurs. Not only do citizens, in the role of victim or witness, call them but so too do various medical institutions. It is clear that not every incident of gang violence is known to the police, but there is no other agency or group that has the amount of information on violent gang incidents. They stand as society's institutional interface in the social construction of gang activities.

Other than members of the communities where gangs live, the police—more so than any other institution or organization—define gangs. However, it is incorrect to assume that the police are the main definers of gangs or gang violence. Researchers from Thrasher to Keiser to Jankowski have done excellent studies with virtually no reliance on the police for defining their topic of inquiry—gangs. They were able to recognize, interact with, and observe various forms of gangs during different parts of the twentieth century. So it is not the case that gangs are a creation of the police solely for political, administrative, or fiscal purposes. To be sure, if there is state or federal money available for antigang units, the police may more readily define certain groups and activities as ganglike. However, since the gangs exist independent of the police, the police can be a resource for locating gang incidents and gangs. The police, much like the researchers, have some idea of what constitutes a gang, and they develop plans to deal with it. Most of the police dealings are with situations and incidents defined by others— victims, hospitals, witnesses—as gang related. With a more precise set of definitions, the police determine whether an activity fits their criteria or not. So while the police may not always agree with citizen definitions of gang activities, they provide clearer parameters and functionally locate the situations and occasions of gang violence. Since the focus of this book has been on those occasions that arguably *define* the gangs, the police are a natural resource. They are contacted and directed to those very occasions that constitute the core of gang activity.

SUMMARY

While the police clearly are involved in the labeling process concerning gang members, they are only one part of the process. Besides the communities and schools, the gang members are self-labeling with tattoos, gang insignia, and hand signs. Without the other parts of the labeling process, there would be no police labeling. Furthermore, while the documentation of gang members used by the police may generate harsher scrutiny of minimally involved gang members, for the most part the documentation work provides investigative information only. Other agencies have very limited access to documented gang members, and so there is not public labeling by the police as such.

The strategies by the police center around proactive intervention and documentation of gang members. The intervention is in the form of attacks on gang sources of income and police presence. Documentation serves the proactive process of presence as well as the reactive work in investigation and witness and suspect identification. Overall, most of the work the police do is reactive in that their options are limited unless the gangs act criminally.

I

Research Methods

At the outset, the research was guided by the question, What are the characteristics of the situations where gang violence occurs? The situation was the independent variable, and gang violence was the dependent variable. The focus of the research was going to be on the situation of violence as the key unit of analysis. Later in the research, questions came up about the nature of the gang organization, and the routines of gangs that gave rise to the situations in question. The new questions required new methods, which were developed and implemented as needed.

As noted in Chapter 1, this enterprise was conducted under the notion that this was to be an "ethnography of situations." Generally, ethnographic research implies living with a group, organization, or culture to understand its beliefs, values, customs, and social structure. Since situations are episodic, it was not possible to live with a situation except momentarily. Moreover, violent situations are difficult to "catch" as data, and it was necessary to rely on reports, interviews, and inferences of situational residues. Since I wanted to "see" as many situations as possible, I decided that the police who were called to situations of gang violence would be the most likely source for data. So the first step involved gaining access to the police.

ACCESS TO RESEARCH AND OBSERVATION NICHE

The access to the research setting was based largely on another research project undertaken at an earlier date. In 1978 I had spent nine months with the San Diego Police Department studying rape (Sanders 1980). Using the contacts that had been made during the earlier study, I was able to gain access to the gang detail, which at that time was in the process of changing from a patrol unit to a investigative unit. The sergeant in charge of the gang detail checked me out with the sex crimes unit and decided that my research would not be detrimental to the unit's activities or goals. So shortly after my initial contact with the gang unit, I was given access to all of the information requested and allowed to accompany investigators in their work. This contrasts with the approximately six months it took when I attempted access to the department with the proposal to research rape.

Once I was allowed access, the police were cooperative in every way possible. Often they went out of their way to get reports, take me places, get information, and generally help in any way they could. In fact there were several occasions where they provided information that I had asked about several weeks or even months before, which had not been available when it was initially requested. There was no interference in anything I did, and while the police had very clear opinions about the nature of gangs, crimes, and criminals, they were very open to outside information and interested in other interpretations. In addition, there was no political pressure from the chief, any of the supervising officers, or the investigators to influence anything I did, said, or wrote.

The observation niche was from the same physical position of the police but clearly not the same perspective. The police had immediate practical matters with which to deal in gathering intelligence, making investigations, and satisfying organizational criteria for doing their work. They also faced the problems of dealing with recalcitrant gang members and the unpredictable contingencies that occurred in work with violent people. My perspective, on the other hand, was from a sociological one focusing on the characteristics of social situations where gang violence took place. So, while I was in a similar position in time and space as the police, we were viewing the same phenomena from wholly different frames of reference.

The only other police department with which I came into contact during the period of research was Scotland Yard in 1984. This occurred while I was at the Institute of Criminology at Cambridge University. A former Cambridge student was a police inspector at Scotland Yard, and I was introduced to him by faculty at the institute. I explained the type of gang violence I was studying, and he sent me to different police districts in London in search of such gangs. During that time in London, the police knew of no youth gangs of the type I described, and so while I gained access to the police, there was nothing they could do to help locate the type of violence under study.

THE OBSERVATION SCHEDULE

The main tool for data gathering was an *observation schedule*. The observation schedule is a cross between an interview schedule, a questionnaire, and participant observation notebook. The idea was borrowed from Reiss (1971) and developed in other research of my own (Sanders 1977, 1980).

Basically, the observation schedule includes two parts. The first part is filled out like an interview schedule or questionnaire. It asks specific questions about a violent gang situation. Most of the questions could be answered by checking fixed-choice categories, but others were left open-ended and later categorized as the categories were discovered. Creation of the observation schedule occurred after some initial observations of gang incidents and interviews with the police. For example, I made up a list of gangs based on my initial observations and then asked the police if the list was accurate or not. Once I had a list that reflected the current reports of gang violence, it was incorporated into the observation schedule as check-off categories. When an incident occurred involving a particular gang, all I or a research assistant had to do was to check off the gang. Table A.1 shows the variables and dimensions in the observation schedule.

Each form also had an observation number, police department case number, and date, day of week, and time of incident. The California penal code number was listed as well.

At the bottom of the question section was a summary section. The summary section provided space where the observer could summarize the event in narrative fashion, very much like field notes. This would enable me to have a qualitative overview of each situation, the contextual background of the incident, and open up the instrument to new information that had not been anticipated in the question part of the observation schedule. The summary section prompted general and specific information. The following headlined the summary section:

> Summary: Include (1) What was happening immediately prior to violence, (2) How violence started, (3) What triggered violence, (4) How violence ended. Make summary brief but provide context of situation Use no proper names.

The observations were conducted while accompanying members of the gang detail. Since the purpose of the research was to understand the characteristics of the situations of violence, it was necessary to come into contact with as many such situations as possible. When called to a gang incident, I could record what could be observed and/or learned through interviewing witnesses, victims, and suspects at the crime scene.

Often not all of the information was available when the observer arrived at the scene of an incident. Therefore, additional information had to be culled from patrol and follow-up reports by detectives, and interviews with investigators. Sometimes it was necessary to use interviews at the police department with witnesses, victims, and suspects to

Table A.1.   Observation Schedule Variables and Dimensions

Type of incident	*Situation*	*Gang vs.*
Drive-by	Hanging out	Gang
Fight	Party/picnic	Nongang
Robbery	Drive-by (driving)	Police
Rape	School	
Assault	Other	*Ethnic configuration*
Other		Ethnic gang
	Access	Black
Weapon	Public	Hispanic
Pistol	Private	Filipino
Shotgun		Asian
Rifle	*Gang[a]*	White
Unknown gun	Logan	
Knife	Logan Calle 30	*Ethnic victim*
Club	Logan Red Steps	Black
Rock	Shelltown	Hispanic
Bottle	Sidro	Filipino
Body	Del Sol	Asian
Other	70s (Setentas)	White
	VELs	
Place	Sherman	*Substances*
	Drug sales	
Inside	Lomas	Drug possession
Outside	Varrio Market Street	Drug influence
	ESD	Alcohol influence
Territory	Be Down Boys	
Gang (name of gang)	Northside Blood	
Neutral	Southside Blood	
	Neighborhood Crips	
Location	Eastside Piru	
Private home	Lincoln Park/Syndo Mob	
Park	Little Africa Pirus	
Recreation center	5/9 Brim	
Street	West Coast Crips	
School	PBI/East Dago Mob	
Other		

[a] Oriental Boy Soldiers, Tiny Oriental Crips, and Oriental Killer Boys were added later.

gather the required information. However, the observation schedule was flexible enough to use any of these sources of information.

Quantitative Analysis. Once the information had been collected, the quantitative data were coded and data analysis was conducted using the SPSS (Statistical Package for Social Science) programs. The frequencies and cross-tabulations presented in this book were the result of that analysis. However, the quantitative data were further compared with qualitative data based on the summary section of the observation schedule and interviews with officers. Overall there were not contradictions between the two types of data, but when there were, the data were reexamined to see if the contradiction could be resolved. For example, the quantitative data showed that the Oriental Boy Soldiers conducted several drive-by shootings against the ESD gang, but ESD had not attacked them. However, in an unstructured interview with an investigator, I learned that the ESD gang had been attacking Oriental Boy Soldiers, but the Oriental Boy Soldiers gang had not been reporting it to the police.

Qualitative Analysis.   The summary or narrative part of the observation schedule was treated the same as field notes. Cases were classified by common characteristics so that it was possible to discover processes in incidents of gang violence. Cases that did not fit into any of the common groups were reexamined to see if they contained commonalties that had been overlooked in some classification or subclassification of incidents. Those that did have features in common were grouped with the appropriate category, and those that did not were either used to start a new category or were treated as deviant cases.

UNSTRUCTURED INTERVIEWS

The final methodological tool used was to interview gang members incarcerated in Juvenile Hall. These interviews were conducted by students who were given specific but unstructured questions to ask and follow up. Especially useful were questions concerning day-to-day routines of gang organization, gang members, and their understandings of what happened in situations of gang violence. The interviewers were college age, and from the responses, there appeared to be good rapport between the interviewers and the subjects.

Some of the more general questions were handled by using essays written by gang members. This technique was partially successful, but either because of lack of communication ability or self-consciousness in writing about criminal activities, some of the essays were of minimal value. However, several gang members used their essays to elaborate their view of gang life, and the writing provided a good indicator of their level of writing ability.

BY ANY MEANS NECESSARY

A disturbing note has sounded in gang research by a new breed of sociological moral entrepreneurs. Having been a long-time advocate and practitioner of participant-observation research, I find attacks on researchers who use data from other methods disturbing especially since these attacks are led by participant-observation researchers. In particular, John Hagedorn (1990:240–59) has decreed that only gang research done along narrow guidelines that he has divined is appropriate. He decries "courthouse criminology" and "surrogate sociology," slogans that summarize research done using "official statistics" and "agency gathered data," respectively. While I concur with Hagedorn that researchers should not rely solely on data provided by law enforcement or other official sources, he should not be so naive (or arrogant) as to believe that those who do use those data are ignorant of the process by which such data are compiled. Indeed, since Hagedorn has not researched the process (official data gathering) himself, he contradicts the very process he decries.

All research methodologies have their limitations and advantages. The issue is not a matter of some version of political correctness in methods so much as it is the questions the researcher asks about gangs. We should look at problems and questions posed by theoretical issues, and then use whatever method can best deliver valid data to answer those questions. To paraphrase Malcolm X, we should attempt to find answers to our theoretical questions by any means necessary. This is very much in the spirit of triangulation, where not only do we look at a problem from different perspectives, but we use multiple methods in examining a research topic so that we do not come away with a single angle.

At one time, and still to some extent today, the survey and statistical analysis were considered the only "truly scientific" method in sociology. Qualitative methods and analytical tools were shunned as inappropriate. This narrow perspective is not only unscientific, it gets in the way of any progress we can hope to make in understanding social life, gang behavior included. Rather than restricting this and the next generation of researchers to a narrowly defined focus in methods as Hagedorn espouses, we should explore and exploit new methodological and analytical horizons, and make ourselves aware of both the limits and merits of different forms of data and methods.

SUMMARY

Erving Goffman once referred to participant-observation research as a "controlled adventure." Actually, such research is hours of exacting, boring, recording-keeping punctuated by excitement, and followed by hours of tedious data analysis rewarded by equivocal insights. Research on the gangs was always interesting, often exciting, but it was systematic and required a good deal of bureaucratic stamina for both data collection and analysis.

The observation schedule focused attention on the pertinent issues, and each one often required more than a single source of information to complete. The questionnaires provided unexpected data that were incorporated into this book to provide a background context for the situations of violence. And finally, the interviews provided data from the perspective of the gang member on what his or her life looked like from the inside of a gang.

I feel fortunate in the cooperation received from the police. Their work is easily criticized from all sides, and to cooperate with a researcher who reports their activities belies their cynicism. Likewise, the gang members interviewed risked self-incrimination in their cooperation. However, the purpose of this work was to shed some like on the issue of gang violence and not evaluate those caught up in it. To that end, I hope their cooperative efforts were not in vain.

References

Allen, John. 1977. *Assault with a Deadly Weapon: The Autobiography of a Street Criminal*. New York: McGraw-Hill.

Bernstein, Walter. 1957. "The Cherubs Are Rumbling." *New Yorker* (September 21).

Boyle, Jimmy. 1977. *A Sense of Freedom*. London: Pan.

Chesney-Lind, Meda, Nancy Marker, Howard Reyes, Yolanda Reyes, and Anna Rockhill. 1992. "Gangs and Delinquency in Hawaii." Paper presented at the Annual Meeting of the American Society of Criminology Meetings, New Orleans, November.

Chin, Ko-Lin. 1990. "Chinese Gangs and Extortion," Pp. 129–45 in *Gangs in America*, edited by C. Ronald Huff. Newbury Park, CA: Sage.

Cloward, Richard A. and Lloyd E. Ohlin. 1960. *Delinquency and Opportunity: A Theory of Delinquent Gangs*. New York: Free Press.

Cohen, Albert K. 1955. *Delinquent Boys: The Culture of the Gang*. New York: Free Press.

Cooley, Charles H. [1902] 1964. *Human Nature and the Social Order*. New York: Schocken Books.

Cummings, Scott. 1993. "Anatomy of a Wilding Gang." Pp. 49–74 in *Gangs: The Origins and Impact of Contemporary Youth Gangs in the United States*, edited by Scott Cummings and Daniel J. Monti. Albany, NY: State University of New York Press.

Fagan, Jeffrey. 1990. "Social Processes of Delinquency and Drug Use among Urban Gangs." Pp. 183–219 in *Gangs in America*, edited by C. Ronald Huff. Newbury Park, CA: Sage.

Garfinkel, Harold. 1967. *Studies in Ethnomethodology*. Englewood Cliffs, NJ: Prentice-Hall.

Geis, Gilbert. 1967. "Juvenile Gangs." Pp. 1–16 in *Report of the President's Committee on Juvenile Delinquency and Youth Crime*. Washington, DC: U.S. Government Printing Office.

Goffman, Erving. 1959. *The Presentation of Self in Everyday Life*. Garden City, NY: Doubleday.

_____. 1961. *Encounters: Two Studies in the Sociology of Interaction*. Indianapolis: Bobbs-Merrill.

_____. 1963a. *Behavior in Public Places*. New York: Free Press.

_____. 1963b. *Stigma*. Englewood Cliffs, NJ: Prentice-Hall.

———. 1967. *Interaction Ritual*. Garden City, NY: Doubleday.

———. 1969. *Strategic Interaction*. Philadelphia: University of Pennsylvania Press.

———. 1971. *Relations in Public*. New York: Harper and Row.

———. 1974. *Frame Analysis*. New York: Harper and Row.

Hagedorn, John M. 1990. "Back in the Field Again: Gang Research in the Nineties." Pp. 240–59 in *Gangs in America*, edited by C. Ronald Huff. Newbury Park, CA: Sage.

Horowitz, Ruth. 1990. "Sociological Perspectives on Gangs: Conflicting Definitions and Concepts." Pp. 37–54 in *Gangs in America*, edited by C. Ronald Huff. Newbury Park, CA: Sage.

Horowitz, Ruth and Gary Schwartz. 1974. "Honor, Normative Ambiguity and Gang Violence." *American Sociological Review* 39(April):238–51.

Ima, Kenji. 1991. *A Handbook for Professionals Working with Southeast Asian Delinquents and At-Risk Youth*. San Diego, CA: SAY San Diego, Inc.

Jankowski, Martin Sanchez. 1991. *Islands in the Street: Gangs and American Urban Society*. Berkeley: University of California Press.

Katz, Jack. 1989. "If Police Call It Gang Crime That Doesn't Make It True." *Los Angeles Times*. September 28, Part II, p. 11.

Keiser, R. Lincoln 1969. *The Vice Lords: Warriors of the Streets*. New York: Holt, Rinehart, and Winston.

Klein, Malcolm W. 1971. *Street Gangs and Street Workers*. Englewood Cliffs, NJ: Prentice-Hall.

Klein, Malcolm W. and Lois Y. Crawford. 1967. "Groups, Gangs, and Cohesiveness." *Journal of Research in Crime and Delinquency* 4(January).

Los Angeles Police Department (no date). *The Crips and Bloods/Pirus*. Unpublished report.

Luckenbill, David F. 1977. "Criminal Homicide as a Situated Transaction." *Social Problems* 25:176–86.

———. 1980. "Patterns of Force in Robbery." *Deviant Behavior* 1:361–78.

Lyman, Stanford M. and Marvin B. Scott. 1970. *A Sociology of the Absurd*. New York: Appleton-Century-Crofts.

Matza, David. 1964. *Delinquency and Drift*. New York: John Wiley.

Maxson, Cheryl and Malcolm W. Klein. 1990. "Street Gang Violence: Twice as Great, or Half as Great?" Pp. 71–100 in *Gangs in America*, edited by C. Ronald Huff. Newbury Park, CA: Sage.

Miller, Walter B. 1969. "White Gangs." *Trans-action* (September):11–26.

———. 1958. "Lower Class Culture as a Generating Milieu of Gang Delinquency." *Journal of Social Issues* 14(3, fall):5–19.

———. 1975. *Violence by Youth Gangs and Youth Groups As a Crime Problem in Major American Cities*. Washington, DC: U.S. Department of Justice.

Mills, C. Wright. 1940. "Situated Actions and Vocabularies of Motive." *American Sociological Review* 5:904–13.

Milovanocic, D. (1993). "The Decentered Subject in Law: Contributions of Topology, Psychoanalytic Semiotics and Chaos Theory." Paper presented at the Annual Law and Society Meetings, Chicago, May 27–30.

Moore, Joan W. 1978. *Homeboys: Gangs, Drugs, and Prisons in the Barrios of Los Angeles*. Philadelphia: Temple University Press.

————. 1993. "Gangs, Drugs, and Violence." Pp. 27–46 in *Gangs: The Origins and Impact of Contemporary Youth Gangs in the United States*, edited by Scott Cummings and Daniel J. Monti. Albany: State University of New York Press.

Pryde, Philip R. (ed.). 1984. *San Diego: An Introduction to the Region* (2nd ed.). Dubuque, IA: Kendall/Hunt.

Quicker, John C. 1983. *Homegirls: Characterizing Chicana Gangs.* San Pedro, CA: International Universities Press.

Reiss, Albert J. 1968. "Stuff and Nonsense about Social Surveys and Observations." Pp. 351–367 in *Institutions and the Person*, edited by Howard S. Becker. Chicago: Aldine.

Sanders, William B. 1977. *Detective Work: A Study of Criminal Investigations.* New York: Free Press.

————. 1980. *Rape and Women's Identity.* Beverly Hills, CA: Sage.

————. 1981. *Juvenile Delinquency: Causes, Patterns, and Reactions.* New York: Holt, Rinehart, and Winston.

San Diego County Deputy Sheriffs' Association. 1990. *Gangs, Groups, Cults.* Nevada: Stuart-Bradley Productions.

Scott, Marvin B. 1968. *The Racing Game.* Chicago: Aldine.

Scott, Marvin B. and Sanford Lyman. 1968. "Accounts." *American Sociological Review* (February):46–62.

Short, James F., Jr. (ed.). 1968. *Gang Delinquency and Delinquent Subcultures.* New York: Harper and Row.

Short, James F. and Fred L. Strodtbeck. 1964. "Why Gangs Fight." *Trans-action* I(6, Sept.–Oct.):25–29.

Spergel, Irving and Ronald L. Chance. 1991. "National Youth Gang Suppression and Intervention Program." *National Institute of Justice Reports* 224:21–24.

Sutherland, Edwin H. 1947. *Principles of Criminology.* Philadelphia: Lippincott.

Sylvester, Sawyer F., Jr. 1972. *The Heritage of Modern Criminology.* Cambridge, MA: Schenkman.

Taylor, Carl S. 1990. "Gang Imperialism" Pp. 103–15 in *Gangs in America*, edited by C. Ronald Huff. Newbury Park, CA: Sage.

Thrasher, Frederick. 1928. *The Gang: A Study of 1303 Gangs in Chicago.* Chicago: Chicago University Press.

Vigil, James Diego. 1993. "The Established Gang." Pp. 95–112 in *Gangs: The Origins and Impact of Contemporary Youth Gangs in the United States*, edited by Scott Cummings and Daniel J. Monti. Albany: State University of New York Press.

Vigil, James Diego and Steve Chong Yun. 1990. "Vietnam Youth Gangs in Southern California." Pp. 146–62 in *Gangs in America*, edited by C. Ronald Huff. Newbury Park, CA: Sage.

Wambaugh, Joseph. 1985. *Lines and Shadows.* New York: Doubleday.

Yablonsky, Lewis. 1962. *The Violent Gang.* New York: Macmillan.

INDEX